MARKETING HEALTH & HUMAN SERVICES

Robert Rubright
Dan MacDonald

AN ASPEN PUBLICATION

Aspen Systems Corporation
Rockville, Maryland
London
1981

Library of Congress Cataloging in Publication Data

Rubright, Robert
Marketing health and human services.

Includes bibliographical references and index.

1. Social work administration.   2. Health
services administration.   3. Marketing management.
I. MacDonald, Dan.   II. Title.
[DNLM: 1. Marketing of health services.   2. Social work.
W 74 R897m]
HV41.R7   361'.0068'8   81-737
ISBN: 0-89443-338-5   AACR2

Copyright © 1981 by Aspen Systems Corporation

Library of Congress Catalog Card Number: 81-737
ISBN: 0-89443-338-5

Printed in the United States of America

2 3 4 5

Table of Contents

Preface

There are hundreds of books about marketing as it is applied to business and industry. From college textbooks to the success stories that enterprising authors just had to put on paper, the serious student of marketing could make a career of reading about the subject. To fill time, the individual could attend seminars, workshops, short courses, and "dialogues," all addressed to marketing. There wouldn't be much time left to practice marketing.

The word "marketing" is applied in various ways. Administrators of hospitals and other institutions refer to marketing as something synonymous with promotion, selling, public relations, a specific feasibility study, a scheme to present an idea, a program to a charitable foundation or to a group of outpatients. To some, marketing is the overall communications program beamed to the general public. To others, marketing is a tool that helps an institution react to public criticism about its rates, services, or policies. We often hear the question: "What is marketing? I just can't define it."

As addressed to the nonprofit, civic, health, human services, arts, fundraising, and government sectors, marketing is in a period of discovery. Those who have introduced marketing to these fields simply have adapted business principles and methods to nonprofit entities, revealing that marketing makes sense and is quite pertinent to any organization that wants to achieve its objectives, resolve its problems, or seize opportunities in a systematic fashion.

The authors bring backgrounds from journalism, planning, fund-raising, and a social work discipline known as community organization. Introduced to marketing many years ago, we were struck with the similarities of marketing principles to our own training and experience. We realized that "social marketing," as some describe it, calls for a sequence of activities and processes that can be understood readily by administrators and managers in our fields and can be put into professional practice by nonmarketing people. The public relations manager's "publics" are translated easily into "targets," though much more individualized attention is demanded. Key techniques of "involvement" and "participation" are recognized as "strategies." Many more comparisons can be made. Much of what we had been taught and had learned through experience has had distinct marketing overtones.

There was, however, a dimension added by marketing that our backgrounds didn't quite satisfy. Marketing, we discovered, is the *disciplined* use of public relations, community organization, planning, and other techniques in an *order of activity*. Without discipline or order, which marketing demands, the execution of most projects lacks continuity and completeness.

We don't claim to plow new ground in marketing. Marketing's tenets have long been established by experienced, competent teachers. Marketing in the nonprofit sector is very new, with few books that deal with its application. Ours is a how-to-do-it publication, short perhaps on the academic side of marketing, but so intended. Our approach is to present the *system* that we have developed and used with our clients.

Marketing, or social marketing if that term is preferred, can be used by:

- Health and human services delivery organizations
- Arts and cultural agencies
- Planning authorities
- United Way and other fund-raising organizations
- Neighborhood associations
- Service clubs
- Various government agencies
- Legislative interest groups
- Personnel and training organizations
- Educational institutions
- Professional associations

Any organization that trades in services, causes, behavioral changes, and education can benefit from marketing's uses. We will refer often in this book to "health and human services," or simply "human services," because most of our direct work has been in these fields. A simple exchange of organizational titles, or some imaginative interpretation for your own organization, should suffice to make marketing applicable for your use, too.

Acknowledgments

A body of literature in the area of health and human services marketing, especially regarding hospitals, is growing rapidly. Our contribution to this blossoming library is to present the more practical applications of marketing and to avoid a concentration on marketing theory.

The authors are deeply grateful for the abiding and understanding support of their wives, Lynn and Hanna, as well as for professional inspiration during the book project from John P. Byrne of St. Louis and Duane Beck of Cleveland. The authors also wish to acknowledge, with much gratitude, the editorial and typing assistance of Christie H. Boyle of St. Louis.

ROBERT RUBRIGHT,
St. Louis, Missouri
DAN MACDONALD,
Indianapolis, Indiana
1980

Chapter 1

An Introduction to Social Marketing

Only recently have health and human services professionals discovered that the use of marketing techniques in counseling agencies, nursing homes, mental health facilities, health maintenance organizations, planning authorities, home health agencies, employment or rehabilitation agencies, United Ways, consumer agencies, character-building, and civic service groups can yield useful benefits, that marketing is an intriguing system with which to implement work or achieve organizational objectives.

Marketing is being experimented with, dabbled in, misinterpreted, fragmented, and studied by managers and boards in organizations of all sizes, settings, and sponsorships. In some respects, marketing has acquired the same status of interest that met management by objectives (MBO) when that system swept the business world some years ago. Like MBO, marketing needs to be understood and applied as a *system* if it is to be productive.

Examples of the misuse of the word marketing are plentiful. A new physician blithely refers to "marketing myself" when what really is meant is that the doctor is available to locate wherever the most attractive salary, patient potential, and professional advantages can be found. A youth agency administrator may refer to the annual work program as the "marketing plan." A children's home administrator describes the efforts of the public relations director in producing favorable publicity as "marketing."

Many persons now borrow the word "target" from the language of marketing. Targets and targeting are set firmly in the jargon of all kinds of professional and nonprofessional people. It is fashionable to target one's own work activities, to list targets, to give people the status of targets. Targeting is as misunderstood and misused as the word marketing. However, until some distinctive term or acronym is coined, we must bear with marketing and, in this book, its special application—social marketing.

In its first decade, social marketing is being explored and experimented with much as was public relations when it was adopted by the health field in the late 1950s. Within ten years, most large hospitals and health agencies had a public relations director and a board public relations committee. Twenty years later, ironically, social marketing's arrival has posed questions for the traditional practice of public relations in voluntary organizations.

Public relations has been the principal conduit of the organization's outward communication. But public relations primarily reflects the problems and concerns of management, not the publics that are related to the organization. Public relations concentrates on publications and news while marketing includes the tools of promotion in a measurably wider circle that also brings in testing, planning, research, targeting, strategies, and much consultation among the organization and its community of relationships.

Since marketing "is a systematic approach to planning the benefits to offer to a distinct public in order to elicit the resources or support that the organization wants in return," it focuses on bilateral communication and exchanges.[1] Ideally, marketing concentrates on one or two problems or opportunities at a time, such as better professional staff relations, client referrals, image enhancement, or new program or facility start-up. Public relations can shuffle easily among more than a dozen projects simultaneously in an unending attempt to attain credibility for the institution on primarily the organization's own terms.

Seminars, workshops, special classes, and retreats are being conducted to investigate, debate, and define marketing and its principles so its users can become acquainted with its offerings and understand the comparison with more traditional industrial marketing. Marketing vice presidents, directors, and managers are being appointed; boards are being asked to approve marketing plans or to hear the results of marketing research; some public relations, planning, and fund-raising staff members are being converted into or redesignated as marketing officers.

DEFINITIONS OF MARKETING

There are as many definitions of the term marketing as there are experts on the subject. Most textbooks are oriented to the selling of products or services and therefore deal with the known, the tangible, the very measurable. Some are valuable because they make it easy to apply marketing principles to any institution or system of management. Marketing books that address human services are few because the use of the system by human services managers is relatively new.

Philip Kotler was one of the first to apply marketing principles to health and social services. His book, *Marketing for Nonprofit Organizations,* published in 1975, drew attention because it highlighted the uniqueness of humanitarian enterprises. Kotler defines marketing as "the analysis, planning, implementation, and control of carefully formulated programs designed to bring about voluntary exchanges of values with target markets for the purpose of achieving organizational objectives."[2]

It is important to understand the key words in the Kotler definition. Marketing is useful in *"achieving organizational objectives."* It is the *implementation* of objectives, doing what one sets out to do. *Analysis, planning,* and *"carefully formulated programs"* are a part of the procedure; thus, marketing becomes very much a *system for implementation of objectives* rather than merely a prescription for advertising, selling, promotion, or other functions; all of the latter are elements of marketing.

"Social marketing is the design, implementation, and control of programs seeking to increase the acceptability of a social idea, cause, or practice in a target group(s)," Kotler continues. "It utilizes market segmentation, consumer research, concept development, communications, facilitation, incentives and the exchange theory to maximize target group response."[3] "Marketing," he says, "can be used to bring products, services, organizations, persons, places or social causes to the attention of a market,"[4] so why not, he reasons, transfer conventional marketing principles to human services organizations; they apply almost equally.

Other definitions of marketing abound. In some of them, readers can substitute health or human services words and terms easily for some of those used.

- "Marketing is the performance of business activities that direct the flow of goods and services from the producer to the consumer or user."[5]

- "Marketing is seen as the task of finding and stimulating buyers for the firm's output. It involves product development, pricing, distribution, and communications; and in the more progressive firms, continuous attention to the changing needs of the customers and the development of new products, with product modifications and services to meet these needs."[6]

- "The difference between simply telling the agency's story and a systematic method of identifying targets and using strategies to influence their response to the agency's problems can be called 'marketing.' It is a key factor in determining whether or not an agency will plateau at some point or continue to grow in many directions."[7]

Many nonprofit health or human services agencies provide tangible products or services to people who need them: day care, hot meals, counseling, contraceptive materials, and so on. Others promulgate ideas and concepts or attempt to achieve behavioral change in people that will result in better lives. For example, a senior citizens center creates service projects involving children and the elderly in the interests of maintaining the self-worth and usefulness of its members. A cancer society campaign aims at getting women in the habit of regular self-examination of breasts in order to detect disease early. A relationship between Big and Little Sisters is intended to have a positive influence on the usually troubled life of the Little Sister. A YMCA or YMHA organizes and promotes jogging clubs for people of all ages as a plank in its physical fitness program. The fact that the form of return for the organization's efforts appears to be different—that is, money is not exchanged or favors received—is not important.

THE PRINCIPLE OF EXCHANGE

Business history is filled with cases of small or run-of-the-mill companies finding glory through applied marketing. Those that have had enduring success have maintained one fundamental principle in their operations that has both a parallel and a lesson for the health and human services agency: a concern for the needs and wishes of the consumer before and after the point of sale. Health and human services organizations must find what it is that patients or clients want from the entity. They also must provide follow-up or maintain a continuing relationship beyond the episode of service.

All of this speaks to an underlying principle, the foundation of all marketing theory. It is contained in one word: *exchange*. Simply put, it means that when two people, or perhaps two organizations, come together in the marketplace to barter, each has something to offer that the other wants. If a transaction is completed, it is implied, though such is not always the case, that there is a sufficient degree of satisfaction in the minds of both parties. Of course, factors such as packaging, effectiveness of salesmanship, or the promise of future benefits might well result in one party's actually coming out ahead.

The theory of exchange in marketing is that there is an equal benefit accruing to both sides in the negotiations and that this should be the objective of the marketer, not only to effect the "sale" but also to leave a lasting impact and fallow ground for future exchanges or transactions. Of course, it is an old ploy of business marketing sometimes to provide the customer with an advantage in the initial exchange in order to pull the individual back again and again with the predictable results of more than equal returns to the company. Exchange means tit for tat or quid pro quo. It is the ability to identify what the mode and method of exchange with potential targets should be that distinguishes the marketer from the public relations counterpart and the ordinary sales campaign. The average charitable organization whose main commodity is providing very personal benefits to people should perhaps be the most skilled in pinpointing the exchanges with its clients.

Before an exchange can be transacted or managed, the marketer must learn as much as possible about the group or individual with whom the exchange is to be made. Such groups or persons are referred to as targets or publics; the better a target is understood, the easier it is to make an exchange. If it is realized that exchange may take many different forms, it isn't difficult to imagine a few examples:

- *A hospital board of trustees creates a special citizens committee to advise it about floating bonds for a new building addition.* What is the exchange between the hospital and the prospective committee? (a) The hospital offers prestige, comfortable meeting rooms, perhaps a new kind of civic experience for most of the members, and the possibility of personal recognition. (b) Committee members provide the hospital with practical knowledge of bonds and financing, some of their personal time, name prestige, and potential leadership that the institution might be able to use on some of its other projects. The exchange appears to be a fairly even one.

- *A nursing home decides to open a hospice section for the terminally ill; along the way, it must inform patients and their families of the new offering.* What exchange is involved between the hospice and the patient/family unit? (a) The nursing home hospice offers space in an existing medical facility, extraordinary concern for the problems of the patient and the family, rigid control of pain and symptoms, a contemporary approach to death and dying, 24-hour support service, and physical and emotional comfort. (b) The patient/family unit receives the benefits of and pays for the service, endorses the hospice concept, possibly makes contributions to the institution, offers encouragement to the staff. Family members may even volunteer their time. With such an exchange (the nursing home gives a little more than the user) it is small wonder that the hospice movement is advancing so steadily in the United States.

- *A family service agency is asked to offer in-depth counseling services to personnel of a large insurance company as part of its in-house employee assistance program.* The exchange appears beneficial to both parties: (a) The company arranges for skilled service it does not have available; it addresses problems of employees in whom it has a respectable investment and for which simple referral to the agency would not be an appropriate action in its view; and resolution of the presenting problem results in a happier, more productive employee. (b) To the family agency, the benefits are threefold: The organization is reimbursed for its services, it is responsive to serving the needs of people who have problems, and it underscores the community responsibility that it accepted when it was organized. The benefits in this transaction are more numerous, of course, but there may be inherent dangers, particularly if the agency overbalances its employee assistance program with its responsibility to serve all clients in need.

- *A private school for handicapped children seeks to recruit its first full time speech pathologist.* The exchange is as follows: (a) The school offers many clients and resources for the professional, a comfortable work setting, acceptable equipment, competitive pay, opportunities for peer contact, and, presumably, a supportive management. (b) The speech pathologist offers professional skills, the promise of a new service and subsequent prestige, a new level of therapy and benefits for students, and new learning experiences for other staff members.

In some of these exchanges, there is obvious parity: one party receives something according to its needs, wants, and desires and gives something according to the needs, wants, and desires of the other party. Some marketers feel that it is incumbent upon the organization to offer more in exchange than it gets from the target. In this approach, the theory goes, an organization can offer more exchanges, manage them better, position itself more solidly against competition, and help its growth possibilities, both in usage and in income. Other marketers, however, are inclined toward balanced exchanges of goods, services or money—whatever is involved to make the exchange equitable.

How can the effectiveness of an exchange be measured? It is difficult since "the values of what is exchanged, as perceived by the parties, are likely to change."[8] Therefore, the most mutually beneficial exchange is desirable, one that has the ultimate attention and respect of both parties. As MacStravic advises, "The value of that which is exchanged is measured in terms of its utility, the real or potential benefits it promises to exchangers, as they receive them."[9]

HESITATION ABOUT MARKETING

Despite marketing's apparent benefits and its systems approach to implementing objectives, many organizations remain wary of it. "Hospitals are not used to the idea of marketing," one critic says. "The word is unintelligible to them. They don't sell their services, they provide them."[10] Marketing sometimes has been thought to be synonymous with advertising, an activity that some persons think to be beneath the dignity of a health or human services agency, a flirtation with questionable ethics.

Marketing's forward progress in the voluntary sector has encountered some detours. In our consulting, the authors have found the words "market" and "marketing" to be objectionable to some people. "That word 'marketing,' it hits me right here," said the physician director of an urban health department as he pondered the idea of a marketing approach for establishing a new "wellness" program. The manager at a large social service organization at first recoiled at the thought of marketing. "Wouldn't it mean that we would have to go out and sell?'' said the executive director, reflecting some disgust. In a Midwest state, when a group of public health nurses was seeking knowledge about marketing, a spokesperson said, ''We couldn't use that word in front of our doctors here.''

In our marketing workshops, sometimes a question is raised about the ethics of marketing. Because there is a strong emphasis on targeting, assessment of targets and the proper application of strategies to deal with them, many persons assume that manipulation is the key to marketing. We disagree. Marketing represents a realistic identification of obstacles and issues as well as opportunities that affect an organization's ability to accomplish its objectives as well as a realistic approach to surmounting them. If an organization's business sense and practice is ethical to begin with in the way it deals with clients, what it charges, its program accountability, its publicity, then it is not likely to abandon its moral principles while practicing marketing. Again, if the goal of equal exchange is a tenet, then any legitimate organization cannot depart from sound ethical dealings for very long and survive.

THE 'PROFIT' IN MARKETING

Marketing, in our view, has profits for the nonprofit agency, too. Only the terms are different. Economically, a proprietary organization sends a share of its net proceeds to stockholders and retains some for development. A nonprofit organization, if it does better than break even on income and expense, can plow all of its surplus back into providing the same services or new ones. Many agencies find that a small margin of financial profit is the most feasible method of maintaining program growth.

For the health or human services agency, the real ''profit'' from its operations is the impact its services have on its clients: the retrained worker placed in a job by Goodwill Industries, the ex-convict who gets a decent new start by living a few weeks in a halfway house, a youngster whose involvement in a boys club was the only thing between him and juvenile court. If marketing is applied properly to reach more people who need to be served, then the agency or institution is fulfilling its original mission.

Social marketing, in its infancy, will continue to receive criticism. ''These kinds of issues or criticisms stem partly from a good deal of ignorance about marketing, a built-in fear of hucksterism, an assumption that our 'public service image' or virginity will somehow be violated and a very understandable feeling that 'marketing,' like management by objectives before it, will be another cumbersome, time-consuming and difficult system to adopt.''[11]

Social marketing has been questioned for its emphasis on adequate research and promotional tool outlays, its intrusions into many management areas, its disruption of tradition, its potential for upsetting public relations practitioners and for jarring planning operations, its imagined links to Madison Avenue, its confusion with long-term and short-range planning, and its relationship to the organization's annual work program. Marketing has been criticized for raising expectations beyond the capacity of the service to satisfy, for tending to neutralize the competition and increase utilization through augmented promotional strategies, and for equating the concept of personal service with the word "product."

PROMISING TIMES FOR MARKETING

Changes are occurring that might explain the reasons for a new and widespread interest in marketing. Competition is growing in every area of personal service, especially among nonprofit organizations that not so long ago enjoyed exclusive service territories. Alcoholic treatment programs are a fast-growing "item;" business firms are contracting with institutions to handle their employees with drinking and related problems. Many employee assistance programs now include casework, financial and marital counseling, preretirement courses, and other services. They are being offered by profit-making groups that become direct competitors with traditional counseling agencies. Many new proprietary home health care organizations are challenging the turf once held securely by visiting nurse associations and public health departments. Hospitals are rushing to establish ancillary services that will replace revenue lost by improved discharge planning and pressures to vacate beds. Sports medicine programs, weight clinics, health education, and other ventures are blossoming.

As in business, rapidly changing conditions mean that there are new classes of purchasers of service, cost-effective rationales for using service, and a far greater number of options for the consumer to consider. Since most organizations, profit or nonprofit, charge for their services, even if by a sliding scale, all but the indigent may make a choice of where to go for assistance. There has long been a body of professional thought that opts for the day when even the poor will be provided with vouchers to purchase services anywhere rather than being forced to accept help from traditional sources.

But as marketing becomes more understood among those who teach administration and planning, who manage service associations, and who serve on chartered or lay boards, there will be less argumentation about marketing and gradual acceptance of its role in health and human services.

The authors offer some assumptions that should meet little disagreement. All health and human services organizations are engaged in one or more aspects of marketing. All are involved in some form of research, in public relations in selling, in promotion. All have some idea of what a market is and some concept of the targets in their marketplace.

Marketing has promises for all nonprofit organizations, small or large. The differences of approach lie in the complexity of the project, the number of persons involved in delivering the service, the financial dimensions of the enterprise, and so forth. A large organization may engage and develop a marketing staff and integrate its planning, public relations, and fund-raising units within the marketing function. In a very small agency, the executive may perform all such tasks or may rely heavily on volunteer help.

Each organization, however, uses the same elements or procedures in its normal service operations, though the levels of sophistication may be different. The same is true in marketing: in a small organization, the depth of market research may be less, the number of targets may be fewer, the tools to be applied may not be so numerous or as polished, the strategies may be simpler. Marketing principles are applicable to any organization; only the way they are managed may be different.

MARKETING'S NINE COMPONENTS

Marketing, in the authors' system, generally consists of nine components:

1. the process of selecting and preparing the marketing project
2. research
3. the market audit
4. setting objectives
5. targeting
6. strategies
7. special promotional tools
8. internal adjustments
9. evaluation/recycling

The components are not always accomplished in the same order, but all of them together contribute to the eventual compilation of the marketing plan.

Considerable care should be taken in *selecting the marketing project and the preliminary marketing process.* It helps management decide the priority among several organizational objectives and then obtain a rough fix on the directions the marketing process should take. Tools for both the selection of projects and for summarizing the preplanning investigation are described in later chapters.

Needs assessment, community surveys, polling, analyses, and interviews are embodied in the *research* component, which is divided into external and internal sections. (Some organizations involve the marketing audit in the internal research section.) A detailed study of the organization's competition often is a third part of the research component.

The *market audit* phase examines the services of the agency or institution and how they are received by users. It analyzes the referral network, how and why the facility gets clients/patients, and what features attract them and their referrers. It also looks at everyone the organization does business with; it sorts through communications tools, questioning their relation to publics; it views the competition as well as its relationships with other providers who are noncompetitors. A completed audit should present a sound assessment of the organizations with which the agency deals.

Independent from organizational goals, mission, bylaws, and charter are those well-articulated *marketing objectives* that can be significant enough to cause agency management to alter some or many of its corporate objectives. "If an organization has an objective of serving the perceived needs and wants of a target public or market, it enhances an organization's chances to survive and achieve its goals."[12] Hence, the time spent in pondering objectives and putting them in writing is crucial.

Targeting is the identification of individuals, groups, or people with special characteristics and with whom the organization wants to initiate and manage exchanges. Patients and clients are logical targets; so are employees, competitors, referrers, third party payers, regulators, and contributors. Targeting is a selective operation, with the organization's attention directed to more important, high-priority targets first. Targets are broken down into primary and secondary categories, then into internal/external groupings; later, they are weighted and ranked.

Imagination and resourcefulness are keys to the next marketing step, the *setting of strategies,* or the action steps taken to reach the targets and fulfill marketing objectives. There are four general marketing strategies: market penetration (increasing the value of services in the area currently served), market development (offering services to new markets), product development (improving present services), and diversification (providing an entirely new service).

Management of *promotional tools* traditionally has been ceded to public relations. In some innocence, public relations people have prepared tools—brochures, slides, films, annual reports, handbooks, signs, forms, news releases, newsletters, and magazines—without carefully exploring how targets are chosen, without marketing research guidance, and with little or no knowledge of either marketing or organizational objectives. In marketing, promotional tools are not unilateral documents that mirror the egos, needs, and opinions of management. Instead, marketing tools reflect the attitudes and needs of those who use or will use the services of the organization and are selectively, strategically developed to do just that.

After the first marketing steps have been taken, it is likely that the organization will have to make some *internal adjustments*. A new staff specialist or a part-time marketing person may be hired, a planner may be converted to a marketer, corporate bylaws and objectives may be revised, or a new board marketing committee formed. New equipment may be needed or intake policies revamped completely.

Evaluation and recycling the marketing operation is the final marketing component. In this phase, the marketer reviews each step undertaken so far and reflects on what has been achieved, at what cost, and with what benefits to the organization and its targets. Adjustments may be made, new strategies added, and ineffective strategies discarded. New targets and new or revised tools may be required.

THE MARKETING MIX

Throughout the planning, the marketer must keep an eye on the four universal elements of marketing, the marketing mix (*product, promotion, place,* and *price*), sometimes called the four Ps. Some add a fifth P, public image, but others feel public image is part of the promotion category.

Product, or service, incorporates the range of the service and the persons who use it; promotion is persuasive communication by the organization to those who use or would use its services or facilities; distribution or place involves the delivery of the services and includes referral arrangements, transportation, the organization's physical plant, and other factors; and price includes both the financial price of the services and all financial activities, plus the "psychic" price experienced by users. The four Ps are fairly controllable factors employed by the marketer in making decisions that lead to setting strategies and following marketing objectives. A successful marketing plan includes all four elements. Although some practitioners regard the four Ps as the key elements of marketing, we believe them to be safety valves to ensure that the marketing system is functioning correctly.

CHARACTERISTICS OF MARKETING

Organizations that discover marketing usually discover something about themselves. There are certain characteristics in organizations that pursue marketing. The more universal seem to be:

- Aggressiveness: an organization must have the capacity to seek new business instead of merely reacting to competition and then taking necessary action. An aggressive organization keeps up with new developments in its industry and takes risks if it can comprehend the ultimate benefits that may accrue to itself and its constituents.

- A continually positive attitude: if the overall agency attitude is character-ized as mainly negative, cynical, or sour, it is almost impossible to achieve a positive climate for marketing.

- Contrariness to tradition: marketing makes things change because its pres-ence means doing things differently, taking chances, discarding old habits, making or seeking new friends.

- Initiative: an organization inclined to market cannot wait for clients to come to it; it can't assume that, just because it exists, it has no obligation to plan and develop its future.

- Responsiveness: a marketing-oriented organization succeeds if it correctly perceives its targets; if it meets the needs of referrers, users, and staff members; if it knows its constituents' psychosocial underpinnings. The organization's response to impacting forces must not be reactive or arbi-trary, but deliberate and calculated.

- Planning: the organization must make this a major characteristic of its op-eration. Marketing is the study of the future, some say, and any bright fu-ture involves the ability to do sound planning.

MORE ABOUT WHAT MARKETING IS AND ISN'T

It is important to clarify any confusion about marketing. First, marketing is not selling. It is a planned system of achieving objectives, quite different from selling. Theodore Levitt comments:

The marketing view of the business process means that marketing does more than simply push products and services. Marketing's job is much more encompassing. Selling tries to get the customer to want what the company has. Marketing tries to get the company to have what the customer wants. Selling is largely a one-way process— sending outward from the company the things it wants the customer to take. Marketing is a two-way process—sending backward to the company the facts of what the customer wants so that the company may develop and send out appropriate goods and services.[13]

Second, marketing is directive in its methods of seeking targets and arrang-ing strategies; it is not generalized or even whimsical—there is a system, not drift. No shotgun approaches to problem solving are used in marketing. It is selective in its use of and investment in promotional tools, making partially obsolete those conventional public relations tools that often embrace the interests and passions of the organization as opposed to those of potential or existing service users. Third, marketing involves skillful management of exchanges and none of the one-sided interchanges with users that frequently are puzzling, patently incomplete, or filled with distrust. Marketing demands that the exchange be a mutual experience, one that concentrates on client desires—a planning with, not a planning for.

Kotler declares:

> The true meaning of marketing is not hucksterism, making it possible to sell persons on buying things, propositions or causes they either do not want or which are bad for them. The real meaning is the concept of sensitively serving and satisfying human needs. Perhaps the short-run problem of business firms is to sell people on buying the existing products, but the long-run problem is clearly to create the products that people need. By this recognition that effective marketing requires a consumer orientation instead of a production orientation, marketing has taken a new lease on life and tied its economic activity to a higher social purpose.[14]

DIFFERENCES IN MARKETING OF SERVICES

There are important differences in the marketing of services as contrasted with products. Most services are intangible, with little opportunity for prospective users to see, use, smell, taste, squeeze, or hear them. Because of this, the offerer instead must provide the potential user a perception of the service and the user must conceptualize the service and its benefits.[15] The less tangible the service, the more need there is for verbal two-way communication.

Rathmell cites five primary characteristics of service transactions in the marketplace:[16]

1. Consumption or use is not possible without the participation of the seller.
2. Services are sold, then produced and consumed simultaneously.
3. The capacity to produce a service must exist before any transaction can occur. Services can't be stockpiled.
4. Universal performance standards are difficult to attain. "Not only do performance standards vary from one service seller to another, but the quality of a single service seller may vary from buyer to buyer."
5. Since most services are paid for after they are performed and cannot be repossessed, service providers are very dependent on the good faith of the buyer.

Finally, there is the advice from marketing teachers that "if there is to be an efficient output of services, there must be marketing channels to secure and keep a sufficient orderly flow of users over both time and space."[17] Without qualification, this viewpoint suggests the critical importance of the communications component of the marketing mix, with careful selection of promotional tools. Social marketing is much more concerned with behavioral changes and attitude shifts than it possibly can be in the hard conversion of cash and the ultimate profit motive, the end product of industrial marketing.

If due attention is given the marketing audit, the preliminary marketing process, and the other steps leading to marketing plans, there should be few reasons for marketing failure. Such a failure results when the health or human services organization pays little attention to competitors, does not keep its services up to date, does not identify its publics accurately, does not match its marketing to its organizational objectives, does not educate its staff or board as to the principles and benefits of marketing, does not work hard enough to obtain facts about the community, hesitates to try new ideas or programs, does not match its publications to its publics, does not discuss the marketing project sufficiently enough in staff meetings, does not put its marketing plans in writing, does not gauge adequately changes in user demands or the position of competition. The general problem in marketing, Thomas L. Berg notes in *Mismarketing*, "is the failure to get the facts and interpret them correctly."[18]

Marketing is meant to spread services to users who need them, achieve better than normal growth for the organization, assist in constructing a credible public image, generate a fair amount of revenue, and meet present and future competition. This book is intended to assist health and human services organizations as they review and challenge their own positions in the marketplace.

This work deals with the very practical aspects of establishing marketing within the organization. Management and the governing boards must have sufficient interest, enthusiasm, and commitment to give it a try. They will demand some demonstration of cost-effectiveness and productivity.

Who is responsible for marketing? Does it fit under the job description of the program director, the planning director, the public relations director, the fundraiser and development chief? Who on staff will be threatened by marketing? Who reports to whom?

All of these are common queries and concerns raised by organizations. From our own experiences, we suggest some ways of approaching the use of marketing, and we express a few cautions, too. Our ultimate purpose is to provide enough information about marketing to make it attractive and promising to the agency that wants to achieve better than normal growth and further its relations with its community.

SUMMARY

This book seeks to help persons in health and human services understand the meaning of marketing as a tool and how it complements their organization's management and planning processes. Social marketing, which seeks to increase acceptability of social ideas, causes, or practices, moves traditional industrial marketing techniques over into human services. Many misunderstand the word "marketing." Many of industrial marketing's precepts apply equally to social marketing, so much so that it is possible merely to substitute the word "service" for "product" and find substance in the interchange.

Exchange is the foundation of all marketing theory. It means that both parties—an organization and its clients, for example—have nearly equal benefits to bestow on each other in the marketing process. How exchanges are developed and managed is crucial to marketing.

Contemporary human services issues, such as rising costs, the role of advertising, competition, and rules and regulations, give rise to social marketing and its capacity to develop the organization's specific objectives into meaningful work plans.

Marketing's nine components are identified as the process of selecting and preparing the marketing project, research, the market audit, setting objectives, targeting, strategies, special promotional tools, internal adjustments, and evaluation/recycling. The four Ps of marketing—the marketing mix—are a beacon to those who build market plans. The mix involves the elements of product (service), promotion, place, and price. It is said that if this mix is absent in a project, no marketing occurs.

Organizations are regarded as prime candidates for social marketing if they are aggressive, present a positive attitude, enjoy departing from tradition, show initiative, are responsive to new ideas, and hold planning in high esteem. Marketing is not selling; it is a planned business system of achieving organizational objectives. "Selling tries to get the customer to want what the company has. Marketing tries to get the company to have what the customer wants," Theodore Levitt says.

Marketing is directive in its methods, selective in its use of tools. It can be employed improperly, especially if the organization does not bother to plumb the marketplace and determine its potential users' wants, needs, desires, and problems. All agencies have the potential for conducting marketing programs for specific projects. Agency size should be neither a deterrent nor an excuse for not using the marketing function.

NOTES

1. Philip Kotler, *Marketing Management* (Englewood Cliffs, N.J.: Prentice-Hall, Inc., 1976), p. 495.
2. Ibid., p. 7.
3. Ibid., p. 495.
4. Ibid.
5. Jay Diamond and Gerald Pintel, *Principles of Marketing* (Englewood Cliffs, N.J.: Prentice-Hall, Inc., 1972), p. 4.
6. Philip Kotler and Sidney J. Levy, *Society and Marketing* by Norman Kangun (New York: Harper & Row, Inc., 1972), p. 62.
7. Dan MacDonald, *A Guidebook for Establishment of a New Agency for Home Health Care* (St. Louis: The Home Health Consultancy, 1978), p. 178.
8. Robin E. Scott MacStravic, *Marketing Health Care* (Germantown, Md.: Aspen Systems Corp., 1977), p. 34.
9. Ibid., p. 27.
10. Christy Mardell, "Hospitals as Marketers: Ads Gain Favor," *Advertising Age*, February 21, 1977, p. 31.
11. Dan MacDonald, "Issues and Implications of Health Care Marketing." Remarks at seminar on health care marketing sponsored by the University of Missouri Health Services Management Alumni Association and the University of Missouri Program in Health Services Management, Columbia, Missouri, October 21, 1977.
12. William M. Pride and O. C. Ferrell, *Marketing: Basic Concepts and Decisions* (Boston: Houghton, Mifflin Co., 1977), p. 9.
13. Theodore Levitt, *The Marketing Mode* (New York: McGraw-Hill Book Co., 1969), p. 231.
14. Kotler and Levy, *Society and Marketing*, p. 64.
15. James M. Carman and Kenneth P. Uhl, *Phillip and Duncan's Marketing—Principles and Methods* (Homewood, Ill.: Richard D. Irwin, Inc., 1973), p. 362.
16. John M. Rathmell, *Marketing in the Service Sector* (Cambridge, Mass.: Winthrop Publications, Inc., 1974), pp. 6-8.
17. Carman and Uhl, *Phillip and Duncan's Marketing—Principles and Methods*, p. 362.
18. Thomas L. Berg, *Mismarketing* (New York: Doubleday and Co., 1970), p. 12.

Chapter 2

Marketing's Challenges to Boards and Administrators

Marketing in many ways is alien to some health and human services organizations, entities that have thrived for years, perhaps decades, by doing things the way they feel they ought to be done.

Robin E. Scott MacStravic wrote:

> Health care organizations . . . have tended to follow a nonmarketing approach or even an antimarketing approach in their planning and developmental efforts. Their basic philosophy has been that they should provide the best possible services as they see them, and—they hope—enough people will make use of those services to make their efforts worthwhile. In other words, the organization decides what it wants to do, and the public is supposed to be willing to have it done to them.[1]

Boards and chief executive officers often have tended to view their agencies as closed, rather than open, groups, preferring to steer a highly structured, autonomous course, making their own decisions and using little input from the outside.

With the development and refinement of mass media, the upsurge in patient and client educational programming, broader community representation among board members, and newer, less restrictive theories and prototypes of organizational models, some changes are very evident in the makeup and operating philosophies of human services groups. Prodded by marketing, with its emphasis on knowing clients and their problems, wants, needs, and expectations, many agencies are evolving into open systems of management.

THE INSTITUTION AND THE COMMUNITY

It is the mission of a hospital to sense the concerns of the surrounding community. The American Hospital Association stipulates that hospital boards define goals and objectives "to meet community health care needs."[2] The governing board of a hospital or a human services agency is asked to establish policies that coincide with community needs, to keep up with current literature and environmental developments that might affect the organization's future, and to coordinate all of the entity's professional interests with administrative, financial, and community requirements.

Enveloped by continuing problems with the economy, staffing, regulations, and planning, the community need factor often has received short shrift in many agencies; community needs are important and real, but internal needs have received higher priority. Marketing challenges this position, stating that there must be a systematic addressing of community needs simultaneously with all other needs and problems so that the organization can function healthily and totally within its environment.

It is a principle of general systems theory that biological and social systems are in constant interaction with their environment. This relatively new principle contrasts with the recent past when "the organization was considered as sufficiently independent so that its problems could be analyzed in terms of internal structure, tasks, and formal relationships—without reference to the external environment," according to Kast and Rosenzweig.[3]

An open system of management isn't possible without inputs in the form of energy, ideas, and feedback, as well as a system to transform the inputs into outputs or effective services. "The open system does not run down because it can import energy from the world around it," Katz and Kahn say.[4] The system converts incoming energy into new services, or training materials, or beneficient policies, or short-term or long-term plans. The services or products that the organization exports into the community "furnish the sources of energy for the repetition of the cycle of activities."[5] An open system draws nourishment from other institutions, clientele, suppliers, employees, regulators, and others. Unequivocally, such a system is not self-sufficient or self-contained.

A critical attribute of both marketing and the open system is reliance on feedback to the organization about the impact of its services. Although understanding the feedback process is vital to the organization's survival, many organizations have been lax in extracting reactions from clientele in any methodical manner. In a way, this oversight has made the job of informing the board of directors or administration about the community's reception of the organization's services much more difficult. Increasingly, boards are asking management to explain how the agency fits into the community and how its services are being accepted.

Marketing requires that management obtain continuous feedback about organizations in the community. Management must know about problems in target areas, demographic shifts, and other changes in the environment that could contribute to the organization's evolution. Katz and Kahn are plainspoken about the value of feedback: "If there is no corrective device to get the system back on its course, it will expend too much energy or it will ingest too much energetic input and no longer continue as a system."[6]

FOCUSING ON THE BOARD OF DIRECTORS

It is the agency board that must deal with the environment, the local community. The board theoretically represents a cross section of the community, especially the business and professional elements, that on request can provide ideas, advice, and services to the administration. For the most part, the board helps to make, and gives approval to, organizational strategies (including marketing) while the chief operating officer is involved with the coordinative aspects (and some of the strategy making). These distinctions are not always well-defined; there are many reasonable exceptions from organization to organization.

In a well-governed health and human services organization, as in industry, the board must be apprised of marketing planning, for marketing is—if accepted philosophically—a part of the comprehensive systems and planning of the agency. The board should be given reading references on marketing; it should be briefed either by management or by an outside expert on the application and benefits of social marketing; it should plan a retreat to discuss how marketing can alter agency programming and services, coalesce top and middle agency management, and contribute to organizational growth and income.

Furthermore, the board should consider the appointment of a marketing committee or the expansion of the public relations or community relations committee to embrace marketing. The committee should:

- offer comments on organizational marketing objectives and goals

- approve project marketing objectives and goals submitted by administration

- respond to invitations to contribute ideas and direction to the preliminary marketing process and initial marketing plans

- assist in writing parts of marketing plans

- counsel the marketing director or appropriate staff member when so requested

- ask for the counsel and advice from the staff marketer or an outside consultant

- inform the board about industrial marketing programs or the marketing of competing organizations

- participate in market research, such as interviewing or visiting potential or existing clients of the organization
- visit similar agencies in other areas to assess their marketing approach
- advocate marketing's presence within the organization
- participate in the marketing evaluation

The board marketing committee should not plan to initiate the draft marketing plans, interfere in the orderly gathering of intelligence and information by staff, or criticize or rebuke staff efforts without supporting evidence or sound alternative approaches. The committee should comment on the first draft of a marketing plan, working with the marketer to tighten, alter, or expand it. In some organizations committee members will team with staff to produce a marketing plan. At times, it will be the board and staff members who will present the draft to the executive director for comment and direction.

Each organization and each board is a different entity, each with markedly different characteristics and personalities. Some boards are extremely liberal in makeup and actions; others are equally conservative. Many are extraordinarily well informed about the programs and activities of their organizations; others have little understanding of their institution's function or impact in the community. Marketing is more or less likely to be championed by organizations that are not so indelibly linked with conservative streams in the community and that have a history of experimenting with new programs and ideas. A Houston-based study by Howard B. Kaplan found that boards that were perceived by the agency executive director as "pragmatically oriented" and as "giving major consideration to the expressed desires of the client population" tended to be associated with agencies "which have histories of more implementation of program changes."[7]

In our years of evangelizing the merits of marketing, the authors have found that governing boards tend to ask tough questions before they are willing to risk money, training, or experimentation for the sake of marketing. Some of our answers are not always clean-cut simply because they depend on the nature of the board, its hired management, and the quality of the program or institution involved.

But the questions remain. Some recurring board member questions, and our generalized responses follow:

Q. *Will marketing cause us to stray from serving those who can't pay to those who can pay for our services?*

A. No, not unless by intent. Marketing is not focused solely on monetary return, on changing client markets, or in any way on destroying the original mission of the organization.

Q. *Won't marketing create an overwhelming demand for our services that perhaps can't be paid for?*

A. Marketing deals with a total picture: promotion of services must be measured against sources of reimbursement; client intake must be tied to staff capacity. Existing overdemand for service can be addressed, too, by a demarketing effort. Marketing aims to fit program components together, not to stimulate one without an equal response from the other.

Q. *Will marketing change the relationship between our organization and clients, our contributors, our various constituencies?*

A. Yes, it should. Most service organizations have not been accustomed to think of clients, contributors, or others in terms of exchange. Marketing forces a reexamination of the needs, wants, opinions, and dissatisfactions of those the organization deals with as well as the shaping of better relationships.

Q. *Is marketing ethical in a health or human services agency?*

A. The question generally is based on past skepticism toward business and industrial marketing practices. Nothing in marketing implies or condones amoral applications; indeed, leading authors stress the necessity of a high sense of moral propriety in order to make marketing more effective.

Q. *Is marketing cost-effective?*

A. Without hesitation, yes, in many ways. Tools of marketing, for example, are stringently examined and used on a limited, target directed basis. Surveys, client assessments, and staff reviews point to the most effective use of agency resources at the lowest possible cost. The agency marketing audit alone should produce savings in several areas.

Q. *Are there other byproducts of marketing besides the successful implementation of a specific objective?*

A. There are many, including:

- knowledge of the agency's marketing environment, its own operations, its competition, all of which can be used in other marketing projects

- a results-oriented implementation program that is satisfying to employees and the board

- satisfied clients or patients

- internal adjustments in operations uncovered by the marketing approach

- more directive public relation tools

Q. *How big does an organization have to be to adopt a marketing approach?*
A. Since we advocate a limited, project-by-project approach rather than a total agency marketing plan, size is no deterrent. Of course, a large agency can hire a marketing director to complement specialized staff in public relations, planning and fund-raising. A one-person (with secretary) operation is another matter, but marketing techniques, if not all of their accoutrements, can be adapted to the service, cause, or project that the agency desires to address. Only the scale of the project differs. The small or medium-sized agency still must do its research, identify targets, and plan strategies.

Q. *What staff capabilities do we need to undertake marketing?*
A. First, a sense of curiosity and inquiry, then a willingness to explore and experiment with new systems. Marketing can be taught and learned. Creativity, imagination, and adventure are innate, not taught. If the agency's chief executive officer will lead the marketing effort, productive efforts throughout the staff usually will be forthcoming.

Q. *What are the dangers of marketing?*
A. Marketing is a discipline that can be abused easily simply by becoming enamored with its process and losing sight of the original goals. When selling becomes the overriding goal of marketing, to the exclusion of maintaining the best interests of clients and consumers, the integrity of the discipline is damaged.

THE ADMINISTRATOR IN MARKETING

If marketing has been accepted as a management tool, the agency administrator must become conversant with marketing principles. The executive should read texts on the subject, attend workshops, and establish a direct reporting routine with the staff marketer.

Although the administrator must rely on the marketer for the preparation of drafts of marketing plans, the chief executive officer (CEO), can interface with the marketer: (1) by forwarding updated short-range and long-range plans and other documents; (2) by including marketing in top managerial councils; (3) by providing rough sketches and outlines of marketing challenges and problems with hypothetical approaches to solutions; (4) by endorsing plans for marketing research and participating in the preliminary marketing process; (5) by meeting regularly with the marketer to work out problems in research, market access, or planning; (6) by endorsing a triad arrangement among marketing, public relations, and planning; (7) by providing marketing entree to the board of directors; (8) by advocating the principles of marketing before the board and its committees; (9) by assisting in carrying out market plan strategies; (10) by participating constructively in the continuing evaluation and recycling of each plan; and (11) by supporting client feedback systems developed by the organization.

The administrator, Kast and Rosenzweig point out, serves as a "boundary agent" between the organization and environmental systems. "The business organization has many interfaces with other systems: suppliers of materials, the local community, prospective employees, unions, customers, and state, local, and federal agencies."[8]

A strong and effective executive director, says Kaplan, knows the community well but often is dissatisfied with the amount of interest that the community shows in the agency. The director is viewed as being ahead of community thinking on social matters, is protected from community pressures by the board, becomes deeply involved in agency program expansion, whenever possible avoids the ramifications of duplicated services, and accepts full responsibility for actions of subordinates.[9] Most of these CEO characteristics coincide with those of marketing: taking the initiative, showing aggressiveness, performing against tradition, responding to the needs and desires of the surrounding environment.

In an open system, "management faces situations which are dynamic, inherently uncertain, and frequently ambiguous. Management is not in full control of all the factors of production, as suggested by traditional theory. It is strongly restrained by many environmental and internal forces."[10] Marketing, then, is a crucial weapon in helping administrators understand the restraints and the opportunities that exist within the internal subsystems of their own organizations as well as in their communities.

"The one enduring objective (of the open system) is the effort to build and maintain a predictable, reciprocating system of relationships," Leonard Sayles notes in his respected book, *Managerial Behavior*.[11] A health or human services organization that agrees with such an observation should strongly explore marketing's contributions to help keep the institution's dynamics in a steadily upward state.

SUMMARY

Some organizations traditionally have been self-contained, deciding which programs and services are best for the community without seeking its wisdom, opinions, or suggestions. Population, news media, and management changes have convinced many executives that perhaps the first law of ecology—everything is connected to everything else—applies pointedly to their own institutions. The significance of this is that there is a growing belief that, with social institutions in constant interaction with their environments, it is highly important to reckon with the appropriate forces in the community.

Since most organizational charters call for board and management to respond to community needs, the inherent characteristics of marketing are appropriate to help institutions carry out charter mandates. Marketing is community oriented and supportive of the open system of management that views the organization as being an integral, working part of the changing, dynamic environment. In an open system that uses marketing, board marketing committees and the chief executive officer have definite roles of advocacy and participation.

NOTES

1. Robin E. Scott MacStravic, *Marketing Health Care* (Germantown, Md.: Aspen Systems Corp., 1977), p. x (preface).

2. Jonathan S. Rakich, Ph.D., et al., *Managing Health Care Organizations* (Philadelphia: W. B. Saunders Co., 1977), p. 187.

3. Fremont E. Kast and James E. Rosenzweig, *Organization and Management: A Systems Approach* (New York: McGraw-Hill Book Co., 1974), p. 109.

4. Daniel Katz and Robert L. Kahn, *The Social Psychology of Organizations* (New York: John Wiley & Sons, Inc., 1966), p. 19.

5. Ibid., p. 20.

6. Ibid., p. 22.

7. Howard B. Kaplan, "Implementation of Program Change in Community Agencies—Studies of Organizational Innovation" (Houston: The Community Council), pp. 86-90.

8. Kast and Rosenzweig, *Organization and Management: A Systems Approach*, p. 114.

9. Kaplan, "Implementation of Program Change," pp. 132-139.

10. Kast and Rosenzweig, *Organization and Management: A Systems Approach*, p. 123.

11. Leonard Sayles, *Managerial Behavior* (New York: McGraw-Hill Book Co., 1964), pp. 258-259.

Chapter 3

Selection of the Marketing Project

Unless an agency has an extremely narrow focus in the type of client served or service offered, it is not practical to develop an organizationwide marketing plan. Properly applied, marketing looks intently at a given situation, develops a detailed set of actions, and requires implementation on most flexible terms. For the beginning marketer, an introduction to social marketing is accomplished best by addressing one organizational objective at a time. Even the experienced marketer refrains from trying to solve every problem simultaneously or to take advantage of every opportunity. In health and human services, there is too much work that requires concentration and, unlike the business world, most institutions do not have enough personnel or money to cover normal service operations adequately, let alone to support innumerable special objectives.

Marketing project selection should be conducted with much discrimination. Selection is a decision by management, which usually can choose from a wide range of objectives, problems, opportunities, or situations. Selection seems to parallel the priority setting in which managers normally are engaged. A manager indicates preference for a project, then applies whatever resources are available. What is unusual is the frequency with which managers who may be engulfed in administrative minutiae, personnel problems, and "fire fighting" require help with organizational priorities and in gaining a perspective on the operational futures of their institutions.

Most health and human services organizations identify certain problems or opportunities that can be translated into potential marketing projects or seek to accomplish, in a marketing sense, specific objectives that may have been suggested by one or more problems or opportunities. Most organizations have short-range and long-range objectives that also can be weighed for their marketing promise.

Among the questions we are asked frequently are: "What is the difference between marketing plans, annual work programs, and long-range planning?" and "How does one determine what should be a marketing project?" When selecting marketing projects, initial reference to a simple glossary can be helpful:

Mission: The basic purpose of the organization—why it exists, who it serves, what its ultimate aims are.

Goal: A general statement of broad direction or intent with no time limit, although usually covering a period of years.

Objective: A proposed result to be achieved that will contribute to accomplishment of a goal; generally, an objective has a specified time for completion and if possible is stated in measurable terms.

Criteria: A series of standards or guidelines that are applied to judgment about the acceptability/nonacceptability of a project.

Priorities: A weighing or ranking of objectives and/or work plans to determine their relative importance, i.e., which should be approached first, which should receive the greater resources.

Work program: Written time-phased action steps and assignments detailing how an objective will be reached.

Marketing plan: A detailed analysis of factors affecting a project contained in the work program, plus identification of targets and strategies necessary to accomplish objectives; an internal management document.

Long-range plan: Generally covers a projection of goals, objectives, projects, programs, facilities, and changes desired in the organization that are to occur in a period of five or ten years, or longer.

Long-range plans necessarily are more general than precise in stating goals and objectives; the longer the span of the projected plan, the more imprecise will be the details and the more it may become a wish list instead of a will-do list. Work programs provide impetus for an organization to undertake tasks or accomplish some objectives within a given period, usually one or two years. A marketing project may well have originated in a long-range plan, been inserted later into an annual work program, then extracted as a simple element for implementation.

Another distinction is in the degree of publication. Long-range plans often are circulated widely to inform various publics about the organization's developmental dreams and intentions. An annual work program contains the tasks—some mundane, some expansive—that the organization will undertake. It generally receives less public attention. A marketing plan, however, is strictly an internal document; its details, which are much more exact, are not meant to be conveyed to just anyone, especially the competition. A marketing plan is related to a specific objective while a work program covers all of the agency's projects. A marketing plan covers who, what, when, where, why, and how; a work program only suggests such details in broad form. A marketing plan is likened to a road map, a work program to the globe.

Whether a work program element or a management objective requires a marketing approach depends on the complexity of existing issues, problems, and opportunities. Examples are:

1. A family counseling agency wants to open a full time, full service branch office in a nearby community. It might develop a marketing plan if:

- there is strong competition in the same marketplace
- there is no competition, but prospective clients need to be informed about services to be offered
- there are negative public or professional attitudes about counseling
- there is a need for the branch to be financially self-supporting by an early date

The family agency might not use marketing if:

- it is concerned that there will be excess demand for its services and wants to avoid it
- it is not concerned about public opinion toward its service, or client acceptance
- it has been begged or coerced by numerous persons or groups to establish itself in the nearby community
- it is financially secure

2. An executive wants to overhaul the entire personnel area of the organization, including policies, practices, salary ranges, and salary administration. The administrator might turn to marketing if:

- employee morale and attitudes have been a problem
- a substantial revision and increase in salary levels would surely be a result
- the board of directors has no appreciation of personnel matters

- an employee union exists

- instances of discrimination in dealing with employees are known

The executive may not need to put objectives on the marketing level if:

- the number of employees is less than 20

- pay scales and fringe benefits are relatively liberal

- the job market for agency employees is heavily on the side of the employer

- open and frequent communication between board and staff exists

PLANNING AGENCIES IN PROJECT SELECTION

Area agencies on aging, health and welfare councils, and health systems agencies (HSAs) are planning bodies whose main business is dealing with problems and the development of projects and programs in the health and human services field. The aging and health systems agencies are required to have annual work programs because most of their support comes from the federal government, which demands program and financial accountability. The health and welfare councils (called by various names such as community service councils, planning and resource development councils, or federations for community planning) are local, citizen organized, and not subject to governmental control. Many of them have been in existence 40 to 60 years, while the agencies on aging and the HSAs are of recent vintage.

Each of the planning organizations could address numerous objectives. Choice of projects is a critical issue. The experiences of health systems agencies in defining their plans are enlightening examples. HSAs must comply with uniform guidelines and regulations with respect to their basic programs as well as conduct regulatory and project review of the financing of all local health services and capital construction proposals. All are required to produce five-year health systems plans (HSPs), updated periodically, that contain analyses of, and prescriptions for, improvement in key areas such as acute bed care, rehabilitation, long-term care, mental health, and emergency medical services. Each HSA must produce an annual implementation plan (AIP), which is mostly an extraction of objectives from the five-year HSP. Theoretically, the AIP represents the HSA's thrust of work and effort.

With small professional staffs and often minimal funding, many HSAs face enormous problems in carrying out all of the objectives in their annual implementation plans. One problem is that of restricting the number of annual objectives so that implementation can be both realistic and digestible.

Although HSAs list anywhere from 20 to 70 annual objectives for implementation, generally only a handful of objectives can be accomplished successfully in a 12-month period. The authors' own informal research among HSA executives in training sessions found that an agency with 30 to 40 distinct work objectives in its AIP would do well if three were completed successfully in the prescribed period. Part of the problem is that high expectations—a surfeit of objectives—rarely are coupled with the pragmatics of funding, staff capability, and unforeseen project barriers.

HSAs are not alone in having insatiable appetites for achieving goals and yet only limited means to complete the job. Any organization in direct service, planning, or fund-raising maintains a list of desired objectives. Its early efforts must be directed at sorting and ranking objectives, an exercise that will help immeasurably to dictate staff activity for a given period. Over several years, we have helped planning agencies, hospitals, nursing homes, counseling agencies, and specialized schools develop some easily applied tools and methods to select objectives, goals, and programs that can be translated into successful marketing projects. Without a trustworthy priority selection process, an organization can disperse its resources so erratically that little or nothing gets done when it should or its effective growth is retarded or delayed.

PRIORITY PROJECT SELECTION SYSTEM

The seven steps the authors suggest in developing a system of priorities for implementing marketing projects are the following:

1. List the stated or publicly known objectives from the annual work program, a new agency study, or any other pertinent organizational document in terms that describe potential projects. Example: A written objective of an HSA might be: "To influence the direction of policy setting and financing of health care services in the state." However, described as a potential marketing project, it might read: "We will assign board members and staff to develop contacts and maintain liaison with key state officials and legislators in order to promote our health program funding goals for next year."
2. Rough sort potential projects into those that will require major or minor commitment of activity, those that will have major or minor impact on the objectives, and those that will be of major or minor importance to the interests of the board of directors and management.
3. Use a program/project profile if more than three or four projects emerge with the classification of "major" to note all pertinent facts that must be part of a decision to begin a marketing project.

4. Develop criteria to rank each proposed project.
5. Identify what are considered to be the most important projects. In the selection process, the marketer will want to combine similar types of projects, discard others that may be too ambitious or costly, and eventually rank the remainder by importance.
6. Apply a preliminary marketing process to each selected project. This preliminary approach should provide the marketer with a quick look at the feasibility of moving ahead before much time or money is invested.
7. Transfer the product of the preliminary marketing process to the form of an initial analysis that may serve as a rough guide to the ultimate marketing plan.

This process is useful only if there are many optional projects to be whittled down. It is not necessary to prepare profiles if the decision to employ marketing is an obvious one.

THE MARKETING PROGRAM/PROJECT PROFILE

The marketing program/project profile is a management tool that can be used in several ways. Most often, a project is proposed by a department head or a staff member or emerges from a committee or board meeting. Usually it is expressed at first as an idea or concept. If the idea or concept appears to have merit, the person might be asked to present a one-page outline at a staff meeting so that it can be discussed at length. If it survives the management discussion as well as other steps that have been outlined, a full description of the proposed project is suggested, and the profile probably is used as a tool.

Profiles usually are prepared by a principal staff member or marketer before the organization's annual work program is determined, but not always. Potential projects seem to have a habit of surfacing after the work program has been adopted. A profile, in fact, may be developed at any time. Its main contribution to organizational decision-making is to list all key factors so that policy makers and administrators can judge the project with similar information and as objectively as possible.

While the authors illustrate here (Exhibit 3-1) only one example of a profile, we have prepared many variations for clients, and sometimes they have produced their own. This form contains 11 sections, followed by suggestions to help in completing the profile.

Exhibit 3-1 Marketing Program/Project Profile Form

COMMUNITY SERVICE COUNCIL

Project No:___

1. Project title: _____ Date: _____

   _____

2. General description (statement of problem or opportunity):

   _____
   _____
   _____

3. Objective of project: _____

   _____
   _____

4. Products: _____

   _____
   _____

5. Justification (document reason to undertake project):

   _____

   A. Source of proposal (who originated and why): _____

      _____
      _____

   B. Bylaws, regulations/guidelines applicable: _____

      _____
      _____

   C. Timeliness and available resources: _____

      _____
      _____

   D. Board, committee or task force (prior recommendations):

      _____
      _____
      _____

   E. Relation to management, informal goals: _____

      _____
      _____
      _____

Exhibit 3–1 continued

6. Previous activity in this project area: _____

_____

_____

_____

_____

7. Project value (applicability of criteria):

	High	Medium	Low	Comment
A. Relevancy to our objective	☐	☐	☐	_____
B. Severity of the problem	☐	☐	☐	_____
C. Support from providers/funders	☐	☐	☐	_____
D. Benefit to service providers	☐	☐	☐	_____
E. Practicability of achievement	☐	☐	☐	_____
F. Council creditability/visibility	☐	☐	☐	_____
G. Cost/service effectiveness	☐	☐	☐	_____
H. Investment in committee staff time	☐	☐	☐	_____
I. Financial investment required	☐	☐	☐	_____
J. Future trade value	☐	☐	☐	_____

8. Feasibility of project:

A. Positive aspects: _____

_____

_____

B. Negative aspects: _____

_____

Exhibit 3–1 continued

_____

_____

9. Initial ranking
   of project: *Comment*

   Scale   1 (high) _____
           2   _____
           3   _____
           4   _____
           5   _____
           6   _____
           7   _____
           8   _____
           9   _____
          10 (low)   _____

10. Action on project:

    ☐ Ask staff for more details or justification
    ☐ Assign to subcommittee for review and recommendation
    _____
    ☐ Refer to board for decision on whether or not to undertake
      project
    ☐ Table project for reconsideration. Date:_____
    ☐ Reject project
    ☐ Recommend to board for inclusion in work program

11. Final ranking of project:

    This project has priority of:
    ☐ A Projects in which sufficient volunteer, staff and other re-
        sources *must* be found and brought to bear for attainment
        of project objectives
    ☐ B Projects in which volunteer, staff and other resources
        should be made available but not at the sacrifice of pro-
        gram projects in Category A
    ☐ C Projects which will be undertaken if and when sufficient vol-
        unteer, staff and other resources are available

Notes on the Marketing Program/Project Profile

Box: (in upper right-hand corner, first page) insert identifying number on each project and date of initiation.

1. Project title: a simple statement that will identify the project easily.
2. General description: no more than one paragraph; state the problem or opportunity to be resolved.
3. Objective: one paragraph describing the primary objective and purpose of the project.
4. Products: expectations such as new service, building, or policies.
5. Justification: quotations, actions, regulations, and recommendations from sources such as reports, legal documents, articles, or memoranda that suggest or mandate reasons for including the project in the work program.
6. Previous activity: past experiences of the agency with similar projects or efforts to deal with one or more elements of the proposed program, described candidly.
7. Project value: based on the organization's own criteria for selecting projects, check one of the boxes and make comments, if appropriate.
8. Feasibility of project: considering the criteria, what are the factors influencing the decision and what are the positive and negative features?
9. Initial ranking: in view of all factors and criteria, how does this project rank? Use numerical estimate of 1 for high and 10 for low; add comments.
10. Action on projects: once the profile is completed, more information or discussion may be needed; a disposition must be made: accept, reject, or table.
11. Final ranking: after all projects have been reviewed, each is given a priority that reflects the relative importance to the organization; use our classification or develop one.

CRITERIA FOR RANKING PROJECTS

Each organization must devise its own criteria to assess how it will rank its proposed projects and to determine what priority will be assigned. The sample form provides a hypothetical listing of criteria suitable for some health and human services organizations, but it may not be suitable for the particular needs of others. Much depends on each agency's maturity, how developed or undeveloped are its service programs, or how prominent are its written goals. Most managers, furthermore, are likely to have a few unwritten goals that will relate to the capacity of their organizations to be truly effective; these become a part of the administrator's personal criteria for project selection and implementation.

An administrator of a large health systems agency once expressed some personal goals that were felt to be critical to the long-term effectiveness of the agency. These were expressed nowhere in official or even unofficial documents; they didn't belong there. But they are worth repeating since they illustrate the quiet agenda that every manager of a health or human services institution develops if the executive is at all concerned with results. This manager had as personal goals:

- Acquiring permanent designation by the then Department of Health, Education, and Welfare as the health systems agency for that region as quickly as possible in order to dispel any question about the ultimate authority of the organization. (In the beginning, all HSAs were given temporary designation until HEW was assured of their ability to function adequately. Although HSAs were created in 1975-76, some were not given permanent designation for long periods of time; in addition, HEW cancelled the funding of a number of them because of dissatisfaction over performance.)

- Finding ways of burrowing within the medical and hospital professional communities that the manager viewed as the seat of power for the control of health care planning and financing in the area.

- Acquiring within the general community a respect for the planning competence of the HSA so that its recommendations and actions would be meaningful and successful.

Another administrator assumed responsibility for operation of a community planning council that recently had undergone self-evaluation and reorganization. Although the council had a record of successful performance as a planning body, the situation was not too dissimilar from that of the HSA. There was a new administration, a smaller board of directors, and an announced aim of broadening its programs and planning interests. These were viewed with varying degrees of concern by constituents.

Neither the reorganized council nor the new HSA had a performance record. Both had to gain initial acceptance from their own internal and external constituencies, then from the rest of their publics. Thus, the selection of program (and marketing) projects is important to new and existing organizations. For the community planning council, the following criteria were developed for the board of directors in making its decisions. (Note that these criteria correspond to those shown previously on the program/project profile.)

1. Relevancy to council objectives: The project's potential contribution to meeting the stated formal and internal (management) objectives of the council is considered to be the primary guideline. Does it have direct

impact on, or is it peripheral to, the thrust to improve human services and delivery?

2. Severity of the problem: The particular problem or issue is of considerable importance. Does it impact on a large number of people, or will its ripple effect create a potentially serious community problem? Does it have a bearing on other problems? Will our involvement serve a remedial purpose?

3. Support from providers and funders: There is a question as to the value of taking on a project if the council is unable to arouse community interest in the particular problem, issue, or opportunity. Are service providers seriously interested in addressing the project? Is there a likelihood that funding can be found if it is required? Can a successful case be made for provider/funder participation in planning and implementation?

4. Benefit to service providers: A criterion in line with our intent to help develop the most effective service delivery system possible is the ultimate effect that the project will have on those organizations that have direct service responsibilities. Will the project eliminate duplicative or obsolete services? Will the quality of service be improved? Will the project help the service provider's own clients or new ones?

5. Practicability of achievement: The council is not, nor will it ever be, able to afford the luxury of taking on projects of huge magnitude or that are purely speculative. We are concerned with both short-range and long-range returns as well as the feasibility of project success. Is a program or project goal readily achievable, or is it more likely to involve years of work with relatively intangible results?

6. Council creditability/visibility: The council is attempting to find its proper niche in the human services planning spectrum because of a relatively new administration and reorganization, its announced interest in conducting community-oriented planning, and the recent amalgamation. We must consider whether a particular project will be likely to enhance our creditability/visibility with our clients and in the community. Will our involvement be merely busywork or of real significance?

7. Cost/service effectiveness: Paramount to the improved delivery of human services are two factors: (a) finding better ways of serving persons and meeting their needs and, (b) improving the dollar effectiveness of the service unit. Will council involvement in the project have a substantial impact in either or both areas? Will efficiency as well as effectiveness be achieved? Can more service be provided at less cost?

8. Investment of committee and staff time: The council's major resources are people (volunteer and professional). The former are key to our system of operation, the latter serve the volunteer committee system and provide expertness of a special nature. Deployment of staff time is a

most critical administrative decision, so we must consider staffing requirements carefully. Do we have the ability to provide competent professionals who have adequate time to serve the project?

9. Financial investment required: We may expect extra expenses that must be included in the project in addition to the normal staff and program budget. Will EDP equipment be a necessity? Will outside consultant services be useful? Will there be products that will require extra financing?

10. Future trade value: Sometimes a project that appears to deviate from our main organizational objectives may be undertaken as a favor to a client. The reasons may be political, but they will be pragmatic. It is important to know whether acceding to the request is nonproductive or whether it will produce an IOU or future support to help reach various other objectives.

The marketing program/project profile allows the marketer to judge whether a project is to receive high, medium, or low marks in relation to specific criteria. This exercise is most useful, especially in judging the project's possibilities for implementation and as a prelude to making a final disposition.

To illustrate a completed profile, we conclude the chapter with an actual project considered by an HSA, an automated management information system. The headings on the form shown are different in this example because they were adapted to the peculiar requirements of the HSA.

The project situation is this: The health systems agency had produced its first five-year health systems plan (HSP) and its first annual implementation plan (AIP). To do so, it had to gather considerable data from many sources. It soon became evident that there were severe shortcomings in some areas; either the data simply didn't exist or service institutions and providers would not release them. The HSP contained several disclaimers that obviously helped to negate the quality of the plan itself. "If they don't have all the facts, how can they make realistic recommendations?" asked one critic.

It became clear to the HSA's management that building and maintaining a sound, automated management information system for health would be essential for its own creditability. It would enhance the professionalism of its work and would help establish its authority as a regional planning agency. The undertaking required additional personnel, equipment, and financing. The project did not stem from an objective found in the HSP or AIP but was on a long list of management objectives. The size of the commitment meant that the management information system had to be measured with all the other objectives and projects for the next year. It was a matter of choosing between long-term research capability or short-term efforts in major program areas such as acute care bed reduction, new rehabilitation services, and others. To help dramatize the importance of the project, management used the profile to assist an administrative committee in setting priorities for work on all projects.

The completed profile for the HSA's project (Exhibit 3-2) contains a few variations from the form exhibited earlier in this chapter that are explained as follows:

- The box on the first page showing the project number indicates whether it originated from the AIP or from management's list of objectives.

- The subheadings under "Justification" refer to the HSA's own sources. For example, "State SHCC guidelines" pertains to the State Health Coordinating Council, a body in each state that is the counterpart to local HSAs and is responsible for setting goals and objectives (and projects) for improvement of health of the total state population.

- The ranking system at the end of the form varies solely to meet the HSA's own methods of priority setting.

Exhibit 3-2 Sample of an Actual HSA Project Form

```
┌─────────────────────────────────────────────────────────┐
│              PROGRAM/PROJECT PRIORITY                    │
│                                    ┌──────────────────┐  │
│                                    │    Project No.    │  │
│                                    │                  │  │
│                                    │  AIP_____      │  │
│  1. Project name: Comprehensive    │                  │  │
│     Management In-                  │                  │  │
│     formation System (M.I.S.) for  │  Org.     5      │  │
│     Health                          └──────────────────┘  │
│                                                           │
│  2. General description: Identify present and potential   │
│     sources of health data; determine needs for data to  │
│     carry out HSA man-dates; design and develop automated │
│     system for storage, retrieval and use.                │
│                                                           │
│  3. Objective: To become the central, authoritative       │
│     source and repository of health data in our planning  │
│     region in order to provide a foundation for the most  │
│     effective health planning program possible.           │
│                                                           │
│  4. Justification (as documented):                        │
│     A.  HSP/AIP citations: Data are lacking in following   │
│         crucial planning areas:                            │
│         —hospital discharge (HSP, pages IV-12-13)          │
│         —inpatient morbidity (HSP, page IV-21)             │
└─────────────────────────────────────────────────────────┘
```

Exhibit 3–2 continued

   —ambulatory health care (HSP, pages VI-13, 22, 27)
   —long-term care (HSP, page VII-2)
   —cost data for health care (HSP, pages IX-3,5,7,22)
B. Federal guidelines: General charge to develop and maintain data base
C. State SHCC guidelines: Of 25 recommended actions from state office, at least 11 require use of information not currently at hand.
D. Board, plan development, task force recommendations: Plan Development Committee has criticized our lack of various data bases, our inability to get all providers and agencies to release information and our manual system of analysis and utilization of what we do have.
E. Management (internal) objectives: Agreement on need for M.I.S. development. Administration views such a program as a primary tool to be used for gaining leverage with primary care providers in particular.
F. Other: Data requests from health care providers are increasing steadily. Have board volunteers who are interested and have the data processing expertise to assist, which makes consideration now most timely.

5. Applicability of criteria/strategies:

	High	Medium	Low	Comment
A. Project visibility	☐	☐	☐	_____
B. Practicability of achievement	☐	☐	☐	Need provider help
C. Benefit to client	☐	☐	☐	_____
D. Benefit to HSP objectives	☐	☐	☐	Strengthens planning
E. Investment of staff time	☐	☐	☐	
F. Potential for staff development	☐	☐	☐	Must add to staff
G. Investment required— new tools	☐	☐	☐	Requires computer access

Exhibit 3–2 continued

H. Community rela-
   tions benefit   ☐   ☐   ☐   ———————
I. Agency planning
    credibility   ☐   ☐   ☐   ———————
J. Future trade-off   Little competi-
    value   ☐   ☐   ☐   tion

6. Judgment of feasibility of project:
   A. Positive aspects: Budget will permit considerable develop-
      ment; have basic staff competence aboard; strong support
      from board of directors; need apparent to most people.
   B. Negative aspects: Size of job is awesome to staff; providers
      with information are concerned about client/patient confiden-
      tiality; must do some original research to achieve maximum
      capability.

7. Initial sort/ranking (as priority):

                                    Comment
   Scale: 1   This program is a *must* for the
           ②   agency in order for us to carry
           3   out our long-term goals.
           4
           5
           6
           7
           8
           9
          10

8. Final ranking (as priority):
           1
           2
          ③
           4
           5
           6
           7
           8
           9
          10

SUMMARY

A marketing plan is prepared most practically for one, two, or a few organizational objectives, not for the total operation and all of its projects and objectives. Selection of which objective or objectives should be marketed eventually is a matter of much prudence, an exercise in which managers must not lose their focus on organizational priorities. Many ideas and concepts for marketing projects arise from existing problems and opportunities known to the agency staff or from written objectives or sections of the annual work program. Others come about well after the work program has been designed and begun. They, too, can be measured against the projects already in the marketing process.

Because they have many objectives to contend with on an annual basis, a health systems agency, an area agency on aging, or a community planning council can provide good examples of how objectives must be sorted and ranked in order for a particular project to gain priority over another and receive the attention it deserves. Most health and human services organizations can follow our guidelines for project selection although all organizations will want to develop their own criteria as they relate to their own surroundings.

A useful tool to begin the selection process is the marketing program/project profile that is applied in order to describe the potential project fully. Both a blank and a completed, varied profile are included in this chapter.

Criteria for ranking projects should be given much attention; some managers also will want to include their unwritten goals or objectives for the future of the organization. Ten criteria for project ranking and selection, developed for a community planning council, are included as an illustration of what an efficient administrator might do before a project is chosen for marketing.

Chapter 4

The Preliminary Marketing Process

Now that the agency has selected projects that may be worthy of the social marketing approach, it is necessary to preplan for each marketing project separately. The proper groundwork can mean success or failure for the entire marketing program. This initial process is the vehicle that brings every element of marketing into proper focus and makes the project tenable. In many ways, the preliminary process is similar to the product development stage of industrial marketing.

A marketing plan is not something that can be given birth to instantly; it does not appear suddenly, the result of a miraculous conjuring. Instead, it is put together carefully and patiently with as much thought applied to the preliminary steps as to the final ones.

In searching for reasons why market plans can't get started or simply fail, the authors have found that the most frequent reason is a lack of planning or preparation, plus a fuzzy concept often held by beginning marketers that once a target is identified correctly and strategies are acceptable, the market plan is impregnable. It just doesn't work that way.

The person who assumes the marketing responsibility for an organization will discover through experience the reasons for much care at the beginning:

- that, at the outset of the project, there is no way in which the individual will have full knowledge of all phases of the organization's program or marketing objectives

- that other people in the organization, from managers to support staff, must be brought along, must understand their roles in the project, and must agree as to how to proceed

- that a little advance preparation will save time and prevent endless searching for a handle to the project

- that the marketer's own self-confidence is heightened when a few signposts can guide the work

In effect, the marketer begins a building process within the organization, a program that uses anyone who can affect the project's ultimate success.

SIX STEPS IN THE PRELIMINARY PROCESS

Mastery of the preliminary process is tantamount to completing a part of the actual marketing plan before writing its initial draft. Good processing can eliminate irrelevant details, identify specific issues, and provide the central direction that the plan should take. Above all, the process is a strong acknowledgment that marketing includes not only the ability to think, write, manage, or ask good questions, it also includes the ability to plan, to forecast, to ask where the organization stands on certain projects or programs, how it will fare in the months or years ahead, and what it will take to make the project achievable.

The six-step preliminary process involves:

1. deliberating within staff about the nature of the project and the marketplace
2. listing of preliminary project objectives
3. identifying obstacles to the success of the project
4. detailing opportunities that may exist
5. establishing general categories of targets
6. outlining an initial approach or plan of work for the project

These steps are not finite. The marketer may wish to add to or remove from them. The inquisitiveness of the marketer and key staff members is more important than the form of inquiry. The six steps in the process now are examined in sequence.

Deliberating within Staff about the Nature of the Project and the Marketplace

The marketer involves certain people from the start: first, the appropriate administrative staff, then other personnel who will be responsible for carrying out various actions. Some organizations as a matter of practice include board or committee members who serve as advisers and advocates.

The reasons for such participation are:

- to be sure all participants understand the nature and ramifications of the project and its objectives

- to acquire as much information as possible from those who are able to provide it

- to discuss the roles expected of various units or departments of the organization

- to fix a preliminary project timetable

- to create an atmosphere of teamwork rather than the impression that the marketer is the sole planner and implementer

Assessing the marketplace is a step perhaps more familiar to politicians and baby food makers than to human services managers. There must be foreknowledge of the marketplace—its geographic and demographic threads, its contours, its character. Regrettably, few organizations are well-informed about their constituencies because, unless forced to go out into the community and ask questions about how their services are received and if they are needed, managers must rely on hearsay, hunches, and staff feedback that may reflect only the positive. To many institutions, this indirect contact has been good enough. It is not sufficient for marketing purposes.

The marketer does not attempt to achieve precision in these early discussions but seeks impressions and clues and enough facts to marshal a plan of attack. If the organization traditionally has been introspective, a recent study of operations or marketing audit may be available. But in most organizations the marketer starts with a minimum of background.

If it were hypothesized that the project would involve the development of a new adult day care and multiservice center by the local council on aging, it would be easy to develop pertinent questions that could be categorized as follows:

Existing Providers and Competition

- What other institutions in our area offer services or programs similar to what we propose?

- How long have they been providing these services?

- How extensive is their penetration of the marketplace?

- How will existing providers (competitors) greet the announcement of our proposed project?

- What are our chances of competing evenly with other providers?

Rules and Regulations

- What rules and regulations will have to be met if our project is to be successful?

- What regulatory bodies must we deal with?
- What future regulatory problems might we face?

Consumers of Services

- Who will be the primary users of our services?
- What will motivate people to use our services?
- Have there been actual requests for new or expanded services?
- How do we characterize the urgency of needs and requests?
- Will our present referral sources support our proposal?
- What are the hypothetical marketing exchanges?

Support and Project Implementation

- Who should we now rely on for project leadership?
- Will our professional staff support us?
- Which professional staffers shall we utilize?
- Will community leaders lend active and, perhaps, financial support?
- Are the necessary funding sources on our side?

Listing of Preliminary Project Objectives

When it was agreed to undertake the project, the sponsors probably had some generalized objectives. Using the hypothetical project of an adult day care and multiservice center, the objectives may have been stated as: "To meet increasing public demand for services to the elderly; to provide adequate and modern facilities and services; to generate income sufficient to cover the costs of services provided."

During the preliminary marketing process, the marketer will encounter additional items, some that are very important, others that might better be placed on a wish list. Sometimes a series of additional objectives that are secondary or peripheral to the main objectives will be set forth. In this case, they might include:

- becoming a formidable and respected resource for serving the elderly
- developing transportation mechanisms for clients
- developing a new model for operation of a day care center

- developing comprehensive services in cooperation with other service providers

- helping the elderly remain free from institutionalization

Identifying Obstacles to the Success of the Project

Some assessment of the realities of implementation is essential. It should be detailed enough so that the marketer can plan some sort of attack or defense in dealing with these realities. In this example, some of them might be:

- We may have a problem in obtaining enough specialists to staff the program.

- We may find that both space limitations and design of our present council on aging facility will require relocation and considerable construction expense.

- We may threaten three church-sponsored programs when we announce our plans.

- We may have an initial image problem because other day care programs have been managed poorly.

Detailing Opportunities That May Exist

There are silver linings in every project, and the marketer should take advantage of them. An initial list might include these points:

- There is no comparable program in our section of the community.

- The city recreation department may be willing to provide land for use.

- Some federal and state funds are available for the center's construction and program operation.

- Our plan will be likely to have the complete support of the area agency on aging.

Establishing General Categories of Targets

Staff members must help assemble a list of potential targets for the service. Targets are persons who actually will use the service or who will refer others to it. Targets also can be financial supporters, regulatory agencies, or even potential opponents of the project. Here are hypothetical targets for the proposed adult day care center:

- clergymen and church groups
- employees
- hospital social workers and therapists
- other human service organizations
- information and referral services
- local news media
- selected physicians
- senior citizens groups
- municipal officials, politicians
- neighbors
- nursing homes
- public health and visiting nurses
- United Way or similar fund-raising entities

Outlining an Initial Approach or Plan of Work for the Project

At this point, the marketer should have a list of preliminary targets, hypothetical questions, a rough description of the marketplace, an idea about objectives, and some indication of obstacles and opportunities regarding the project's chances. Information and opinions from these areas should provide sufficient material to start. Not to be forgotten is the necessity of obtaining approvals along the way, such as from the chief executive officer, an executive committee, or a project task force, all in the interests of retaining organizational commitment to attaining full agency involvement.

The preliminary marketing process may be equal in importance to the writing of the market plan. It is an opportunity to discuss in detail one or more segments of the project, a unit or objective that either shows promise or might be continuously troublesome. From the melding of staff (and committee) ideas, a consensus will emerge that will guide planners in isolating key components of the future marketing plan.

As suggested earlier, a product of the preliminary marketing process is the initial analysis, an optional tool that may be used in winning internal approval as well as serving as a takeoff point for those who will work on the project. If the organization is small and informal, there may be few problems. However, the larger the organization, the more layers of administration must be worked through, the more bureaucratic its procedures, the more people who will be affected by the marketer's work. It is best to have some focus and agreement on procedures. This generally means that something must be put on paper. Hence, the use of the initial analysis.

The initial analysis is optional and is useful only for the short term. Its purpose is to present as much of the total job to be done as is possible to allow the development of a rational agenda and sequence of studies by those charged with planning for the organization. It is not a full-blown institutional study like those normally undertaken by a health or human service agency and, most certainly, it is not a marketing plan.

Some of the uses of the initial analysis are:

- to achieve a consensus among staff members about the methods of attack on the project objective

- to synopsize for the board of directors the issues surrounding the marketing project and perhaps to introduce the realities of success or failure for the first time

- to list as many obstacles and opportunities as can be perceived

- to identify the major research tasks required to prepare the marketing plan

- to suggest some immediate changes in programs, policies, or personnel that would help to reach the objective

- to help decide whether outside consultants should be employed on the project

- to present options on procedures before too much time, money, and planning are invested

To illustrate some of the effects of the use of an initial analysis, the authors cite the following from our experiences:

Case 1

The situation: A community fund board directed its staff to undertake a merger between two member agencies on the premise that they were very similar in nature and that substantial economies could be effected from the marriage. An initial analysis revealed that: (a) a shotgun marriage would affect clients and quality of service adversely; (b) the political clout of one agency was enough to hurt the community fund's annual campaign; (c) the programs, though similar, were not duplicative; and, (d) the possible savings would not be equal to the public relations damage that might result.

The outcome: The merger plan was abandoned. The community fund board was happy to have avoided what could have been a wrong move. The initial analysis helped uncover a number of political booby traps prior to possibly long and fruitless negotiations.

Case 2

The situation: A federation of community centers, owning a dozen facilities, decided to embark on an energy conservation program. It was prepared to use a part of its endowment fund for whatever plan was proposed by the staff. The project officer in presenting the initial analysis to the board suggested that one approach was to join with other property owners in the same field in a collective project to seek grants from government for such a purpose.

The outcome: A local planning agency took the lead and much responsibility for developing a program in energy conservation and the financial resources for its operation. Local foundations became interested and offered support. The federation of community centers saved a sizable portion of its permanent reserves.

The depth of the initial analysis depends on the size and complexity of the project and, of course, its use. If a committee or board must monitor progress, the initial analysis provides a better starting point and a checklist of beginning activities.

Exhibit 4-1 is a short-form version of the initial analysis that the authors used as an instructional tool in a training program for staff members of a large social service organization. The purpose of the instruction was to introduce social marketing. Some of the program participants were selected for assignment to a team charged with development of a new service venture, an employee assistance program (EAP). Since most of the staff were unfamiliar with EAPs, much of the initial analysis was intended to be educational. Later, a detailed market program was developed. Within a year, the new program had begun.

Exhibit 4-1 Short-Form Initial Analysis

INITIAL ANALYSIS: DEVELOPMENT OF AN EMPLOYEE ASSISTANCE PROGRAM—HUMAN RESOURCES CENTER

The Project:

The center's objective is to establish a contractual program of direct service to employees of local business and industry. Such

Exhibit 4–1 continued

services have been known as employee assistance programs (EAPs), industrial social services, or occupational programming.

Description:

EAPs have been in existence for 30 years or more, but only recently have they attracted widespread interest in the business world. Originally founded as alcoholic treatment programs, they have been enlarged to deal with other employee problems such as money management, marital difficulties, drug abuse, and retirement adjustment. There are four general types of EAP sponsorship:

- *In-house services:* provided by specially qualified personnel who are on the company payroll

- *Union-sponsored programs:* union staff members who are specially trained to assist unionized companies to deal jointly with employee problems

- *Proprietary services:* provided by commercial firms that offer special management training, information, referral, and counseling services

- *Nonprofit agencies:* voluntary or publicly supported programs that can provide some or all of the services required by a company

An EAP venture would be compatible with the service goals of this organization, which has as its central purpose "the strengthening of family life and assisting in the development of the human potential of children, youth, adults, and older persons."

Previous Actions:

A committee of the local community planning council, in November 1977, issued a statement, "Recommendations on the Provision of Employee Assistance Services by the City's Voluntary Nonprofit Agencies." It said:

Employee assistance programs are desirable and should be expanded . . .

Voluntary nonprofit human services agencies should be encouraged to provide . . . services . . .

Exhibit 4–1 continued

One or more locally-based voluntary agencies should sponsor an entry into what is a proprietary-dominated field . . . in which nonprofits can provide better and more extensive services at lower costs . . .

One agency, considered as a possible lead organization, was consulted but found to be incapable of organizing an effective and comprehensive service. The planning council has recommended that the center undertake establishment of a program and has pledged various forms of support.

The Project Environment (Marketplace):

In the metropolitan area, the center has not explored potential markets. It has been encouraged by the United Way and has other advocates with influence in business and industry. Until now, there have been no formal considerations of the project idea by the board of directors. There is *no* detailed prospectus either for management or the board.

In terms of present competition, the following have been identified:

- Several *in-house* programs exist in local government, a few banks, and manufacturing companies.

- Two local *proprietary* organizations mainly provide information and referral services to four or five very large corporations. (There may be more proprietary providers, but they are hard to identify because they advertise other kinds of services.)

- Area Labor United is a *labor*-sponsored agency that conducts union counseling training programs and provides information and referral services. It serves only one major segment of organized labor and only unionized firms.

- Alcoholism Central is a nonprofit rehabilitation service that has expanded its programs beyond the alcoholic worker. It appears to be primarily a counseling program.

While the center's staff has been discussing the potential of an EAP venture for many months, it has not gone to the business and industrial community to determine the degree of interest

Exhibit 4–1 continued

there might be in its entering the field. Thus, the marketplace is presumed to be sizable and wide open.

Obstacles:

The following have been identified as obstacles to the proposed project:

- Management and policymakers lack a full commitment to entering the field.

- No staff member has been assigned yet to the project because of commitment to other programs and lack of staff time to plan and develop the EAP.

- No agency personnel are experienced in industrial counseling or in dealing with management on contractual service matters.

- Any procrastination will result in loss of time and opportunity to exploit the market.

- Some persons think that the program might threaten the "free enterprise" of proprietary firms.

- Some feel that employee assistance services should not be "sold," but "given" to anyone who needs them.

Opportunities:

- No existing EAP provider has a comprehensive service program.

- Additional center services may be used separately or in conjunction with an EAP.

- There is a minimal need for seed money for start-up of operations.

- Considerable training capacity within the center can be applied to programming to help train industrial supervisors in dealing with troubled employees.

Initial Analysis:

The center must decide either to begin a strong planning effort for the EAP or withdraw as a potential major provider. It is

Exhibit 4–1 continued

far better equipped than any other nonprofit organization in the city to undertake and successfully provide EAP services. It has outside support and enough funding to permit an investment over a three-year period, an investment that will not jeopardize the financial status of the organization. Its entrance into the field will serve the interests of the United Way from which it receives a substantial annual allocation. It should be pointed out, however, that if the center fails to conduct sound planning, provides inferior services, or in any way fails to live up to its contractual promises, it will be placed in double jeopardy. It not only will lose contracts but also will affect its image seriously.

Initial Approach:

Several steps are suggested in order to start the program:

1. Assign one senior staff member to explore feasibility and assume responsibility for development of the program.
2. Utilize the services of a consultant experienced in EAP development.
3. Develop a first draft of a prospectus for internal management and board consideration.
4. Establish a step-by-step implementation schedule.
5. Develop research on potential marketing targets.
6. Establish priorities for contacting targets.
7. Establish an advisory committee consisting of board members and outsiders familiar with corporate personnel operations and who can help open doors of prospective clients.
8. Begin active discussions with major competitors to explore possible cooperative service arrangements; consider involving other agencies as service subcontractors (e.g., consumer credit counselors).
9. Seek the establishment of two or three programs with local firms to serve as a pilot effort.
10. Aim for a *comprehensive* or full-service program that would be unique among all current service providers.

SUMMARY

Each project selected for marketing must be evaluated on its own merits. Preliminary planning can eliminate problems later; indeed, most market failures can be laid to shoddy planning or the marketer's lack of imagination. To guide the transition of a project into a concrete marketing program, a preliminary marketing process can be useful. Components include staff discussion about the nature of the problem as well as known factors in the marketplace. Obstacles and opportunities are examined critically. The process asks the organization's principals to produce an extended list of objectives, tentative targets, and some suggestions for an initial approach to the marketing procedure or continuum.

The initial analysis, a product of the preliminary marketing process, is a management tool to provide background information to an agency about a particular problem or marketing objective. It helps management gain a perspective on the issues at hand; it keeps its focus narrow and to the point. It aids the organization in deciding to proceed on a project or withdraw from it in order to devote time to more profitable, useful undertakings.

Flexibility is a key benefit of the initial analysis. The analysis can muster staff enthusiasm for a project, serve as a basis for development of a full marketing plan, become a major resource document for staff decision making, and provide a platform for obtaining relatively quick summaries of the main points in any proposed project.

Often, the initial analysis is used as a logical culmination of the preliminary marketing process; more often, it can be used for obtaining the approvals needed from a board of directors or the chief executive officer.

Chapter 5

Researching the External Environment

The discussion in Chapter 4 found that the preliminary marketing process helps to weed out projects that do not require a complete marketing approach and permits a clearer perspective of the nature of the project. The initial analysis offers approaches for developing the marketing plan. The marketer has emerged with a decision about which projects will warrant application of social marketing techniques. That is the point where the formalized system begins; the components of the marketing plan are tackled one by one.

The essential difference between the preliminary process and subsequent activities lies in the depth of the investigation. Work becomes much more precise, particularly in examining the marketplace and the operations of the agency or institution. It will become apparent that:

- hard facts will be relied on more than supposition and guestimates

- much more time and money will be invested in studies

- organizational resources will be utilized more carefully in implementing the objective

How to go about establishing responsibility for the marketing process within the administration and staff is the subject of Chapter 15. The ways and means will vary considerably depending on size, the kinds of persons employed, and agency finances. The authors contend that most organizations can use marketing, and size should be neither a prerequisite nor a deterrent.

This component of social marketing is labeled as research. It also is called market assessment or market analysis. It represents the collection of the information that a marketer must have to plan a course of implementation for the marketing objective.

Marketing has been referred to earlier as a system that is applied to a given situation. Discipline is an ingredient essential to the success of any system and, within marketing, research implies and requires the use of discipline. It is the use of time, attention, and, most of all, thoroughness. The results should be worth the effort.

Research is separated into three parts: external environment, internal environment and competition. The external environment is the marketplace where the organization currently conducts its business or where it might want to do so. The internal environment is the marketer's own organization. Competition refers to other agencies, institutions, or business firms whose activities have a direct or indirect effect on ability to grow and prosper. All three are put under the microscope here with as much interest as would scientists looking for clues that will lead them to realizing their own objectives.

If any organization in the nonprofit sector has any weakness or handicap in its marketing potential, it would be a tendency to overlook the opportunities or obstacles in its marketplace, the external environment. There are notable exceptions, but most would agree that the average service organization was created to meet certain needs of specific population groups or geographical areas and would not expect it to conduct its operations like a proprietary firm whose very existence depends on knowledge of, and ability to exploit, the marketplace. Almost every organization has competition but the edge is with those who know how to "work the territory."

The marketer can be likened to a photographer using a camera with a zoom lens. The photographer extends it to get the wide view and gradually pulls into focus on certain subjects. From time to time, the lens widens or narrows until the marketer is satisfied with the scene.

Where to start? How much has to be done? Is there information already available, or must it be located? The answers depend on the breadth and complexity of the project objective but the average service organization must cover several standard areas of examination. The marketer will find that these same areas will suffice for several projects; in other words, once the information is gathered, it will be found useful again and again and will make it possible to take a few shortcuts in future marketing tasks. The basic elements of the external environment include:

- geographic, demographic, and economic characteristics
- needs, problems, and service delivery perspective
- the political scene atmosphere
- present or potential clients or consumers
- resources and reimbursement for services
- information sources for the marketing research

GEOGRAPHIC, DEMOGRAPHIC, AND ECONOMIC CHARACTERISTICS

The geography of the marketplace is studied first. It is necessary to know where the project objective is applicable, whether service boundaries are fixed or flexible and if adjustments in the territory are to be an eventual consideration. Often, there are variables between what is a defined service area and an actual service area. To illustrate:

- A county welfare agency that has an objective of promoting use of food stamps and nutrition programs among the elderly may be confined legally to a single county.

- A community multiservice center designated to serve a general residential territory may find that it actually is confined because an interstate highway bisects its neighborhood.

- A large teaching hospital typically draws its patients from many counties and perhaps other states, rather than just the local area, because of the diversity and quality of its medical services.

- A voluntary agency that provides counseling to the mentally and emotionally ill may accept clients from a larger area than what its bylaws stipulate simply because there are no similar services in that area. Conversely, the same organization may be empowered legally to cover the larger area if it so desires but in fact may serve only a single community.

It is important to know the legal boundaries affecting the project. If there are no such restrictions or if they can be changed, then what are the possibilities for expanding the project area? Or, should a large service area be adjusted into a more realistic and manageable territory? Obviously, this requires study of the organization's charter and bylaws and any applicable certificate-of-need laws.

Once the service boundaries have been examined, they may be classified into two types: legally defined service areas and potential service areas. These are of utmost importance to the organization with expansion in mind, as is the actual service area.

Next, the focus is on people who live and work within the present and potential territory. Population makeup has many dimensions. Is the population growing or waning? How much? Which groups are of most concern to the project? If the population appears to be shifting, why? In what directions is it shifting? What kind of occupations are represented—white-collar or blue-collar? How large are the middle-income and upper-income classes in relation to lower-income families that consume a disproportionate amount of human services? What is the racial, ethnic, and religious breakdown of the population?

Economic characteristics seem to have a strong bearing on the nonprofit sector's ability to operate simply because there is a limit to the amount of charity it can provide without continuous reimbursement sources. Nor can government provide unlimited funding or services. The vagaries of federal financing of health and social programs are well known to any agency or institution that has depended on grants for existence.

Exploration of economic conditions should cover several questions. Does the defined service area parallel the normal commerce or trade area? What is the growth rate of local business? What is the unemployment rate, and what has been the trend? Which industries are expanding, and which are losing business? What are the unique economic conditions that will impact on the project's objectives?

Each of these will provide some indication of the response to the marketing problem or opportunity. A nursing home operated on a nonprofit basis might want to consider relocation or establishment of a new facility in an area that appears economically stable and where the population consists of a relatively high percentage of senior citizens. A for-profit institution of the same type might aim at a very affluent area without consideration of the age of the population because it believes younger people will want their parents in a "good" neighborhood, with cost not a significant barrier. The marketplace for the direct-service organization rarely remains stable. People make up the marketplace; they are mobile, they age, they change their preferences often and unpredictably. Whether creating a new program or revitalizing an old one, the marketer must understand the characteristics of the environment thoroughly.

NEEDS, PROBLEMS, AND SERVICE DELIVERY
   PERSPECTIVE

Again, the marketer puts the zoom lens on full to look at the needs and problems of people. Needs and problems are not synonymous. "Need" means "to be in want." A problem is either "a situation or question raised for solution." There is a further distinction between need, want, and desire. As an example, a ghetto area may have a very high infant mortality rate. It is a serious problem that demands solution. There is a need for preventive and remedial services to reduce the incidence of death. Whether there is a desire on the part of the affected population to do something about it is quite another matter, conditioned by past history and cultural attitudes.

In a middle-income neighborhood in the same community it would not be unusual to find venereal disease approaching epidemic proportions. It is a problem to be reckoned with, but a need for special services may not exist because middle-income individuals have ready access to private physicians. The population also might lack any desire to deal with the matter because it is unwilling to admit it has a problem. In short, the marketer must distinguish between needs, problems, and desires solely because there has to be a precondition of acceptance and a willingness to respond on the part of the people who are to receive the services, be they free or for payment. Service organizations are need oriented and problem oriented and are responsive to these factors. They must cater to consumer or client desire, often stimulating such interest; to this extent they do not differ from their for-profit brethren.

The market researcher develops an inventory of the problems and the identified, emerging needs of the population as a prelude to fixing the boundaries of the project. The chances are that much information already exists, compiled by someone else. (Such sources are discussed later in this chapter.) One more step is making an inventory of the kinds of service agencies and institutions that exist and deal with specific problems and needs in which the organization is likely to be interested.

To provide an understanding of the application of these ideas, an experience of a hypothetical health systems agency in a northwestern state that wanted to deal with the problem of alcoholism is examined. This was the situation and how the HSA tackled the matter of inventorying the existing resources and those that might become useful:

> The geographic area involved 40-plus counties of a highly rural and thinly populated character. State health department sources identified a high rate of alcoholism in the adult population, with evidence that it was growing rapidly among teenagers. The department's analyses attributed the cause to a very harsh climate and widely changing weather conditions during most of the year, isolation of rural areas because of limited roads, hard manual labor conditions in local industries, a general acceptance of drinking habits, and few public education programs stressing the consequences of alcohol abuse.

> A narrowed study of the problem indicated that the population most affected was employed in mining, oil field exploration, and ranching. A profile of the average alcoholic pictured a male between 30 and 45 years of age, limited in education, well paid, independent in nature, and highly mobile in residence (thus not strongly community-oriented), and without major health problems. The teenage alcoholic was described as one in whose family alcoholism already was prevalent and whose circle of friends considered hard drinking as "the only thing to do around here."

> In examining existing services, the planning agency made some interesting observations: Some persons held the view that alcoholism was

a moral weakness rather than a disease, and thus they were intolerant of programs aimed at alcoholism. Some hospitals followed the practice of not identifying alcoholism as an admitting diagnosis but listed other ailments without reference to alcoholism. If hospitals provided any service, it was to dry out the alcoholic. Patients were discharged with little effort made to recommend follow-up treatment or counseling. Law enforcement agencies considered the problem so common that they largely ignored it. Churches in the area, with few exceptions, limited themselves to preaching about the evils of drink.

A local bright spot was an interest on the part of two large employers in the mining industry. Their concerns centered on losses in productivity. Each provided limited programs of treatment and counseling within company medical programs.

An inventory of alcohol treatment and education services provided the following:

- A state hospital provided acute care services in one wing of its facility—approximately 75 beds.

- A private hospital (just outside the HSA region) served alcoholics exclusively.

- Two local hospitals provided isolated wards but did not advertise their limited services.

- Two halfway houses for male inebriates were sponsored by Alcoholics Anonymous.

- There were several A.A. and Alanon chapters in nearby counties.

- Three voluntary agencies and a regional mental health center had specialists in alcoholic counseling.

- The areawide health training center provided alcoholic education programs for professionals.

- There was one nearby chapter of the National Council on Alcoholism, which was concerned primarily with public education.

During its inventory the planning agency uncovered latent resources, including:

- the availability of state alcohol tax funds that could be used for education and treatment purposes upon application by county officials

- a consortium of organizations under the umbrella of a voluntary health and welfare council with an interest in dealing with the problem

- a philanthropic foundation interested in providing funds for treatment facilities

- a nursing home operator with one facility who was willing to convert it to care of alcoholics

- a program developed by the state department of education and health that could be used in public schools

- a liberal policy toward reimbursement of health care for alcoholism on the part of the major health insurer in the region

As can be surmised, the process lends several possibilities to the marketing plan; the intent is to find as many clues as possible for dealing with the project. In this case, the objectives were to develop some kind of coordinated, comprehensive attack on the broad problem of alcoholic education and treatment services.

A second stage of the inventory is an assessment of professional personnel. It is important to determine the numbers and kinds of service personnel in the area. For example, development of a sophisticated community mental health program is dependent on the availability of certain professionals such as psychiatrists, psychologists, psychiatric social workers, and others. If the agency is dependent only on its own area for drawing trained persons, it can have a serious problem.

The marketer identified expert personnel resources by residence and service location. If specialized employees cannot be maintained internally, where are they and are they available to the program? In today's health personnel market, for example, there is a universal shortage of physical therapists and, in some localities, of registered nurses. Board-certified child psychiatrists are very limited; most often they reside in large urban areas. It is a buyer's market for teachers and social workers in most communities.

Another task for the marketer is to learn which professional organizations and individuals tend to have a major impact on the development and delivery of services in the area. Who are the decision makers when it comes to development of a new program? Can one organization or individual provide access to or block a new venture? Knowing professional attitudes toward the agency, a service, or the problem often is of crucial importance.

Not to be overlooked are the historical records of the particular project. What efforts were made in the past to deal with the problem? What programs were started and failed? Why did they fail? What studies have been made in the last five years that have a bearing on the matter? What were their recommendations, and what was done about them? It is very desirable to learn from past mistakes in order to avoid covering the same ground and perhaps meeting the same fate.

THE POLITICAL ATMOSPHERE

The marketer, armed with as many facts as possible, now moves to test the political waters before plunging in. There are three general sectors to explore: regulatory, the professional hierarchy, and real politics.

Regulatory agencies cover every aspect of operation from the birth to the demise of a program. Many approvals have to be obtained to start most new agencies or programs and most institutions cannot be closed without also encountering rolls of red tape.

The writers once assisted a client in establishing a new home health care program. Months were spent in a feasibility study with much concentration on dealing with principal reimbursement sources. The process involved dealing with several layers of government and at least half a dozen third party payers, all with different compliance requirements. Our client was pleased to learn he could hurdle the financial barriers, could meet the state's certificate-of-need specifications, and had the full blessing of the regional HSA. Being new in business, however, he was somewhat disconcerted to find he had climbed the regulatory ladder only part way. He still had the following items to deal with:

Federal Government

Department of Labor

- Fair Labor Standards Act: minimum wage and overtime

- Welfare and Pension Plans Disclosure Act: pension plans

- Occupational Safety and Health Administration: safety and health of physical premises

- Age Discrimination in Employment Act: protection of employees aged 40 to 65

National Labor Relations Board

- National Labor Relations Act: potential unionization and good faith bargaining

Equal Employment Opportunity Commission

- Title VII of the Civil Rights Act of 1964: protection of employees from discrimination because of race, color, creed, sex, national origin, or physical handicap

Internal Revenue Service:
- FICA, withholding tax, profits, and tax exemptions

State Government

Licensure
- Control of quality of care by mandating staffing patterns, supervision, staff ratios

- Taxes on services performed, profits, telephone

- Unemployment Compensation Fund

- Workmen's Compensation

- Vehicle and operator registrations, licensing, and insurance

- Various medical practice acts; health professional licensing

Local Government

- Occupational licenses

- Safety codes and zoning

Besides pure regulation, there are more sides to the political scene. It is in understanding the professional environment and being able to work well within it that may determine the success of a venture. There is no more complex or controlled arena than health care. One of the most perceptive analyses of recent vintage is in the 1975 book, *The White Labyrinth,* by David B. Smith and Arnold D. Kaluzny. They dissect the roles of institutions and professionals who control the health sector:

> No institution in the health sector is an autonomous agent. There is a tight network of interrelationships, overlapping interests and memberships among professional schools, associations, and medical suppliers and among hospitals, physicians, and the third party mechanisms. Deans of medical schools and top officials in the Food and Drug Administration become executives in pharmaceutical companies.

> The pharmaceutical and medical supply company advertising subsidizes most of the professional journals. Hospital associations and medical societies have often been indistinguishable from Blue Cross

and Blue Shield Plans. In effect, this means that hospitals determine by themselves how much they should be paid. The various professional and trade associations shape most of the health-related state and federal legislation and, at least as importantly, the implementation of that legislation. It is this kind of inter-dependence that makes the labyrinth a system.[1]

Changing a program or institution or establishing a new one is not possible without being somewhat adept in coping with the politics of health care. The field is more tightly controlled than social services but both must be appraised with some astuteness. It is necessary first to understand the pecking order within the health care community before that of the health care or human services institution.

Medical societies dominate professional associations in terms of influence or changes in the delivery system. Smith and Kaluzny note that in organized medicine there are different weights or levels of influence among specialists. A widely publicized study ranked the relative prestige of 22 medical specialties and found that neurosurgeons, internists, and general surgeons topped the list while those in preventive and occupational medicine were near the bottom. Medical administrators ran a dead last 22nd in peer prestige.[2]

The influence of other professionals depends on the relative prestige of the specialist, which stems in part from the complexity and length of training required but perhaps even more so from the respect for and acceptance of the particular practice by the doctor of medicine. As an example, the acceptance of osteopathy has been relatively slow. In larger cities it is not unusual to find few relationships between M.D.s and D.O.s. However, in rural areas, particularly where this is a shortage of medical personnel, the two specialists work quite well together, often serving jointly on the same hospital staffs.

The field of nursing, subject to years of dispute over minimum standards and length of training, has depended on the individual physician's concept of nursing rather than the nurse's own determination of what services can be provided to patients. Underscored by federal regulations for reimbursement of health care, most nursing services must be prescribed and supervised by M.D.s. Certain fairly new specialists, such as nurse practitioners, find relatively more respect and influence in medicine than their peers.

There is an increasing conflict between nursing and medical schools over their respective roles in the production of what are described in accurate, if somewhat grotesque, terms as "physician extenders" .... Both the nurse practitioner and nurse specialist programs are attempts to move nursing in the direction of specialization similar to that which exists in medicine.[3]

The influence of the nurse, therefore, depends a great deal on the extent of training but perhaps more often on placement within the system. The nurse in the doctor's office often is given more leeway than the visiting nurse who may treat the same patient. The head nurse in the hospital's surgery or intensive care unit will make decisions not entrusted to counterparts on a general care ward.

In social services, the master of social work professional dominates a counseling agency or multiservice center. Doctoral specialists are found more often in teaching positions than in practice. Psychologists may be more influential than M.S.W.s in a school setting, less so in a mental health clinic. The marketer therefore must know the touchstones of professional power.

A third sector that may or may not be significant to a project is the real or body politic. It is distinct from the regulatory sector that deals after the fact, when laws and policies already have been established. So much of the health and human services field is impacted today by legislation or financial appropriation. Dealing with elected and appointed officials is commonplace and mandatory. Elected officials can change laws or make new ones that may help enlarge an organization's service area and potential, restrict its operations, or perhaps protect it from encroachment by a competitor.

Legislators can dictate whether a mental health clinic can be built, a union can organize human services employees, a welfare department can pay higher Medicaid rates, or a children's home can be renovated. Pleas for financial support are annual occurrences; legislators provide core or matching support for retardation programs, child care centers, senior citizen programs, and vocational rehabilitation facilities.

The marketer must identify various levels of political relationships critical to the cause involved. A neighborhood recreation center would be ill advised to ignore its alderman when appealing for city support. City and county council members set tax rates for funding the public health department. The regional council of governments, made up of elected officials, has the final say in the A-95 review process (the federal government's procedure for screening expenditures for capital projects). The state legislature is the body that creates a legal base for delivery of almost all services of a public nature even though the federal government enacts and funds the major programs. Congress shapes the general course and content of all public health and social service programs. Occasionally, the marketer will direct efforts there, but more often will turn to an individual senator or representative who can help resolve a local problem.

If this suggests that the marketer must contain a little of the "political animal," it is intentional. The marketer also must have some of the instincts of a good manager who knows what power is, where it is, and how to set it to work for the organization.

The relevancy of the political spectrum, from regulatory to the body politic, can be illustrated by the following experiences:

- A homemaker-home health aide agency withdrew its plan to seek certification as a home health care agency when it found that its referral sources (some of whom already were certified by Medicare) would create their own service if threatened with competition.

- A merger between two vocational counseling agencies was opposed bitterly by the staffs of both agencies but was consummated when influential board members of the two programs decided it was feasible and something they wanted to see happen.

- A community planning council in a major city objected to the construction of a recreation center in a neighborhood whose population had been decimated by highway and industrial development. However, it could not overcome the power of a single alderman who had been promised the facility for his ward in exchange for past political favors provided to the mayor.

- Construction of a new hospital in a small town, although strongly opposed by the HSA and the Medicare intermediary, was accomplished by a consortium of business executives, physicians, and elected officials who successfully appealed the decision to the governor and other state officials.

- A nursing home operator of questionable repute was successful for many years in operating substandard facilities because of his ability to deal with and neutralize licensing and program regulators in state government.

PRESENT OR POTENTIAL CLIENTS AND CONSUMERS

Depending on project objectives, marketers will focus attention on the people, organizations, and institutions with whom they now do business or whom they want to serve. If the marketplace has a geographical focus, then it has market groups within it. It is necessary to identify all those with whom an exchange of some sort is appropriate.

One necessity is to determine if there are enough people to buy or support the service and to allow steady growth. A home health care agency might determine the number of Medicare enrollees in its area since reimbursement is readily available. A neighborhood health clinic might depend on Medicaid financing and thus is concerned about Medicaid-eligible persons. A public health department may have special funds to deal with rat infestation in certain neighborhoods; its success may well depend on a sociological knowledge of the residents since their cooperation and concern is needed. Analysis of sociological factors often is as important and critical as an anaylsis of demographics.

The practice of market segmentation is critical, too. Kotler says it is:

> . . . important to list the markets that (the organization) sees as important and the relative importance of each in the total scheme of the organization's objectives. Each market, in turn, consists of distinguishable market segments. It is a central tenet of marketers that *market segmentation* is an essential step to analyzing and planning for markets. Organizations are not able to serve whole markets effectively, and the organization is wise to choose a segment to serve or at least differentiate its marketing programs for the different market segments it serves.[4]

The researcher organizes markets by category, beginning with present clients or consumers. The intent is to determine who is being served and what is being provided. This leads to the questions: Is the organization serving all of those who are eligible or who might use its services? Is it providing all of the services that it can? What new groups of clients are there to be served? How can it vary the kinds of services provided?

The following case is an example of a marketer's examination of this type:

> A vocational and rehabilitation service had the ability to provide extensive diagnostic testing for the physically handicapped, to provide occupational rehabilitation services, to give continuous counseling to trainees, to provide short-term housing facilities, and to place rehabilitated graduates into positions in community businesses. Its program was considered comprehensive and effective. Its principal markets consisted of the following client categories and estimates of its share of client percentage in each category:
>
> - Persons suffering physical disabilities from job-related injuries (80 percent)
> - Selected referred clients graduated from sheltered workshops for the mentally retarded (20 percent)
> - Female public welfare recipients assigned from Work Incentive Programs (WIN) (15 percent)
> - "Problem" (but not physically handicapped) CETA workers who required special adjustment training prior to or after their placement in public services sector jobs (90 percent)

Somewhat later, after assessing its program potential, the agency raised its sights on the percentages of market share it felt it should serve. It did reduce its intake of CETA employees by more than half because of the establishment of a similar program in another agency and its admitted failure to get workers to adjust to working in surroundings with the physically handicapped.

When potential client markets were examined, they were segmented and an estimate was placed on the numbers to be sought and served (in parentheses):

- Patients discharged from a state mental hospital and placed in halfway houses (300 annually)

- Patients from three hospital-based alcoholic treatment centers who required short-term job adjustment experience (550 annually)

- Employers interested in the 1973 federal mandate to implement "equal rights for the handicapped" legislation (unlimited)

Other, smaller markets were identified and later assessed as to their feasibility and attractiveness.

A creative approach was applied to the question, "What kinds of new services should we provide?" With staff help, the marketer produced the following service ideas:

- Establishment of a separate, nonprofit subsidiary to construct apartment housing for the handicapped.

- Development of a special communitywide transportation program for handicapped citizens by expansion of the agency's existing fleet of specially equipped buses and vans.

- Provision of a special team of industrial/vocational counselors to consult employers who were unfamiliar with ways of implementing handicapped rights laws.

A decision to enter into any new market or provide a new service is made only after appropriate study. Another organization might have quite a different set of markets, and its services might take other forms. For instance, one state health planning and development agency (SHPDA) sought passage of a certificate-of-need law that would control health facility equipment and program growth. Since it was not a direct service agency, its products and markets were of a different order. Its product was planning; its markets were persons who would accept its planning recommendations. The latter included:

- elected representatives of the state legislature

- the governor, appointed department heads, and citizen advisory boards

- statewide professional associations and trade groups (e.g., medical associations and nursing home councils)

- civic and special interest groups (including League of Women Voters and state AFL-CIO)

- communications media

- third party payment organizations

RESOURCES AND REIMBURSEMENT FOR SERVICES

No less than in business, the search for dollars among human services is compelling and continuous. To some administrators this would be first priority. The nonprofit agency that says it will serve anyone regardless of ability to pay really must limit itself to helping on a first-come-first-served basis. Public agencies do not have unlimited resources, either. The availability of funding is dependent on many factors.

An older population means more Medicare clients and some assistance from other programs helping the elderly under auspices of the Older Americans Act. Support provided through local government taxing units generally is higher for health and mental health services than for social services. Proposition 13-style programs have reduced further the availability of resources; there is no program with unlimited funding. However, Blue Cross, Blue Shield, employer-run health plans, health maintenance organizations, and others gradually have broadened their services. Alcohol, mental illness, dental care, and even legal services have become subjects for third party reimbursement—indeed, they are becoming more and more a part of collective bargaining in the workplace. As an example, the United Auto Workers nationwide health plan provides many advanced benefits for members, their dependents, and retirees.

Some communities have supplied general revenue sharing dollars for the provision of human services. Community Development funds, allotted through the Department of Housing and Urban Development, are available to target neighborhoods but most often are limited to hardware or capital items. Continuity of this type of financing is a risky matter, particularly since target areas are apt to change from year to year.

Cataloguing potential, as well as existing, financial resources and reimbursement mechanisms is essential. All conditions of reimbursement, such as eligibility and service limitations, should be known to the marketer.

Each marketing project requires other questions, other explorations. The marketer will shape the extent of the work according to the weight each marketing decision will have on the future. When a sizable financial investment is contemplated in a project, it is easier to discipline one's thoroughness. A human services organization may afford one financial mistake, but another could put it out of business. Researching may appear to be endless, but the experienced marketer learns to do only what the project requires.

INFORMATION SOURCES FOR THE MARKETING RESEARCH

The less original research the marketer has to undertake, the better. An abundance of information may be available already for the asking. An experienced researcher knows sources and systems, what organizations and individuals to turn to and, just as importantly, how to extract what is wanted in an economical way.

For a demographic study, a good starting point is the local council of governments (COG) that serves a multicounty area. The COG usually specializes in the physical arena, such as zoning, water use, highways, and environmental studies, rather than in human services. The COG maintains current information on population trends and changes. State planning agencies usually rely on metropolitan COGs for their own file information. COGs are likely to have considerable economic data.

Chambers of commerce usually have business development departments. They are excellent resources for information about types of firms, numbers and skills of employees, wages, and other data. City planning departments often are overlooked but many of them employ personnel who are extremely knowledgeable about local human services. Some perceptive cities have linked their physical planning with human services planning because of its importance and because the planning departments have a role in determining the disbursement of community development and other federal funds.

The health systems agency, of course, maintains much data about health services, needs, facilities, and personnel. Such information is its stock-in-trade, the basis for its health systems plan. State health and welfare agencies with licensing responsibilities have information on all kinds of services and facilities. Some associations maintain registries of professional personnel and a number of states have made extensive studies of such needs and resources. Every state, and most metropolitan areas, have medical, dental, and specialist organizations that will supply information.

Often overlooked are public utilities, which maintain excellent data because their own growth is dependent on forecasting population changes and business development. Local universities, particularly business schools, have a different perspective to offer. Other departments such as sociology, public health, social work, and special research units provide data. In rural communities the agriculture extension division of the state university is a key resource. County farm agents maintain close ties to these programs. Community service councils or United Ways often maintain extensive inventories of human services programs of all descriptions; areawide agencies on the aging know of facilities and special services, maintain rosters of senior citizens organizations, and much more. Perhaps more overlooked than any other resource is the local public library, often the recipient and collector of a variety of studies of human needs and services.

A surprising amount of information can be obtained at little or no cost or simply for the photocopying fee. Most organizations provide free advice and limited consultation on proposed projects but generally are unable or unwilling to undertake original research. Sometimes a trade-off can be made with each group gathering information that both can use.

Timeliness is important to the marketer. Extensive surveys are costly and run the risk of being outdated rapidly. Data must be as current as possible. Because federal grant programs may require use of perhaps outdated population data, such material often is incompatible with other available information.

Sequencing of research can dictate the effort to be expended. If, for example, the picture of potential reimbursement sources for a new service is too discouraging, the marketer may decide rather quickly to go no further. On the other hand, exploration may uncover a gap in services. As mentioned earlier, the marketer enters the project as a result of a perceived problem or opportunity and almost always encounters new obstacles or opportunities along the way. The final direction the marketer takes is dictated after, not before, the research task is complete.

SUMMARY

The first subdivision of market research is examination of the external environment: where the organization is going and expects to do business. It is essential to know this marketplace thoroughly before refining objectives and pursuing their implementation.

For the health and human services agency, its initial examination should involve the people and their characteristics in the defined service marketplace. Age, income, type of employment, cultural heritage, and racial mix all are important. Their needs and problems come next—what are they and how are they being met? A perspective on the delivery of services helps greatly.

Politics, with both capital and lowercase p, has a bearing on the marketer's investigation: it affects the organization's chances to change, grow, and even to relocate. At one end is simple regulation and, at the other, legislative influence that may be mandatory to a marketing project. Professional politics, too, often is of consequence to any health and human services institution.

The clients, patients, and customers being served must be placed into perspective with other potential clients, patients, and customers. Who is the organization serving? What does it do for them? How much of the market do they constitute? Are there others who should be served?

Financial resources in the marketplace obviously are crucial to the marketer. It is important to inventory and assess such resources at an early stage, to know the potentialities and the limitations.

While the research task seems most imposing, many resources are available to the marketer that should serve to shorten the workload. The marketer, becomes adept at locating and using them. Some ideas of where to look for help are suggested.

NOTES

1. David B. Smith and Arnold D. Kaluzny, *The White Labyrinth* (Berkeley, Calif.: McCutcheon Publishing Corp., 1975), p. 51.

2. Ibid., p. 8.

3. Ibid., pp. 15-16.

4. Philip Kotler, *Marketing for Nonprofit Organizations* (Englewood Cliffs, N.J.: Prentice-Hall, Inc., 1975), p. 57.

Chapter 6

Researching the Internal Environment and the Marketing Audit

If attaining the best possible perspective of the marketplace is an initial research goal, it is no less important to know everything about the organization and its operations. There is an added, most essential ingredient that is required: objectivity. It means to be able to view something without distortion. When marketers look at their own organization, assuming they are members of it, they must take on a certain detachment, be as critical as if they were outside consultants and be willing to "call 'em as they see 'em."

In the health and human services field, the authors have found some characteristics common to a great many organizations:

- Statements of goal and purpose are generalized or vague.

- Measurable objectives by which to judge the effectiveness of services delivered are lacking.

- Few agencies have annualized written work programs.

- Standards and procedures for accounting for program or service results are absent.

- Many have managers who "grew up in the business" as specialists or technicians but without previous training in administration.

These traits are not indigenous to human services agencies; thousands of organizations of all descriptions, in and out of the business world, start informally, address customer and client needs for a time, and hope to establish a permanent spot in the marketplace. Health and human services institutions of the nonprofit type are founded under different circumstances. These agencies are in the public domain, using tax monies or contributions, and thus have a special kind of accountability. In the past, the public was rather lenient, accepting good intentions and demanding little in the way of proof of the effectiveness of most human services programs. But times are changing rapidly. Charitable donors and taxpayers have become more sophisticated in their knowledge of human problems and needs and much more selective about what they will support. The abuse of the public trust by a few bad actors has resulted in hard questioning of all public institutions, regardless of size or past contributions. All are being scrutinized and subjected to the kind of examination that their founders never would have imagined.

Until a few years ago, there was much inconsistency in the accounting of fiscal affairs of nonprofit organizations. Today uniform standards are used widely, and in some communities where licensing is required, there are extensive fiscal reporting procedures. Full disclosure of finances is a condition for participation in United Ways. Governmental agencies have been subject to such auditing for many years. However, both sectors have lacked program accountability to any significant degree.

Millions of dollars have been spent to develop evaluation techniques to be applied to the delivery of human services. Because of the very complex nature of human services and the unpredictability of, and difficulty in measuring, human behavior, no perfect evaluation systems have been devised. Evaluation of most programs is largely a matter of subjective judgment. Nonetheless, program evaluation has an unmistakable future in agency management. As the number of service organizations multiplies, expenditures increase, and the severity of social problems seems to rise unabated, the public has realized that human services is big business and, consequently, should be examined and regulated so that its existence can justify continued support.

THE SIGNIFICANCE OF EVALUATION

What significance does evaluation have for marketing? Why should the marketer be concerned about program effectiveness?

Social marketing offers a strong benefit to those who use it. It should lead to improved administration and improved services because self-evaluation is a prerequisite. In examining the internal environment (the agency or institution itself), the marketer looks for the flaws and strengths with an eye to the organization's capability of achieving its particular marketing objectives. Thus, the ability to deliver services effectively, efficiently, and competitively is most important. And if exchange between the client/patient and the service provider is to be kept in reasonable balance, providers must be able to carry out their end of the bargain.

Marketers are most useful to their employers (or clients) when they put the organization through a marketing audit. Honestly done, the result almost always is a prescription for some adjustments or rearrangements of the service pattern and methods of service delivery. There is a rationale for changing the operation, particularly if the audit indicates that an objective can't be attained without meeting client/patient needs or demands in a better fashion.

Before approaching the audit in more detail, a few simple questions should be asked.

What Is the Organization's Mission?

The marketer begins with the legal roots of the organization: charter, articles of incorporation, bylaws—the documents that convey the authority to operate as a service body. These lead to other materials: written objectives, long-range plans, studies, or other directives. Few organizations ever take time to reexamine their missions, let alone do it with regularity, perhaps once every five years or so. The agency's descriptive brochure may catalog a number of services and functions but rarely mentions why it exists. Many agencies have no formal statement of mission. Meritt L. Kastens, in *Long-Range Planning for Your Business,* says that, "The mission statement tells you where you are going to concentrate your resources, where you are going to look hardest for new opportunities, where you are going to try to build the success of the enterprise."[1] Knowing where the organization wants to go is the first thing the marketer seeks to determine. For background, the marketer probes the legal foundations of the agency, then reviews board policies and board and committee meeting minutes, and questions administrative staff. Such inquiries can well lead to the rewriting or restatement of mission and objectives.

What Are the Organization's Service Capabilities?

The bread and butter of any service organization are the people it employs. In human service agencies, personnel consistently comprise 70 percent or more of operating budgets. While the board of directors, committees, and volunteers may account for a substantial part of a service program (a typical youth agency, for example, may employ only one professional staffer for each 50 volunteers), it takes paid staff to maintain the organization and keep service operations flowing smoothly. The more complex the type of service, such as counseling a patient bent on suicide or researching causes of family dysfunction, the farther removed is the volunteer from the supervision of personnel or actual service delivery.

The field staff deals day to day with the client or patient public. It is staff performance that dictates agency receptivity, use of services, and the extent of income, and affects productivity and profit. Staff personnel are more important, perhaps, than the manager simply because the executive's success depends upon their competency and effectiveness.

First, a look at the trained professional staff. What is the mix of service disciplines? For example, in a school for handicapped children, it is necessary to explore the academic and field experience of teachers. Have they had special training to work with autistic children, the palsied, the emotionally disturbed? Does the school have a speech pathologist? Are there qualified counselors to assist parents with out-of-school situations that bear on educational objectives?

Though a skilled nursing home may be required by state law to have a registered nurse on duty 24 hours a day, the rule has little bearing on what the patients' real needs may be. What other staff members are available for their care? Is there a physical therapist who visits regularly? Is the activities program run by a qualified occupational therapist?

It is not necessary, of course, that staff be full time. Contractual arrangements for sophisticated and short-term professional care are commonplace. It is the range of services, the competency of the service people, and how they are deployed that concerns the marketer. Paraprofessional staff are scrutinized just as carefully in the evaluation. In some organizations, large numbers of clients or patients, as contrasted with limited numbers of professionals, may mean that paraprofessionals have far more contact with clients or patients than does the professional staff. Aides in a day care center or home health aides in a visiting nurses association are regarded as the real pulse of the agency. The training and patient rapport of these employees is no less important than that of professionals.

Next in review is the managerial element of the organization. For example, a neighborhood multiservice center may employ a director of intake, a person who supervises assignments of work to all professional staff. The marketer examines that person's ability to maintain the order of requests and referrals for service and the output of all services. A sense of organization, the ability to control productivity, and an eye to quality of care are very important. In a Meals on Wheels program, the program director may be the one responsible for finding clients and arranging to help them. In marketing, anyone managing a division of persons who directly provide services comes under scrutiny.

Support personnel, from the clerk in the mailroom to the comptroller, add to the efficient flow of work or can cause chaos. If billing procedures and the handling of accounts create a cash flow problem, then the agency has a business handicap that won't be compensated for by a high standard of service delivery. Poorly operated print rooms can slow the movement of the mountains of paper required in today's service world. The switchboard operator's personality may be the reason why the volume of service might be 5 percent higher. The attitude of the first person in the agency to be contacted is known to affect and influence business.

Eventually, marketers work back to the chief executive officer since the image of an organization often is viewed in terms of the person who manages it.

Marketers look to the administrator for an understanding of their work, support for their proposals, and follow-up on their recommendations. Such is the ideal; it is not necessarily so in practice. On more than one occasion, the authors have been invited by a client organization to develop marketing plans, only to find the administrator opposed to faultfinding. One defensive-minded manager spent considerable time and skill in keeping us at a distance from the trustees of his organization who needed to know that some fundamental changes were necessary in the front office. Obviously, marketing was not fruitful for that agency as long as that management endured. As a general rule, however, if examination of the total staffing situation turns out to be positive, the chances are that top management is positive, too. Successful managers are not threatened by marketing analysis. They accept the fact that they need new pairs of eyes through which to see their programs.

Who Does the Organization Serve Now?

Helpful to the marketing assessment may be the construction of one or more profiles of the clients or patients served. A certain men's magazine will describe its prime reader as being a male, between the ages of 30 and 36, white, college-educated, professional, with an income of $37,000 annually, drives a late model foreign sports car, and so on. Its advertising department thus can target its sales efforts and advise potential advertisers about the products they should feature. The lesson can be transferred easily to the human services agency. By knowing the types of people who seek its services, the agency learns something about how it is perceived and how to isolate potential target markets for new clients and services.

It is good business for any service organization to maintain a continuing analysis of its clients/patients. Admission records should be designed for use of the marketer as well as the program director and accounting office. Agencies tend to leave out the kind of information that could provide clues for the marketing plan. For instance, a home health care agency may record the name of a patient's physician and note that the referral was from a hospital that had just discharged the person. Typically, the agency would not provide information that would indicate who in or out of the hospital caused the referral, recognizing that most of the time it is someone other than the physician. Sometimes a patient's family will request service a few days after discharge. Unless the person who influences the referral is identified, the agency proceeds blindly, not knowing if its educational and promotional efforts are being directed to the right people.

Many United Ways, which raise money for a variety of human services, have arranged for member agencies to keep simple statistics on client residence, place of employment, sex, race, and age. Without revealing confidential information, the United Way then can tell employers and donors about the numbers of individuals in their organizations and the extent of services being provided. Such data can play no small part in the annual employee campaign for United Way.

In addition to routine information, agencies should consider some of the following:

- recording precise reasons for rejection when a prospective client is turned away

- noting what efforts were made to get the rejected client to another service agency

- keeping account of admission trends, such as the hours or days in which applications were heaviest

- asking whether other members of the client's family or circle of friends have received the agency's service

Study of the origin of client referrals and the results of the service experience generally is desirable, sometimes mandatory. The purpose is to establish a framework of knowledge about actual practice to apply against what the organization thinks it should be doing or how it perceives itself.

If a rehabilitation facility, for example, finds that it is serving mostly persons who are over 50 years of age (or perhaps a high percentage of Medicare enrollees) when it has the capacity and desire to help younger patients, then it knows it can make some adjustments. Its public image, its prime sources of referrals, its reimbursement mechanisms, and other factors may dictate that it is not in its right niche. Changes in admitting patterns may signal the possibility of new markets, too.

The marketer should develop charts to show the service picture over the previous three to five years. They should reveal:

- growth rate in total services, by major categories

- referral sources and cycles of referrals

- chronological peaks and valleys in service demand

- funding source trends and their impact on services

As the existing market appears more distinct, the organization is likely to perceive one or more new markets to enter or groups of clients it might want to acquire. If there has been a decline or leveling off in growth, it is natural to consider providing alternative services. Instead of a simple decline in potential clients, it may be that the service being offered no longer is needed.

What Services Are Needed or Wanted?

If anything is a hallmark of marketing, it is the deliberate search for consumers' personal preferences. Great sums of money are spent by business and industry to seek reaction to products or to discover what products or services clients want. The human services professions often have not copied the business practice of seeking advice from clients or patients. Programs and services often are designed solely on the basis of the professionals' perception of client needs, sometimes with disdain for clients' ability to articulate their own wants.

Seeking the ideas and opinions of clients before the new program is started also is important. Providing a hot meal at a community center may well meet the nutritional needs of senior citizens in its neighborhood, but if they are afraid to walk the streets at dusk, then the program might be better off if meals were delivered at home or provided only at midday. A family counseling agency engaged in group therapy courses might find that parents are reluctant to hire babysitters as well as pay the cost of the sessions. In response, the agency could set up a playroom, hire young people to supervise activities, and cover the extra cost by a minimal increase in the class fee.

There are many ways to assess client/patient opinions. Postservice mail questionnaires or interviews, personally or by telephone, are most common. They are helpful in making continuing adjustments in a program or discovering new service needs. To maintain objectivity, surveys should be conducted by someone not directly involved in providing the service. Mail surveys of selected population groups, interviews with professional and other personnel in those organizations apt to make referrals, and studies of information and referral agency intake data can be most useful.

In small communities, the authors sometimes have sought input on special projects from local thought leaders by using simple questionnaires filled out at meetings of civic service clubs, women's clubs, or professional associations. Questionnaires inserted into daily or weekly newspapers generally have minimal research value, but they do have unique benefits to offer in the agency's public education efforts.

Small grassroots discussion groups or cluster interviews with clients are an excellent sounding board for the marketer. Groups of housewives, students, business executives, or other special interests are brought together for structured discussion about a product or service. Their reactions can help shape the marketing effort of the sponsor. Such a technique can be used easily in health and human services organizations.

Some organizations have included clients on program planning committees and boards. The concept is democratic, but the benefits sometimes tend to be short range because client objectivity can be clouded by the change in relationship that occurs with deep involvement with the provider agency. Besides, the opinions of all clients cannot be expressed by only a few. An organization that provides a mechanism for regular client/patient participation should not let itself be lulled into thinking it understands all the needs and wishes of all the people it services.

THE INTERNAL MARKETING AUDIT

Once a general picture of the nature of the organization becomes available, marketers turn to inside areas that influence marketing objectives. They look more precisely at the organization's methods of operation. What makes it tick? What marketing and promotional techniques does it employ? Can it change direction and pursue new opportunities? This exercise, the internal analysis of the organization, is the marketing audit, an essential operation to capitalize on the potential in future operations.

"The purpose of the audit is to define problem areas in terms of questions to which marketing managers (or administrators) should direct attention and specify information required to answer the questions competently," Ben F. Enis writes.[2] Putting the auditing function in sharper perspective, and in the language of Voltaire: "Judge of a man by his questions rather than by his answers."

"Before determining that the job is done right, it's essential to determine that the right job is done," comments David F. Linowes, who adds that a right job is done when "a right need has been focused on and the right goal is being met."[3] Linowes chides those who plan on a large scale by making assumptions about what people want (without supporting data), with misjudgments and misappropriations due to guesswork, and little understanding of probable acceptance of projects. "Clearly, more research, analysis and experimentation are needed in all our social institutions and services," he says. "Until needs are adequately determined, resources will continue to be allocated on a hit-or-miss basis. Goals will either be lacking or haphazardly established. The monitoring of performance and progress will be correspondingly ineffective."[4]

A marketing audit may be applied to any health or human services organization, large or small. An audit is not exclusively the domain of large or monolithic social services organizations that may have a dozen or more branches. Any organization can benefit by asking penetrating questions about its actions and activities. Most textbooks on marketing concur that auditing is key to market plan preparation, the foundation of such a plan, many say; but there are varied approaches to auditing, from simple to complex.

A central goal of the audit is to examine the organization's marketing and promotional position broadly and deeply. Oxenfeldt prescribes an audit with six distinct components: objectives, policies, organization, methods, procedures, and personnel.[5] Enis views the audit with two main parts: diagnosis (where are we now?) and prognosis (where are we going?).[6]

To Kotler, the audit is "a periodic, comprehensive, systematic, and independent internal examination of the organization's marketing environment, internal marketing system, and specific marketing activities, with a view to determining problem areas and recommending a corrective action plan to improve the organization's overall marketing effectiveness."[7] Kotler divides audits into three parts: (1) marketing environmental review, which reveals the current and anticipated marketing environment of the organization and includes an examination of markets, customers, and competitors; (2) marketing system review, which examines the objectives, programs, implementation, and structure; (3) detailed marketing activities review, which examines the marketing mix—products, prices, distribution, personal selling, advertising, publicity, and sales promotion.

The authors' own audit has eight elements: competition, constituency (markets and/or publics), documents, fees, management functions and philosophy, new business mechanisms, promotional tools, and basic services. Other marketers have equally useful and plausible approaches to the audit, suggesting unequivocally that in marketing no one pathway is necessarily the only route. An audit should be constructed creatively, with some helpful guidelines and suggestions from books and manuals, but with the problems, hypotheses, traditions, styles, and peccadilloes of each organization clearly brought into focus.

In its early use by industry, the audit often was considered as a last-chance analytical device to save a company from financial ruin or from being swept up by aggressive competition. Today, says Abe Shuchman, the audit "is the practice of preventive as well as curative marketing medicine," meaning that it is applied when an organization is well and not when it is visibly sliding downhill.[8] Hartley adds that, an audit can be useful as an aid to future decision making, such as evaluating various alternatives before the decision is reached.[9] It can be used to identify strongpoints or highlights or directions in the organization so that these can be capitalized upon. "If used to its fullest potential, a marketing audit could lead to new vistas and to innovative thinking," Enis says.[10]

In approaching the marketing audit, these criteria should be considered:

- An audit is performed best by outsiders who are independent of the organization.

- Management and employees of the audited organization should view their work with the auditor as a teamwork effort.

- An audit probably should be conducted every other year or so, although some larger organizations perform annual audits.

- A written checkoff list should guide the auditing. "My strong opinion," Enis says, "is that every marketing manager (or administrator) should use (an auditing) framework explicitly as a foundation for marketing decision-making in the same sense that an experienced pilot always uses a checklist."[11]

- The audit should be completed before the marketing plan or plans are developed.

- Audit questions should be formulated within the framework of local or regional environments as well as acceptable professional standards.

- The organization should be prepared to learn from the audit about where it is weak and deficient, not just where it is strong and dominant and where it deals most effectively with its competition.

- The average auditing process should take three or four weeks.

- Each audit must be followed by the auditor's recommendations as well as proposals as to suitable tools and approaches to improve the organization's marketplace access.

The marketing audit example (Exhibit 6-1) is a composite of audits that the authors have performed. This example by no means is a final approach, but it does provide basic questions that most agencies will want to ask themselves.

Exhibit 6-1 A Sample Marketing Audit

THE MARKETING AUDIT

Documents
Does the organization have:

1. A written statement of mission? ___ Yes ___ No

   If Yes, state its most specific mission: _____

   _____

   _____

2. Bylaws that specify or suggest the mission? ___ Yes ___ No

   If Yes, which sections of the bylaws relate to mission?

   _____

   _____

   _____

Exhibit 6–1 continued

3. A charter that specifies or suggests the mission?
___ Yes ___ No
If Yes, summarize charter sections that relate to the mission: __

_____

4. Any other documents that allude to the mission or the purpose of the organization? ___ Yes ___ No
If Yes, please detail:_____

_____

5. A short-range or long-range master plan? ___ Yes ___ No
Are marketing plans or marketing elements contained in either planning document? ___ Yes ___ No

Date the plan prepared: _____
Explain: _____

_____

6. A publicity or public relations plan? ___ Yes ___ No
Date plan prepared: _____
Explain: _____

_____

7. Marketing plans for individual projects? ___ Yes ___ No
Explain: _____

_____

8. A set of organizational goals and objectives? ___ Yes ___ No
Explain: _____

_____

9. A set of marketing objectives? ___ Yes ___ No
Explain: _____

_____

Constituency of the Organization

10. List in priority order (from most to least important) the main

Exhibit 6–1 continued

publics, groups, targets, markets, or constituents of your organization:

_____	_____
_____	_____
_____	_____
_____	_____

11. Specify how the organization communicates with *each* of its publics or markets (through memorandums, letters, newsletters, speakers, advertisements, television, radio, newspapers, brochures, orders, or directives):

Public or Market   *Communications Channels*

12. Detail how each public communicates its needs and wishes *to* your organization:

Public or Market

Communications Channels to Your Organization

13. Estimate the attitude toward your organization on the part of each key public or market (i.e., negative, positive, or neutral):

Public or Market

Attitude toward Your Organization

14. List the publics or markets that your organization has surveyed, polled, or sampled in the last two years; state how survey results were used by your organization:

Exhibit 6–1 continued

> *Public or Market* *How Survey Results Were Used*
>
> ——————————— ———————————
> ——————————— ———————————
> ——————————— ———————————
> ——————————— ———————————
>
> 15. List the publics or markets your organization wants to survey; state reasons why a survey should be conducted:
>
> *Public or Market* *Reasons for Survey*
>
> ——————————— ———————————
> ——————————— ———————————
> ——————————— ———————————
>
> 16. Which publics or markets would your organization like to know more about; what information is sought about each public or market?
>
> *Public or Market* *Information Sought*
>
> ——————————— ———————————
> ——————————— ———————————
> ——————————— ———————————
> ——————————— ———————————
>
> 17. List the publics or markets with which there are *known barriers* to effective communication. What are those barriers?
>
> *Public or Market* *Barriers to Communication*
>
> ——————————— ———————————
> ——————————— ———————————
> ——————————— ———————————
> ——————————— ———————————
>
> 18. Is there a recent communitywide survey conducted by either your own organization or some other group that purports to indicate the overall health or social welfare status of area residents? ___ Yes ___ No
>
> If Yes, how has the organization used the survey results?
>
> ———————————————————————
> ———————————————————————

Exhibit 6–1 continued

19. List all organizations or individuals that refer patients/clients to your organization, starting with heaviest referring groups or individuals:

20. Is your organization satisfied with the time it spends with, and the communications it directs toward, its referral network?

___ Yes ___ No

Comments:_____

21. How does your organization provide feedback to referrers?

___Written forms
___Letters
___Telephone
___Personal visits from staff
___Other:_____

22. Is your organization satisfied with its feedback system?

___ Yes ___ No

Explain: _____

23. What is the annual turnover, if any, among sources of referrals to your organization? ___%

Comment: _____

24. Are reasons for turnover among referrers known or analyzed by the organization? ___ Yes ___ No

Comment: _____

Exhibit 6–1 continued

25. What changes or shifts in client or patient needs or service patterns have been noticed by the organization in the last two years?

    Explain: _____

    _____

    _____

26. Where does the organization obtain information about how its services are received by users?

    ____Telephone surveys of users
    ____Written questionnaires via mail
    ____Written questionnaires via hand distribution
    ____Face-to-face interviews with individuals
    ____Cluster surveys
    ____Feedback from referral sources
    ____Letters or telephone calls initiated by clients
    ____Rumors and gossip
    ____Other sources: _____

27. What does the organization do with information it receives from clients or patients?

    ____Circulates to management
    ____Sends written response/acknowledgment to clients
    ____Uses it to expand, modify, or drop services
    ____Uses it to praise staff
    ____Uses it to admonish staff
    ____Uses it for short-range or long-range planning
    ____Uses it for public relations purposes
    ____Uses it for marketing purposes
    ____Uses it for staff orientation or inservice
    ____Nothing

Basic Services

28. List alphabetically the services of the organization, breaking them down to smallest components:

    _____   _____
    _____   _____
    _____   _____
    _____   _____

Exhibit 6–1 continued

29. Do the organization's services reflect its purposes as found in the mission, bylaws, charter, or other documents?

__ Yes __ No

Explain: _____

_____

_____

30. After reviewing the complete list of services, is it your opinion that the organization's mission, charter, bylaws, or other documents require revision?   __ Yes __ No

Comment: _____

_____

_____

_____

31. What new services have been started by the organization in the last five years?_____

_____

_____

32. Are the new services started in the last five years growing in acceptance by clients? Please explain by service:

New Service	Approximate Annual Growth Rate (or Rate of Decline)
_____	_____
_____	_____
_____	_____
_____	_____
_____	_____

33. Which new services begun by the organization in the last five years have failed or seem to be failing?

New Service	Reason for Failure
_____	_____
_____	_____
_____	_____
_____	_____

34. Which current services bring the organization the most revenue?

Exhibit 6–1 continued

| | *Income Per Year or* |
Service	*Percent of Revenue*
_____	_____
_____	_____

35. Which services bring the organization the least income?

| | *Income Per Year or* |
Service	*Percent of Revenue*
_____	_____
_____	_____
_____	_____

36. Which services seem to be the most popular with users?

Service	*Why Are Services Popular?*
_____	_____
_____	_____
_____	_____

37. Which services appear to be the least understood by users?

| | *Possible Reason* |
Service	*for Misunderstanding*
_____	_____
_____	_____
_____	_____

Competition

38. List all known or potential competitors of the organization. Include size of staff, ownership, services, service area, fees, caseload size, and annual growth rate:

Competitor	*Supporting Information/Data*
_____	_____
	_____
_____	_____
	_____

39. Describe the one agency or group that is thought to be the chief competition of the organization:

_____

_____

Exhibit 6–1 continued

_____

_____

40. How does your organization learn about its competition? State methods used:

_____

_____

_____

_____

41. If our own organization were the competition, how could we best compete with it?

_____

_____

_____

_____

Management Functions

42. Does the organization have a spokesperson? __ Yes __ No
   If Yes, who is that person and what is the position's title?

_____

43. If the organization has a spokesperson, does it also have an alternate spokesperson?   __ Yes __ No
   If Yes, who is that alternative spokesperson; title?

_____

44. Is there an organization public relations director?
                                                          __ Yes __ No
   If Yes, who is PR director?_____

_____

45. Is there an organization marketing director?   __ Yes __ No
   If Yes, who is it?_____

46. Is there someone who does part-time marketing for the organization?   __ Yes __ No
   If Yes, who is it?_____
   How much time does that person give to marketing functions?

_____

47. Is there a board public relations committee?   __ Yes __ No

Exhibit 6–1 continued

48. Is there a board marketing committee?   __ Yes __ No

49. Is the executive director or administrator sympathetic to market-
    ing?   __ Yes __ No

    Explain: _____

    _____

50. Has the board discussed marketing?   __ Yes __ No

    Comment: _____

51. If the organization has not had marketing research or planning,
    how has it determined the needs of users in order to expand or
    add new services?

    Explain: _____

    _____

    _____

Promotional Tools of the Organization

    Does the organization have:

52. A written press relations policy?   __ Yes __ No

    How is it employed?_____

    _____

    How has the policy benefited the organization in the last two
    years?_____

    _____

    Who has copies of the press policy?_____

    _____

    _____

53. A basic brochure that explains most of the organization's serv-
    ices?   __ Yes __ No

    When was the brochure last revised?_____
    Which publics get the brochure?_____

    _____

54. An internal newsletter or publication?   __ Yes __ No

    Which publics receive the newsletter or publication?

    _____

    _____

Exhibit 6–1 continued

55. An external publication or newsletter?   __ Yes __ No

Which publics receive this publication?_____

_____

56. Which publics or markets generally do not receive your external publication(s)?

_____

_____

57. Direct mail operation?

___for fund-raising purposes?
___for information distribution?
___other purposes:_____
___no direct mail program

58. Regular news release program?   __ Yes __ No

59. A newspaper clipping service?   __ Yes __ No

60. A radio or television news recording service?   __ Yes __ No

61. Radio public service announcements?   __ Yes __ No

To which publics are radio PSAs directed?_____

_____

Which benefits of the organization are highlighted in radio PSAs?_____

_____

62. Television public service announcements?   __ Yes __ No

To which publics are TV PSAs directed?_____

_____

Which benefits of the organization are highlighted in TV PSAs?

_____

_____

63. Slides?   __ Yes __ No

If Yes, to which publics are slides addressed?

_____

Do slides reflect the needs of clients?   __ Yes __ No
Or do slides, on the other hand, reflect the wishes of the organization?   __ Yes __ No

64. Annual report?   __ Yes __ No

Exhibit 6–1 continued

If Yes, to which publics is it directed? _____

Are representatives of any public or market consulted while preparing the annual report?   __ Yes __ No
If Yes, which publics? _____

If annual report were not published, how would the organization direct the flow of information that normally is found in it?

65. Speakers bureau?   __ Yes __ No

Which publics are addressed in activities or promotion of the bureau? _____

Which main messages are the organization's speakers conveying to audiences? _____

What determines subject matter of speeches? _____

66. Print advertising?   __ Yes __ No

To which publics or markets are your ads addressed?

Which benefits of the organization are mentioned in ads?

Do the ads bring the organization new clients or patients?
          __ Yes __ No
How do you know? _____
How many new clients have been obtained through ads in the last 12 months? _____

67. Suggestion systems by which employees or clients can communicate upward to management?   __ Yes __ No

From a communications viewpoint, what does management learn from the suggestion system? _____

Exhibit 6–1 continued

68. Community seminars, symposia, or lectures? ___ Yes ___ No
    What benefits does the organization derive from such events?

    _____

    _____

    _____

69. What are the general themes or directions of the organization's news releases? Check main items:

    ___New personnel (particularly managers or department heads)
    ___New services
    ___New equipment
    ___Revised policies, procedures
    ___Announcements of special events
    ___Recruitment of employees, volunteers
    ___Financial or statistical data/information
    ___Feature stories
    ___Other:_____

70. How does the organization determine how well its purposes, objectives, problems, mission, and news distribution policy are understood by the news media?
    Comment: _____

    _____

    _____

New Business Mechanisms

71. Is someone in the organization designated to:

    ___Find new business (patients, clients)
    ___Find new referral sources
    ___Find or recruit new employees
    ___Find new contacts in the community
    ___Find new sources of funding

72. Is casefinding a practice of the organization? ___ Yes ___ No
    Explain: _____

    _____

    _____

73. Do auxiliary members or volunteers perform community relations functions for the organization?   ___ Yes ___ No

Exhibit 6–1 continued

If Yes, how? _____

_____

74. Do the community relations activities of the auxiliary or volunteers result in more users for the organization? ___ Yes ___ No

   Explain: _____

   _____

   _____

75. Does the organization attract or encourage walk-in users?

   ___ Yes ___ No

   If Yes, how do such users discover the organization?_____

   _____

Fees of the Organization

76. Compared to similar organizations, are your own organization's charges in line, high, or low?

   Comment: _____

   _____

   _____

   _____

77. How does the organization characterize client attitudes toward its fee structure (acceptable, unacceptable, no feelings one way or another, etc.)?_____

   _____

   _____

78. If your organization turns away persons who cannot pay for services, how is the announcement of this practice conveyed to clients?_____

   _____

   _____

79. Does the organization convey an impression to some people that it can provide more free or reduced fee care than it actually can deliver? ___ Yes ___ No

   Comment: _____

   _____

   _____

Exhibit 6-1 continued

80. What questions about your fees do referral network representatives ask?_____

_____

81. How does the organization communicate the main points of its fees to its key publics or markets?

_____

_____

82. How often in the last two years has the organization raised its fees?_____

83. Characterize the reaction from key publics upon announcement of your latest fee increase: _____

_____

_____

When the audit is complete, a comprehensive picture of organizational strengths and weaknesses should be available. It is helpful in the wake of the audit to summarize the insights that have been gained so that both policymakers and managers will have some guidance. The form of such a summary is a matter of style and preference. The authors use various formats with an eye to what will make a client listen and respond to our assessment. We prefer the liberal use of visual material so as to convey key ideas and infiltrate the client's memory.

An elementary yet useful idea for transmitting the substance of the audit is the balance sheet format. Take a large legal pad and draw a line down the middle to create two columns. Label the first column Assets, the other Liabilities. The subheadings in each column should be similar: staff, financing, services, or any other pertinent areas. Subheadings under each main category will lead to refinements. Begin by listing one-sentence statements under each heading until the subject is exhausted. Performed at a staff or board meeting, the effect of the balance sheet can be memorable.

A cautionary note: if the assets considerably outweigh the liabilities, the objectivity of the exercise might be questioned, although perfection seldom is found in any organization. On the other hand, if the liabilities outweigh the assets, marketers might conclude that their attention should be directed to agency reorganization.

A balance sheet for a hypothetical client might appear as in Exhibit 6-2.

Exhibit 6-2 The Market Audit: Balance Sheet

Assets	Liabilities
Accounting Program	*Accounting Program*
1. Forms and records are up to date; understandable to staff.	1. Service data error rate is too high; result is frequent reimbursement delay.
2. Staff size is sufficient for handling billing/accounting operation.	2. System becoming too complex; no professional accountant on staff.
3. New computer program will be on line within three months.	3. Management does not know how to use computer for maximum development of financial program.
4. Design of accounting system appears sound for type and size of program.	4. Cash flow problem exists partly because there is no policy on fee collection.
	5. Accounting system is not used to make trend analyses or projections.
	6. Agency has not taken advantage of federal prepayment reimbursement program.
Staff Development	*Staff Development*
1. Agency has adequate inservice training standards for professionals.	1. Agency makes no provision for training of clerical and support staff.
2. Agency has good educational leave policy.	2. Regular staff meetings are lacking.
3. Budget for staff development program is adequate.	3. High absentee rate exists at scheduled inservice training meetings.
4. In-house library is good, with ample materials for self-study courses.	4. Format for training programs is standard, rather pedestrian.
5. New, well-qualified director for inservice training has just been employed.	5. Little use is made of outstanding local professional resources.
	6. Top management provides no support or enforcement of inservice policies.
	7. No provision is made for staff critique of inservice training.
PR/Communications Program	*PR/Communications Program*
1. Agency has visible attractive service that lends much opportunity to publicize program.	1. Management's concept of public relations is: "Get our name into the paper."
2. Free consultation is available from a top local PR firm.	2. Good internal communications are lacking among various staff levels.
3. Adequate budget is provided for public relations.	3. Several recent incidents of insensitive staff handling of clients have been reported.

Exhibit 6–2 continued

4. Good relationships with local news media exist.
5. PR staff is bright and able.

6. In-house print and production facilities are excellent.
7. Support for development of communications program exists within middle management.

4. Telephone and reception system is inadequate.
5. Budget is spent on hodgepodge of printed materials and advertisements.

Service (Business) Development

1. Agency has monopoly on providing some services (accounting for one-third of total service volume).
2. Agency is recognized for quality of its care.
3. Several new markets for present services are readily identifiable.
4. Reimbursement potential is high for some new services that could be provided.
5. Staff for new business development will be hired soon.
6. Board has given mandate to examine future service directions.

Service (Business) Development

1. Demand for some traditional services is diminishing.
2. Agency fails to maintain system of liaison with its major referring sources.
3. Agency has no precise knowledge of current clients/patients.
4. Attitude of "let the business come to us" is prevalent in administration.

With this balance sheet approach, the marketer will be able to pinpoint images the agency is conveying to publics, markets, and targets. Clients have told the agency about their wants; examination of agency managerial and professional attitudes has produced another view. Staff morale and performance is as much a concern as its size, makeup, and competency. The board of directors, the auxiliary, committees, and other friends of the agency have something to add. The agency's competitors, the regulatory bodies it deals with, its major financing resources have their own perspectives. Rarely is the combined evidence totally flattering to the institution. Nor should it be, since the marketer seeks only the truth.

With the auditing phase completed, the marketer knows which tools are available to work with, whether to use a hand saw or power saw, a brace and bit, or an electric drill. Especially, the marketer will know what help to expect, and from whom. The marketer knows much better what can or cannot be done and has reached those conclusions systematically.

SUMMARY

Marketers need to take a penetrating look within their own organizations, especially at statements of goals, purposes, and mission to make sure that the agency is providing the services it has promised to deliver or is capable of delivering. A continuing program of organizational self-examination is necessary to detect flaws, discover strengths, and plan the future. Everything from the wishes of the founding fathers to the organization's services and service potential must be scrutinized and charted so that the marketer can know the organization first before proceeding to ask clients and prospective clients their opinions.

A device to obtain a searching picture of internal operations and the organization's image, both inwardly and outwardly, is the marketing audit. If it does not apply an audit or a similar introspective device, an organization will find it more difficult to develop internal sources to plot and build successful operations. A completed audit provides clues about the organizational potential or success in marketing, promoting, and dealing with a constantly changing environment.

NOTES

1. Meritt L. Kastens, *Long-Range Planning for Your Business* (New York: AMACOM, 1976), p. 24.

2. Ben F. Enis, *Marketing Principles: The Management Process* (Santa Monica, Calif.: Goodyear Publishing Co., 1977), p. 178.

3. David F. Linowes, *Strategies for Survival* (New York: AMACOM, 1973), p. 135.

4. Ibid., p. 140.

5. Alfred R. Oxenfeldt, *Executive Action in Marketing* (Belmont, Calif.: Wadsworth Publishing Co., 1966), p. 746.

6. Enis, *Marketing Principles: The Management Process*, pp. 178-179.

7. Philip Kotler, *Marketing Management* (Englewood Cliffs, N.J.: Prentice-Hall, Inc., 1976), p. 448.

8. Abe Schuchman, "The Marketing Audit: Its Nature, Purposes and Problems," in *Analyzing and Improving Marketing Performance—Report No. 32* (New York: American Management Associations, 1959), p. 14.

9. Robert F. Hartley, *Marketing: Management and Social Change* (Scranton, Pa.: Intext Educational Publishers, 1972), p. 619.

10. Enis, *Marketing Principles: The Management Process*, p. 180.

11. Ibid., p. 180.

Chapter 7

Researching the Competition

Competition is said to be whatever business executives have to do to take business away from rivals and vice versa. In health and human services, this definition has similar applicability, although many agency heads will deny that they compete or are competitors. Often, the word "competition" is unmentionable to those in the nonprofit public service sector.

Competition exists, nonetheless. Energetic, honest competition—vying for referrer allegiance, developing friends in the community, seeking the same fund-raising dollars, or making overtures to the same potential service users—occurs continually. Competition provides clarity and force to marketing decisions, helps to depress or contain costs, encourages service innovation, and generally results in better agency services.

In health and human services, competition is not pointedly price oriented. "Because a service organization cannot demonstrate a service, its reputation for dependability, skill, and perhaps creativity becomes its chief promotional aid," David J. Schwartz says.[1] To illustrate, two hospital rehabilitation clinics offer about the same services but compete in service quality; reputation; location; street access; waiting and treatment time; staff availability, depth, and attitudes; billing policies; and promotional tools. Price is not a major factor, although operational costs are important to hospital administration. Nonprice competition holds promise of longer payoffs, embodies the greatest opportunities for creative distinction, and probably is less likely to precipitate reprisals, according to Ronald R. Gist.[2]

Through sound marketing planning, a health or human services organization must convince potential users that its staff is experienced, skilled, knowledgeable, caring, ethical, and sensitive since it can't blatantly promote low service fees, offer guaranteed results, or conduct special sales. Also, it can't overrun its competition overnight. It must develop its reputation gradually, using rational, honest marketing strategies.

DIFFERENCES IN COMPETITION

How do competitors differ? Mostly in how users perceive the benefits of their services. Such perceptions might involve:

1. a perceived objective performance provided by the physical aspect of the service—promise of a completed adoption procedure or resolution of a parent-child conflict
2. perceived social benefits represented by the use of the service—well-designed counseling areas, well-educated staff members, contemporary testing or analytical equipment
3. psychological benefits delivered by an association with the service—a feeling of physical improvement, a healthier or relieved state, a positive attitude change
4. objective benefits and subjective satisfaction conferred by the location, manner, and timing of the service
5. instructive, informational, or technical material or data furnished through the service
6. an assurance of dependability or quality imparted by the service
7. an assortment of benefits, such as having a variety of services from which to choose.[3]

Some characteristics of a strongly competitive situation are: conscientious and direct selling activities, such as personal visits to referring groups; an interest in capitalizing on the quality and contemporaneousness of the agency's service; generous spending for research; above-average curiosity in what competitors are doing; and possible active efforts to obtain patients or clients from the competition.

There are three ways to react to new competition: ignore it, imitate it, or adopt some of its main features.

COMPETITION: POSITIONS AND PARALLELS

Nearly all marketing planning is shadowed in one way or another by a competitor's actions or reactions. "One must remember that each competitor or potential competitor has both strong and weak points that must be considered in evaluating and developing market strategies for any given target. Knowing and understanding one's competition, whether existing or potential, is vital in planning market segmentation strategy."[4]

An institution continually seeks a favorable place to stand—not merely immediate profits, notes Perry Bliss, who compares competition to "a succession of military campaigns rather than to the pressures and attrition of a single battle."[5] A competitor, he adds, "may gain ground through a successful campaign based on new product features or merchandising ideas. It may lose ground or be forced to fall back on its core position because of the successful campaigns of others." Alderson and Green remind us, on the other hand, that: "The parallel to military action is not complete since the marketing strategist is not always free to choose startling innovations but is restricted by legal limitations and considerations of trade relations and consumer attitudes."[6]

Every institution occupies a unique position in its marketplace: there are differences in its services, management philosophy, location, policies, promotions, and clients. These differences, once they are known by management, must be emphasized as part of the organization's special character.

In health and human services, at least three competitive categories exist: (1) generic (institutions operate in the same general area); (2) service-related (one agency offers services that are or can be offered by another agency); and (3) direct (agencies provide the same services).

How can new competition impact on an established human services organization? It can: (1) compete for the clients who represent the existing institution's market core; (2) compete for the attention of referring professionals or for capable volunteers to serve on its board, task forces, or committees; (3) compete for employees, especially professionals who seek better salaries, fringe benefits, or quicker advancement opportunities; (4) compete for the attention of community interests such as politicians, news media leaders, bankers, and service clubs. A new competitor may offer different services, such as extended daily or weekend coverage, new specialties, computerized billing, influence with third party payers, chain ownership, less paperwork, or better office location.

REACTION TO RIVALS

No matter how overpowering the threat by new rivals, some existing agencies faced with competition will stand aside, ignoring the newcomers. A year or two may elapse before the rival managers talk; sometimes they never get together, since some organizations are content to coexist leisurely with competition and in nearly complete ignorance of the newcomer's motives, mannerisms, or potential impact on their services. This "live and let live" posture, with each organization fairly comfortable with its market share, violates no rules of competition. It does, however, tend to make each agency less robust than it might have been had natural competitive elements been actively at work.

"For competition to remain effective, contestants must be able to continue in the competitive process as long as they supply a commodity (or a service) that is accepted in the marketplace," Wasson declares.[7] Action by one organization that places another at a measurable disadvantage destroys the purpose of competition, he adds.

Competition often favors the new or the smaller agency. Alderson and Green assert:

> . . . the firm with smaller resources can sometimes let its larger competition incur all of the costs in pioneering a new field and then seize some of the benefits for itself. It can offer to do the same thing for less after its competitor has made the investment in showing how to do it. It can add minor refinements to a basic innovation or add improvements in processing or marketing to what someone else has accomplished in basic design.[8]

Corwin D. Edwards writes:

> In a competitive system, the rules of the game should be like those that govern a competitive sport: that is, while they set limits within which the play must take place, and in so doing necessarily affect the character of the play, they should allow choice among a large number of alternatives, including all those that make for a good game.[9]

PRINCIPLES OF COMPETITION

In health and human services, understanding the competition can enhance the marketing effort. Some observations:

1. Each service organization offers a unique bundle of services to satisfy various groups of potential clients. In its bundle, for instance, United Way will tout its cost-effective umbrella form of community solicitation, or a vocational counseling service might accent its number of sheltered workshop contracts with industry. Stressing specific components of the bundle can assist in the development of objectives and strategies with target groups.
2. Markets are never static; they're transient. A health or human services organization continually reexamines its place in the community, redefining and reconfirming its niche. Less than the total market, a niche is a segment of the market. Many organizations can be weakened permanently by not understanding the fickleness of the marketplace.
3. Although other organizations may be firmly established in the area, a new health or human services organization must be allowed to enter the marketplace without any barriers other than those prescribed by planning laws or practices.

4. Opportunities for new health and human services organizations tend to proliferate. New groups successfully imitate established groups. The imitating agency often can find its niche in the community while barely competing with the more established entity since most markets seem to be large enough to support organizations offering similar or nearly comparable services. Risks to the newcomer are reduced because of the successful experience of the original agency. Furthermore, so long as original agencies survive in the marketplace, more potential operators will deliberate on the possibilities of their own entry into business. If the original service organization abuses its good fortune of being the first or the only such agency in the area (perhaps by charging exorbitant rates or delivering shoddy services), the marketplace entry by others is enhanced sharply.

5. Both the buyer and the seller seek each other out in the marketplace. Buyers of contrasting backgrounds and qualities fill the marketplace. A heterogeneous situation such as this means that a health or human services organization and its clients may search endlessly for the best match-up. In this bilateral search, the agency's promotional tools are important, especially in communicating elements of the service bundle.

6. A competitive action needs creative elements and innovation. If not, the rival will emulate the competitor's program too easily.

7. If there are few competitors, each should be individually identifiable to the other.

8. Each competitor in a small market is important enough that any significant marketing changes that it makes will have a direct impact on competitors.

9. All areas of marketing decision are influenced to some extent by competitors' actions and possible reactions.

10. Every business or service organization must have a chunk of the market for itself. The chunk is the market core, the repeat business an organization obtains.

11. If the health and human services agency's marketing strategies are successful, the competition is likely to retaliate.

12. Each organization should be able to respond to competitive retaliation. Marketers must prepare alternative strategies.

Established organizations ought to be curious about newcomers or potential rivals for several reasons: they may learn from the newcomer's approach to business (service modifications, rate structuring, staffing, fringe benefits, promotional stances); peers or constituents may question established agencies about the new rival; an established agency may be asked to explain or defend its own policies, procedures, and services in contrast to those of the new rival.

The established agency always will require basic information about the new agency to help it respond to its programs or promotions. Part of the intelligence gathering is a survey form (Exhibit 7-1) to assist the established agency in organizing its knowledge about the new rival so it can formulate its revised marketing objectives, strategies, targets, and tools.

Exhibit 7-1 Checklist for Competitors

1. Name of competitor:_____

2. Address of competitor:_____

3. Date competitor opened for business: _____

4. Describe the nature of competitor's business:
   _____
   _____
   _____

5. Who sponsors the competitor's agency?
   _____
   _____

6. Describe competitor's financial backing, if known:
   _____
   _____
   _____

7. Name and title of competitor's chief administrative officer:
   _____

8. Previous employment of that chief administrative officer:
   _____
   _____

9. Name of competitor's chairman of the board:
   _____

10. Names and business titles of other volunteer board members:
   _____
   _____
   _____
   _____
   _____

Exhibit 7–1 continued

11. Names, titles, immediate past positions of key members of competitor's administrative staff:

   _____

   _____

   _____

   _____

12. Did a community survey precede the competition's formation?

   ___ Yes ___ No

   If Yes, describe the survey and state who conducted it:_____

   _____

   _____

13. Did the new program facility undergo a formal project review through a community planning council or any other central planning agency or authority? ___ Yes ___ No

   If Yes, what agency and when?_____

   _____

   What were the final recommendations?

   _____

   _____

14. Is the competition's program or facility licensed? ___Yes ___No

   If Yes, when and by whom was the license issued? _____

   _____

   Was a license ever denied? ___Yes ___No

   If Yes, by whom was the license denied and for what reason?

   _____

   _____

15. Was a certificate of need (CON) issued? ___Yes ___No

   If Yes, when was it issued?_____

   Any unusual qualifications or conditions attached to the CON?

   _____

   _____

16. In your opinion, are clients of the competitor's program or facility being recruited from (circle one)

   your own agency's service area,   a new service area,

   a combination of both?

Exhibit 7–1 continued

17. Who on the new competitor's staff is the contact person with clients and referring sources in the community?

_____

18. What services are offered by the competition?

_____

_____

_____

_____

19. Do any of the competitor's services differ from those your own agency offers?   __Yes __No

    If Yes, how do they differ?_____

_____

_____

_____

20. Does the competition have any striking features to help it attract clients?   __ Yes __ No

    If Yes, what are those features? _____

_____

_____

_____

21. What are the competition's costs and charges in comparison with your own?_____

_____

_____

_____

_____

_____

22. What socioeconomic, psychic advantages do you think the competitor has over your own operation?_____

_____

_____

_____

23. What disadvantages does the competitor face in the community?_____

_____

_____

Exhibit 7–1 continued

24. Does the physical location of your competitor offer any advantage over your own location? __Yes __No

    If Yes, what advantages?_____

    _____

    _____

25. What are the competitor's main marketing targets?

    _____

    _____

    _____

26. List the competitor's marketing tools and how they are used:

    _____

    _____

    _____

    _____

    _____

27. If your competitor were to make a major marketing change in the next several months, to which markets or targets would the rival shift? _____

    _____

28. What challenges does the competitor face from your agency?

    _____

    _____

    _____

    From other competitors in the area?_____

    _____

    _____

29. In a paragraph or two (use a separate sheet of paper if necessary) describe how the competition might characterize your own agency from a competitive viewpoint:

    _____

    _____

    _____

30. What does your organization need to do to protect itself from the new competition, both immediately and long range?

    _____

    _____

APPROACHING THE COMPETITION

Gathering information and data about a new rival is bound to frustrate an established agency, but the results should be worth the effort. In the authors' experiences, we have found that the competition usually is receptive to its rival's questions. A rival's answers usually will be forthright since the competitor can learn something in turn from the interrogator; this is helpful because the newcomer usually has a need to be accepted early by established agencies. Here is one way to approach the new rival:

1. Phone the rival and extend a welcome. Share some background about your own agency; start asking some questions about the newcomer in order to feel your way.

2. Ask for the competitor's brochure and other literature it is distributing. Tell the rival you'll send your brochure if it does not have one.

3. Determine who the competitor's key managers are, as well as their backgrounds. If the agency is small, there may only be one or two. It is not unorthodox to discuss staffing during the first visit.

4. Set up a session to get to know the newcomer better. At that point, obtain an understanding of the agency's owners, sponsors, financial angels. Though the competitor might volunteer such information by telephone, go ahead and arrange for the social meeting anyway.

If answers are hard to obtain:

1. Shop the new facility as a prospective user or delegate the task to someone else.

2. Telephone the new facility's switchboard or intake section and ask appropriate questions.

3. Ask colleagues what they've heard about the newcomer.

4. If there is a known parent organization, obtain its last annual report for clues about the newcomer's objectives, goals.

5. Contact appropriate licensing agencies to determine more about the organization's origins and makeup.

6. Talk with professionals who may have had dealings with the newcomer.

If there are unreasonable roadblocks in your way, and there is some legitimate concern about the competition, try the following, but cautiously:

1. Use the Freedom of Information Act to gain access to information about the competitor's ownership, financial strength, and management.
2. Contact a Better Business Bureau for information.
3. Ask an attorney to assist in gathering facts.

It may not be possible to compile a complete profile on a competitor, but if the existing agency's efforts are applied systematically, it can determine enough to reassess its own marketing strategies and strengths, estimate how the newcomer may seek entry into its core market, and calculate how successful it might be in becoming a part of the professional life of the community.

The careful study of competition, established or new, is one of the most beneficial facets of marketing. It forces the marketer's agency or clients to evaluate its own operations in the light of the strengths and weaknesses of its rival. It is likely to reveal marketplace gaps that neither agency is serving properly. It removes the tendency to grouse about the other entity and its tactics. It opens opportunities for improving or developing one's own product or service, to stay a step ahead. Sometimes it brings about a judgment or conclusion that it might be better to join 'em than fight 'em, thus leading the way to consolidation of interests and objectives that can only benefit clients or patients and the community.

SUMMARY

In most ways competition is a healthy activity, constructive rather than destructive. Competition may aid marketing decisions, keep costs more constant, invite service innovations, and result in better service delivery to clients. Most health and human services groups are in some form of competitive position, not so much as to price but as to service bundles as well as to the perceived social, physical, psychological, and other benefits of their agency. Institutions react to competition in three ways: they ignore it, imitate it, or adopt a variation of the rival's main service features.

Gauging the strengths and weaknesses of competition is encouraged, as is the agency's own introspection. New competition can influence existing organizations variously; by contacting the existing agency's constituents, referring sources, employees, or managers; or by offering a markedly different service bundle. If threatened, existing agencies must determine their reactions and form retaliatory strategies.

Newcomers often can flourish at the expense of older, more established organizations. All competitors discover that their markets are changing continually, that awareness of change is a requisite for survival. Opportunities for new health and human services agencies seem to proliferate, creating niches for newcomers that understand the professional and political environment. Competition is natural since buyers and sellers continually seek each other in the marketplace. Most areas of marketing decision are influenced by competitors' actions or possible reactions. The act of retaliation, as has been stressed, is natural. It can be expected and must be prepared for systematically.

NOTES

1. David J. Schwartz, *Marketing Today* (New York: Harcourt Brace Jovanovich, Inc., 1977), p. 539.

2. Ronald R. Gist, *Marketing and Society* (Hinsdale, Ill.: The Dryden Press, 1973), p. 254.

3. Chester R. Wasson, *Research Analysis for Marketing Decisions* (New York: Appleton-Century-Croft, 1965), p. 258.

4. P. Dudley Kaley in *Marketing Strategies—A Symposium,* ed. Earl L. Bailey (New York: The Conference Board, n.d.), p. 58.

5. Perry Bliss, *Marketing and the Behavioral Society* (Boston: Allyn and Bacon, 1967), p. 569.

6. Wroe Alderson and Paul E. Green, *Planning and Problem Solving in Marketing* (Homewood, Ill.: Richard D. Irwin, Inc., 1964), p. 461.

7. Wasson, *Research Analysis for Marketing Decisions,* p. 102.

8. Alderson and Green, *Planning and Problem Solving in Marketing,* p. 465.

9. Corwin D. Edwards, *Maintaining Competition: Requirements of a Government Policy* (New York: McGraw-Hill Book Co., 1949), p. 3.

Chapter 8

Setting Objectives in Marketing

An objective is "something that one's efforts are intended to attain or accomplish"[1] and a "specific description of an end result to be achieved."[2] The process of setting objectives is built around three factors: hierarchy, work and assignments, and accountability.

One positive result of the research phase of marketing is apt to be a revision of the original objectives of the project simply because so much more becomes known about the marketplace. The primary objectives may remain the same but subobjectives will be revised, added, or dropped. The preliminary marketing process helped to identify and sort preliminary project objectives, scan the marketplace and the internal operating environment, and place objectives in some initial order. The result usually is a hierarchy of objectives for each specific project. This means that to achieve the primary goal, there are one, two, or more subobjectives that must be met first, and for each subobjective there are an equal number of sub-subobjectives. Like a stage erected for a great drama, a framework of imagined poles and braces supports the platform on which the show is performed. In the marketing project, each brace is a subobjective; each is aligned with another, each holding its share of the project's weight.

"Objectives," says Drucker, "are the basis for work and assignments. They determine the structure of the business, the key activities which must be discharged, and, above all, the allocation of people to tasks. Objectives are the foundation for designing both the structure of the business and the work of individual units and individual managers."[3] The same can be said for a marketing project.

To accomplish a marketing goal, the manager or marketer showing sound managerial talent first must break the primary marketing objectives into various pieces, assuring that appropriate levels of the organization are assigned specific parts. As the ringmaster, the marketer simultaneously must keep an eye on several rings that are the scene of controlled, synchronized actions. Each gets the spotlight occasionally but all contribute to the achievement of the first objective. Failure on one assignment might mean the failure of the whole project.

"If objectives are only good intentions they are worthless. They must degenerate into work. And work is always specific, always has—or should have—clear, unambiguous, measurable results, a deadline and a specific assignment of accountability."[4] Accountability means control over the marketing project. Because the marketer is not likely to be the administrator as well, the individual needs the backing of the administrator to see that subobjectives (tasks) are accomplished. The marketer also needs the cooperation of lower level managers who, unless wholly committed, can circumvent carefully planned intentions. To satisfy all parties, the assignment for implementation—and control over implementation—must be utterly clear and acceptable.

Chapter 1 suggested that the various components of marketing followed a logical sequence and that the process should be extremely flexible. For example, the marketer may identify a group of potential clients for a counseling agency quite some time after the research phase is completed because of a new and previously undiscovered opportunity: the willingness, for instance, of insurance companies to pay for services that are provided to employees with mental or emotional ailments. This change could necessitate, of course, a revision and new ranking of targets for the counseling agency. With a major change in potential reimbursement sources, the agency also must reconsider its service objectives.

CHANGING ORIGINAL MARKETING OBJECTIVES

Objectives may be added, subtracted, or amended at various stages. An exception is the primary objective, which is the capstone of the project's pyramid of goals. If that objective is changed, the entire project also is changed.

In the following situations, the organizations changed the original objectives of their projects.

Case 1

A large physical rehabilitation organization adopted, as the primary objective of its marketing project, the prevention of the loss of approximately one-third of its business because two hospitals planned to establish their own competing programs. Both hospitals always had sent their patients to the rehabilitation facility. After researching the marketplace and studying the agency, the marketer (an outside consultant) persuaded management to revise its primary objective from a negative stance (and one almost impossible to defend) to a far more positive position. The change: The organization agreed to seek client referrals from many more referral sources, to diversify its services, and to consider merger with similar agencies. The effect of the change was to spread the operations so that the loss of any major source of business would not have an adverse financial impact on the total program. Further, the facility discovered that a positive objective had far more psychological or morale benefits than one that was defensive in nature.

Case 2

A family planning council serving a metropolitan area decided that a great opportunity lay in expansion of its geographical service area. It set a primary objective of absorbing a half-dozen smaller, similar agencies so that the result would be an organization serving more than half the state. After the marketing audit and a two-day staff retreat to consider future directions, the expansion objective was demoted from first to twelfth place on the list of goals. In its stead, the agency's staff adopted two other objectives, both leading to expansion of service but at a fraction of the investment and risk of the original. The moral: Objectives must have a degree of practicality about them; an agency must be ready to pull in its horns when realities so dictate.

Case 3

A regional council on aging operated an information and referral service for senior citizens. It decided to take a marketing approach to the objective of broadening the program to 24-hour, seven-day-a-week coverage in order to serve the elderly better. However, its marketing research revealed the following: True emergencies after normal business hours were handled by a local crisis telephone hot-line and the police department, which manned the 911 emergency telephone line. Other calls were received by the local United Way's information and referral program. A limited marketing survey of senior citizens revealed that there was little or no interest in the expanded program. The survey did uncover another interest: a telephone calling system directed to homebound persons (telephone reassurance). The investigation persuaded the council to abandon its original objective and to create a new program. It found that a network of volunteers calling the homebound brought far more benefits than simply having a few staff persons available for assistance. This example illustrates that the organization occasionally may change its primary objectives, and perhaps should, if it will consult the people it serves before deciding that it knows what is good for its constituents.

In none of these examples was there any departure from organizational principles. There were no reasons to be ashamed of switching from original intentions; the agencies, in fact, were applauded for being responsive and pragmatic. They did not terminate their marketing projects but proceeded in their revised objectives with far more confidence.

THE SIMPLICITY OF OBJECTIVE SETTING

Objectives can be classified in various ways. There can be strategy, innovation, development, results-centered, productivity, financial, and operational objectives, to name a few. External and internal (or management) objectives have been referred to earlier. Unless one has a penchant for clearly sorting and labeling objectives for one's own use, the authors prefer to make objective setting as simple and painless as possible

Writing a clean, clear objective takes both practice and skill. Long and rich experience in a profession does not always qualify a person to write well-honed objectives. The key undoubtedly is the ability to be able to measure the objective by time, quality, quantity, or any other dimension. What must be avoided is the tendency to be too vague, to refer to "doing good" without saying how or how much and when it will be accomplished.

One of the authors reviewed a document prepared earlier for a nonprofit planning organization with a traditional interest in human problems and services. Supported mostly by private monies, the agency possessed a strong volunteer base. In the throes of reorganization, it was seeking to develop a community-oriented or broad base of planning in cooperation with other planning and funding authorities.

The agency wrote the following management objective: *"The Council will seek to be an effective agent to help resolve problems and improve the delivery of human services."*

In critiquing this objective, there is nothing that says *how* the organization will be effective, *what* problems will be addressed, *when* the objective is expected to be accomplished, or *which* human services are involved. Such a statement is more like a New Year's resolution; even then, it hedges by using the term "will seek." The objective should have been written to reflect more clearly what would be needed to be "an effective agent to help resolve problems . . . " (for example, "by strengthening its staff capability and enlisting key volunteers during the first half of next year . . . "). More clarity could be added by mentioning the areas of planning to be addressed and the service providers with which the organization would work.

Manager or marketer, supervisor or department head, all have a difficult and challenging responsibility in setting objectives. We suggest that a few guidelines are useful for any organization faced with such a challenge.

GUIDELINES FOR WRITING OBJECTIVES

1. *Objectives should be written.* Unless they are, everyone in the organization will have a different idea of what must be accomplished, and individ-

uals will operate at cross-purposes. In addition, some important objectives may be left uncovered.

2. *Objectives should be adopted formally.* Some may require approval by the board of directors, a policy committee, or top management. Others are of most importance to departments or program units. Adoption implies a commitment to action.

3. *Objectives should be stated positively.* This means the agency will do something that has an affirmative rather than a negative effect. Instead of stating that, "We will cut down client complaints about long waiting times in the casework section by adding more staff," it would be better to state that "We will increase caseworker personnel so that no client must wait longer than 10 to 15 minutes before receiving services."

4. *Objectives should be quantified or measurable.* If stated in terms of dollars or dates, objectives are elevated beyond just "doing good." Instead of stating, "We will expand counseling and education services in Dodge County next year," why not say: "We will conduct 12 family life classes, provide two half-time counselors, and open an office in Central City in Dodge County in the first quarter of next year."

5. *Objectives should help facilitate work assignments and accountability.* As the primary objective is split into components, someone should be assigned to each part. It would be desirable to have each department or individual establish one or more subobjectives. Thus, in the Dodge County example, the objective could be assigned to a particular department or person: "The Client Education Unit will conduct 12 family life classes . . . " and "The administration will open an office in Central City . . . "

6. *Objectives should avoid philosophical or imprecise terms.* Consider the word "quality." Every organization tends to think of itself as delivering quality care or maintaining quality in its performance. The problem is in the definition of quality. Are there standards? Has the organization been accredited as a quality operation? It is better to avoid ambiguity than to be trapped by a phrase that cannot be proved. Vagueness in objective writing leads to philosophical meanderings. Avoid the temptation.

7. *Objectives should be ranked by priority.* Each objective is important to the organization and in the scheduling of activities. If one objective is "to open two branch offices" and another is "to employ and train four new vocational counselors," which comes first? Why hire and train persons if their worksites aren't in operation?

8. *Objectives should be pragmatic, attainable.* If objectives are established by persons at various levels of the organization as part of personal work programs, as we believe they should be, it is important that the objectives be realistic. Performance, salary increments, and promotions are based on

achievements. Objectives should require staff to extend themselves but not beyond what reasonably can be expected.

OBJECTIVES AND THEIR HIERARCHY

Forming a hierarchy means putting objectives in a sequence of actions that, when summed up, will result in accomplishment of the primary objective. A hierarchy is a vertical, top-to-bottom arrangement. When looking at marketing objectives' placement in such an arrangement, the hierarchy is pictured as in Figure 8-1. The marketer starts with the intentions of the organization, develops a time-limited (usually on an annual basis) prescription of objectives that are coupled with management's special (and compatible) objectives, then develops an array of marketing objectives.

To carry out the marketing project objectives, the marketer can either extend the triangle or create new ones to establish a hierarchy for each project (Figure 8-2). Assume that primary objectives have been prepared for each project. The primary objectives then are split into logical, timely actions and responsibilities are assigned to the appropriate persons.

Figure 8–1 The Hierarchy Triangle

Organization

Goals   Objectives

Annual Program
Objectives

Management's
Objectives

Marketing Project Objectives

Figure 8–2 Hierarchies for Individual Projects

There are, in fact, six or seven subobjectives under the . . . primary objective. You know that if each of these subobjectives is achieved, the primary objective will be achieved automatically. You know further that if any of the subobjectives is missed, it is most unlikely that the primary objective will be achieved. This is the "necessary and sufficient rule." At any level in the hierarchy of objectives the sum of the subobjectives must be *sufficient* to automatically achieve the next higher objective. If any of the subobjectives could be missed without impairing the next higher objective, drop it out. It is not *necessary.*[5]

All managers and marketers agree that development of objectives below the primary level probably will be more successful if they are negotiated with the individuals who must carry out work activities rather than if they are assigned automatically. The lower level managers will have had a share in the setting of the primary objectives. They also must help decide the sequence of subobjectives. Kastens suggests that managers "let . . . subordinate(s) cascade the hierarchy of objectives down the ultimate action level."[6] McConkey notes that "continuous care must be exercised to prevent the preceding process," setting objectives by the levels described, "from ending up in a top-down approach. Obviously, one of the ways to prevent this is to ensure that each team member is given the greatest possible voice in recommending and debating the objectives at the higher level."[7] McConkey refers to the hierarchy as the "link-pin" concept.

Kastens analyzes the actual operation of a hierarchy:

In describing the process of cascading objectives down through a hierarchy, one can't avoid making it sound more simple than it is. In the first place, the process is not so linear as it sounds; it doesn't go all in one direction, from the top down. . . . The normal sequence is: The information flows up the organization to where the high-level objectives are set. Then the discussions move down the organization until they get to the point at which the work will actually be done. Finally, the details of a myriad of individual actions are aggregated and passed up the hierarchy to see whether they will all hang together and still add up to the attainment of the primary objectives.[8]

The hierarchical message is that managers and individuals in the affected departments, by their participation in negotiations, have outlined their own individual workplans. The results of creating the hierarchy are work assignments. If written according to the suggested guidelines, they are quantitative, time defined, and specific in terms of actions.

With work assignments determined, the marketer has at least a framework for accountability or control over the marketing project and can report on progress to the administrator and prod others to perform their work. If a breakdown occurs, the marketer can take remedial action of a different kind: using managerial backing for getting performance, revising the strategy, or developing a new tool for staff to use. The marketer is the expeditor, the traffic cop for the entire project. This individual's role is to stimulate enthusiasm, to get people to look at their objectives as opportunities to build toward something of which they can be proud.

Drucker writes: "An organization will have a high spirit of performance if it is consistently directed toward opportunity rather than toward problems," (or the negative). "It will have the thrill of excitement, the sense of challenge, and the satisfaction of achievement if its energies are put where the results are, that means on the opportunities."[9] If anything, the marketer must possess a highly developed sense of opportunity as well as the ability to convey such a sense throughout the marketing plan implementation.

EXAMINING THE HIERARCHY EFFECT

The hierarchy of objectives can "cascade," as Kastens puts it, from primary objective to five or ten subobjectives on down to 50 or 100 sub-subobjectives. This theory is illustrated with a relatively simple project with a hierarchy, work assignment, and control points.

Rockwell YMCA Sports Health Program

The board of directors of a progressive YMCA decided that it wanted to establish a program in sports health and medicine in its area. It was led to this venture because of a highly successful athletic program for its members, its good working relationship with a hospital next door, available space that could be readily converted to different uses, and the interest of a group of young physicians associated with both institutions. A study of the financial feasibility cleared the way for the Y. The hospital's trustees agreed in principle to share in the program if benefits would accrue and there was no loss of funds to the hospital. The *marketing objective* was stated as follows:

By the end of the next fiscal year we will establish the Rockwell YMCA Sports Health and Medicine Program which will specialize in providing in-house physical testing and therapeutic services, promoting programs of wellness and physical fitness among groups and individuals, and arranging for acute-care treatment of sports-related and occupational injuries through Community Hospital.

An initial analysis of the project led to the development, by an in-house marketing team, of a prospectus or plan for operation of the new department. The implementation period was calculated to be 18 months. Seven primary objectives were drawn up as a result of the team's efforts:

Objective A: Design a complete program of service offerings, including equipment and facilities needed.

Objective B: Acquire $235,000 for renovation of space and purchase of testing equipment and related program materials (as determined from financial feasibility study).

Objective C: Develop appropriate arrangements for payment and reimbursement of services to be provided.

Objective D: Renovate and equip first floor of north wing of YMCA to accommodate the program.

Objective E: Acquire clients/patients in sufficient numbers to enable fiscal operations to be self-supporting within one year after opening the program.

Objective F: Negotiate for participation of Community Hospital in program, including use of facilities and staff.

Objective G: Acquire and develop a staff complement that will operate the Y's program.

Subobjectives were developed for each of these objectives and placed in a Gantt chart format as a guide and control sheet for the marketer and those responsible for each of the subobjectives. The chart is sequenced vertically with the list of tasks to be undertaken; horizontally, it is time-related by days, weeks, or months, depending on what suits the marketer. It also can include

Table 8-1 Gantt Chart for Implementing an Objective

Objective A: Develop Service Plan

Month 0	3	6	9	12	15	18	Assigned
Subobjectives:							
A-1	Research state of the art in sports health and medicine.						Team
A-2	Employ consultants to assist in design.						CEO
A-3	Organize and utilize staff advisory group.						Mkt. Dir.
A-4	Prepare comprehensive service plan by target groups.						Team
A-5	Determine appropriate geographical service area.						Team
A-6	Obtain appropriate regulatory approvals.						CEO & Mkt. Dir.
A-7	Write policies/guidelines for operations.						Team

other information of the marketer's choosing such as designation of the department or individual responsible for the task or a checkoff system to show completion of tasks. Rather than detail the entire list of Rockwell YMCA subsubobjectives in chart form, Objective A is used here in broad form (Table 8-1).

It should be noted that the marketing team established by management was to be responsible for implementation of the program. Although there might be arguments about the placement of any of the responsibilities for Objective A or, for that matter, the appropriateness of the objectives (abbreviated in this example), results are the main consideration.

For the remaining primary objectives, the following subobjectives were outlined (not shown in chart form):

Objective B: *Acquire funding*
          B-1 Prepare program prospectus to be used with concerned parties.
          B-2 Submit proposals to appropriate foundations.
          B-3 Obtain loans or guarantees from lending institutions, if necessary.

Objective C: *Develop reimbursement capability*
          C-1 Negotiate with Blue Cross and other insurers.
          C-2 Seek contracts with local employer health plans.
          C-3 Establish membership fee system for program.

C-4 Provide low-cost medical underwriting benefit in membership plan.

C-5 Tie member care to hospital's outpatient services.

C-6 Solicit contracts with other institutions.

Objective D: *Renovate, equip facility*

D-1 Prepare architectural design.

D-2 Solicit and let competitive bids for renovation.

D-3 Purchase newest testing/therapeutic equipment.

D-4 Provide plans for development of program support materials.

Objective E: *Acquire clients/patients*

E-1 Identify target client member groups.

E-2 Develop selective promotional tools.

E-3 Prepare group/individual membership plans.

E-4 Develop personal contact plan for enrollment.

E-5 Assure participation from high schools/colleges.

E-6 Obtain news media support for program.

E-7 Participate in public events to promote program.

Objective F: *Negotiate Community Hospital participation*

F-1 Establish joint planning/liaison group.

F-2 Establish terms for mutual client referral.

F-3 Develop joint working arrangements—staffs.

F-4 Provide joint equipment use.

F-5 Plan joint public relations approach.

F-6 Develop joint cost accounting program.

Objective G: *Acquire staffing*

G-1 Ascertain ideal staff needs for program.

G-2 Employ key operational staff.

G-3 Make contract arrangements for part time specialists.

G-4 Train staff for operations.

G-5 Make staff service trade-offs with hospital and other agencies.

It also is obvious that the objectives in one or more areas, of necessity, are linked to others. Again, it is the marketer who determines the linkages and ties them together.

To illustrate the "cascading" of objectives, Objective E, the acquisition of clients and patients, is used, with the following further breakdown:

Objective E: *Acquire clients/patients*

E-1 Identify target client/patient groups

    E-1-a Determine extent of population to be served.

E-1-b Identify athletic/occupational groups with potential interest in program.

E-1-c Identify groups concerned with physical fitness and wellness programs.

E-1-d Place priority on contact with each group.

E-2 Develop selective promotional tools

E-2-a Identify tools needed for each target group.

E-2-b Establish budget for promotion.

E-2-c Develop basic graphics for all programs.

E-2-d Set priority for development of print, media, and other tools.

E-2-e Write basic theme copy for use in promotion.

E-2-f Establish total written communications plan.

E-3 Prepare group/individual membership plans

E-3-a Calculate capacities for service programs.

E-3-b Write statement of benefits and terms of membership.

E-3-c Calculate costs and charges by class of membership.

E-4 Develop personal contact plan for enrollment

E-4-a Identify ways to solicit group enrollments.

E-4-b Utilize departmental staff for part time membership enrollment activity.

E-4-c Enlist support of prominent athletes for program endorsements.

E-4-d Develop complete list of prospects for group enrollments.

E-4-e Prepare personal letter campaign.

E-5 Assure participation from high schools/colleges

E-5-a Identify all academic and athletic authorities in each school.

E-5-b Make presentation to various coaches' associations.

E-5-c Provide special preventive health courses for student classes.

E-5-d Provide free physical examinations for sports teams prior to season start.

E-5-e Create program advisory committee of athletic coaches.

E-5-f Provide special rates for student participation in off-season programs.

E-6 Obtain news media support for program

E-6-a Hold clinic for sportswriters and editors to explain program.

E-6-b Provide free fitness and exercise prescriptions to selected media personnel.

E-6-c Provide kit of informational materials for media.

E-6-d Seek editorial support for new department.

E-7 Participate in public events to promote program

E-7-a Hold monthly clinics for joggers.

E-7-b Provide booths at local public events (county fairs, bike-a-thons, etc.).

E-7-c Help organize health fairs or demonstrations for preventive health care.

E-7-d Hold annual coaches' clinic focusing on preventive health measures for athletes.

A further breakdown of objectives is possible and appropriate. It is worthwhile repeating Drucker's admonition that objectives must *degenerate* into work, that "unless objectives are converted into action, they are not objectives; they are dreams."[10]

Writing objectives in hierarchical order, affixing deadlines, and assigning responsibilities is tantamount to creating the workplan or implementation schedule for the marketing project. The process is subject to occasional revision as new strategies or tactics are revealed as promising.

SUMMARY

Not only is the primary objective for the marketing project of great importance, but careful application of the marketing research, targeting, and strategizing may compel its revision. Objectives constitute elements of the work program for the project; they are placed in a hierarchy of importance and timing so that the project can be achieved.

Proper objective writing requires discipline and sometimes approaches an art form. The marketer must follow guidelines in establishing objectives. Ideally, objectives are not imposed upon the organization but are negotiated so that agency personnel not only feel a part of the project but also are enthusiastic about carrying out their own individual portions of the task.

NOTES

1. *Random House Dictionary of the English Language* (unabridged ed.) (New York: Random House, 1973).

2. Dale D. McConkey, *MBO for Nonprofit Organizations* (New York: AMACOM, 1975), p. 53.

3. Peter F. Drucker, *Management: Tasks, Responsibilities, Practices* (New York: Harper & Row, Publishers, 1973), p. 102.

4. Ibid., p. 101.

5. Meritt L. Kastens, *Long-Range Planning for Your Business* (New York: AMACOM, 1976), p. 110.

6. Ibid., p. 116.

7. McConkey, *MBO for Nonprofit Organizations,* p. 49.

8. Kastens, *Long-Range Planning for Your Business* p. 116.

9. Drucker, *Management: Tasks, Responsibilities, Practices,* p. 460.

10. Ibid., p. 119.

Chapter 9

Targeting

Any organization or individual that can affect the outcome of the marketing project objective for better or for worse is a marketing target. If our calculations are correct, you the reader are a target for the authors and the publisher of this book. You are an object of the book's marketing, much as you would be for any specially prepared text or guide in a specific subject.

As a target of our efforts to transmit information, you were selected from an exceptionally large market—the health and human services field. From the larger market, we examined certain criteria, reexplored the book's contents, and worked with the publisher to divide or segment potential reader markets as methodically as possible, even suggesting different messages to different industry segments so that we (1) might have a stronger appeal and (2) cause an exchange to occur: you want to buy or read this book; the publisher wants to sell you the book.

Determination of our targets hinged on some objectives that were set out for the book originally. A key objective was: "Develop, chapter by chapter, a guide for people working in health and human services on how to use marketing as a method to achieve workplans and complete projects." Three subobjectives were: (1) outline chapters to show progression of a marketing idea through its eventual implementation; (2) use words and terms likely to be familiar to people in the industry; and (3) explain each step in the marketing process.

This chapter underscores the importance of thoughtful selection of targets and their relationship to other parts of marketing, particularly objectives and promotional tools. Understanding and distinguishing between publics, segmentation, and targets is an appropriate place to begin.

A public is any group with common interests "affected by the acts and policies of an institution or whose acts and opinions affect the institution."[1] Organizations contain at least nine separate publics. "There are three input publics (supporters, employees, and suppliers); two output publics (consumers and agents); and four sanctioning publics (government, competitors, special publics, and the general public)."[2]

Thus,

> The organization is viewed as a resource conversion machine which takes the resources of supporters, employees, and suppliers and converts these into products that go directly to consumers or through agents. The organization's basic input-output activities are subject to the watchful eye of sanctioning publics such as government, competitors, special publics, and the general public. All of these publics are targets for organizational marketing activity because of their potential impact on the resource converting efficiency of the organization.[3]

A segmented or divided market is a collection of persons with similar (homogeneous) wants, needs, and desires, with a potential for exchange with the marketing institution. A marketing target results from a marketer's breaking down each segment into nearly irreducible parts, determining which groups or individuals within a segment can make an exchange with the marketer. Thus, a homemaker agency might identify the elderly as a public it wishes to embrace, but the elderly by themselves are too broad a public to handle practically. As a result, the agency must determine which segments of the elderly public it wants to address with its programs, services, and information. Following marketing objectives, past experience, and research findings, the agency's managers determine that its appeal should be to recently hospitalized elderly 65 years and over who live on the north side of the city. These senior citizens, segmented from the larger public, thereby become targets of the homemaker agency, targets that can be reduced further so that the agency can assure itself that its ties with the chosen target will be mutually beneficial.

Marketers often use a three-step approach to targets:

1. They determine the total market for their services.
2. They divide or segment the market into identifiable, homogeneous submarkets that can be related with some logic and persuasion to any or all of the organization's marketing objectives and subobjectives.
3. They create marketing strategies and tactics to reach the targets.

Many times in the past, managers in health and human services have squandered funds on poorly defined targets. It has been too easy for an institution to regard the total market as a target and then discover that it is very difficult to penetrate that wide area with traditional promotional tools. Wasted time, a distortion of agency objectives, incorrect staff work assignments, managerial and staff attention diverted from the real targets—all can result from mistakenly defined targets.

CRITERIA FOR TARGET SELECTION

Few, if any, organizations oppose expanding their services to accommodate the needs of constituencies. But the idea for expansion must be tempered by a rational marketing approach. For instance, does the organization have the resources with which to successfully effect an exchange with a new target, and can such resources be developed easily? What about the organization's technical and managerial capacities? Will they be overtaxed as a result of delivering services to a new target?

Will the objectives of the organization be met by working with the selected targets, or will they be distorted, blurred, sidetracked? Can the organization develop and execute strategies to reach the new targets? Can appropriate promotional tools be developed feasibly? How will the newly selected target respond to agency strategies and tools? Is an equitable exchange foreseen? Can the organization's management state that efforts taken to reach targets will be worthwhile from a cost, labor, and benefit viewpoint?

Increased client satisfaction—a worthwhile marketing exchange, in other words—is the final destination of segmenting and targeting.

> Satisfaction is the result of *product benefits,* which in turn result from product use. *Product usage* is related to certain customer characteristics—*state-of-mind* (attitudes, values, perceptions) and/or *state-of-being* (geographic location, demographic characteristics). These four factors, therefore, form a hierarchy of possible segmentation bases leading to customer satisfaction.[4]

(The reader must substitute the word "service" for "product" in the preceding paragraph.)

GUIDELINES FOR TARGETING

To understand the targeting process, these guidelines should be kept in mind:

1. *Marketing targets never are stable.* They change, shift, grow, erode, evaporate. Targets must be reexamined and audited constantly for signs of danger and of opportunity for target expansion or penetration.
2. *Each new service proposed or developed by the agency must have a marketing target or targets before the service can be delivered to clients.* It sometimes is said that a new service will generate a new target automatically. Nevertheless, before the service is operable, the marketer must define the target or targets and develop strategies to reach them. (It is as-

sumed that the proposed new service is responsive to the research findings and organizational objectives.)

3. *If target selection is erroneous, development of strategies or promotional tools cannot occur.* Strategies and promotional tools are related directly to target selection. For example, it would be wasteful to develop a brochure on how a mental health facility is meeting the needs of the area's elderly unless careful targeting has determined in advance that those segments of the elderly the agency wants to reach are over 75, male, ill at home, but not living alone. Furthermore, strategies or plans of action can't be assembled practicably without some specific indication as to whom the strategies should be directed. Marketing, as has been emphasized, is the often slow process of taking one step after another until the final marketing plan is put in writing and the marketer can carry out the steps as systematically as possible.

4. *It is axiomatic that each organization must decide if it wants to segment its publics or address its publics as a whole.* A typical question from a human services organization executive to the marketer is: "We have 12 different programs in our organization. Should we have one overall image or 12 different images?" To answer the questions, the organization first must decide on a policy of market segmentation. If it segments its publics, it most likely will cast multiple images. If it maintains all 12 programs but doesn't segment its publics deliberately, its image will be singular and at times confusing to many people.

5. *Segmentation into targets provides the organization with a continuing scanning device.* Through careful targeting, the organization can be tuned to any changes in the total market, to competitors' thrusts, to possible marketplace erosion, to new opportunities. Creating a new target or updating the status of an existing target is similar to an exercise in market auditing. There is ample reason to conclude that the shifting nature of a well-chosen target will assist the organization in taking a closer look at every aspect of its services. A target is likely to change its nature first; then, the service also must change if it is to keep pace with the needs, wants, and desires of the target.

6. *Despite everything else, individual tastes and personal preferences of administrators and managers can influence the selection of most targets.* The managers of any organization retain the right to decide not to serve certain target selections. On the other hand, a well-developed rationale for target service delivery usually should overcome most personal objections or biases by managers.

7. *Targets may be organizations, small groups, individuals, or specific areas of interest or concern, such as fund-raising sources, reimbursement*

sources, or information and referral channels. Segmentation's goal, says David J. Schwartz:

> is to isolate birds of the same feather. Understanding how people differ is helpful in identifying what some people—a particular market segment—have in common . . . a marketing manager is a practical social scientist in the broadest meaning of the term. A knowledge of human differences helps him sell products (or services).[5]

It is important to remember that targets may be designated not only for acquiring new clients or business. They also can be designated for their assistance in getting legislation passed, funds raised, or programs begun.

UNDERSTANDING MARKETING DIFFERENTIATION

Most organizations that use marketing employ a process known as differentiated marketing. When an organization "sets out to serve more than one target group, it will be maximally effective by differentiating its product (service) offerings and communications. Groups require different appeals and frequency of solicitation and communications. There is no one message for all groups."[6] Furthermore, "in considering different ways to reach target groups, an organization is advised to think in terms of seeking a differential advantage. It should consider what elements in its reputation or resources can be emphasized or exploited to create a special value in the minds of potential customers."[7]

Under differentiated marketing, as contrasted with concentrated marketing that promotes an organization's services to one market only, there is opportunity for health and human services groups to tailor their marketing to each separate target with the hope that the client or referral source, for instance, will be impressed by the overall strength, depth, and versatility of the agency and find some cue either to use personally or to recommend the use of agency services.

Within differentiated marketing, there are obvious cautions for marketers. Costs of marketing and the marketer's work schedule increase as each target is added. Each target is reached by specific promotional tools, another budget consideration. Depending on the size and sophistication of the organization, increased costs for marketing research, planning, and administrative paperwork are budgetary factors. Nevertheless, differentiated marketing should prove beneficial enough that the organization will want to expand its services to more targets.

EXAMPLES OF TARGET SELECTION

As simple as the operation purports to be, target selection needs to be walked through for the first time because steps not taken cause waste and frustration. The target example here is a job counseling agency in a medium-sized city.

An established agency that provides vocational counseling and testing, on-the-job training, homebound work programs, work evaluations, skills training, and preretirement counseling seeks to reestablish itself in the community after years of decline, weak management, and the rise of several aggressive competing agencies. Agency contracts, agreements, and cooperative programs in the community are almost nonexistent. The agency board feels instinctively that it should market its services to both the professional community and to targets within the community at large. One objective is: "To increase by 30 per cent in the next 12 months the number of contracts to use agency services." Which targets must the marketer develop or expand to meet this objective? The following process is used:

1. Identify target organizations that existing research data, objectives, managerial experience, and intuition indicate must be reached if the agency is to attract more contracts. Target possibilities are local industry, school system officials, government agencies, foundations, peer organizations, the state legislature, the local United Way, and labor unions. Some of these are existing but uncultivated targets; some must be developed for the first time.

2. Rank each target according to an assessment of its impact on service delivery and the ultimate benefits to the organization and the users of agency services. Since it is impossible, and very perplexing, to reach each target at once personally, priority is assigned to the most important ones. It might take a year or more to contact or visit all targets. By then, the organization may have decided that it does not need to reach every one since it may be accommodating all the clientele it can, and may have met most marketing objectives.

3. List individuals within each target who will influence or make the decision to use or recommend the agency's services. Any target organization's name by itself is meaningless without determining which individual or individuals within it can unlock the gates and provide the agency with information, money, ideas, or clients. List each influential person beside each target; update the list quarterly. (This list also helps cultivate feedback communications with targets.)

4. Identify the exchange that should occur between the organization and the target. If an exchange cannot be determined easily, the potential target

may be a mistaken choice and needs to be reassessed for its promise or benefits.

5. Establish the sequence of target approach and exchange. In other words, when should the target be approached and when will the exchange be expected to occur? This step asks of the marketer: How much investment in time and money should be put into this prospective target, and when should the entity be approached in view of the other targets selected?

TARGETING THE AGENCY NEW CONTRACT PLAN

The targeting process for the job counseling agency is outlined in Exhibit 9-1. Targets and subtargets were developed from the apparent needs of users and what marketing research data reported. (Another organization might prepare a different set of targets, depending on the results of its own research and objectives and its interpretation of the results.) This illustration indicates: (1) primary targets, (2) reasons for selection, and (3) projected exchanges with each target.

The secondary targets in Exhibit 9-2 were selected for the counseling agency's contracts project. Anticipated exchanges are omitted in this list since many of them are implied in the target designation.

Undoubtedly, cases can be made for more secondary targets, but the primary and secondary targets listed here should suffice to systematically bring new contracts to the agency and reverse its long period of decline.

Of course, primary and secondary target selection must be broken down further. Each projected target must be ranked in order of its impact on the marketing objectives as well as its probable influence on potential clients and the probability of effecting an exchange. Thus, it is possible to rank and give a numerical weight (ten being the highest ranking, one the lowest) to the primary targets identified for the job counseling agency:

Local CETA program	10
Local industry	8
Agency board of directors	7
School system officials	7
Peer organizations	6
Foundations	5
United Way	5
State legislature	3
Labor unions	3

In rationalizing the primary target ranking, it was assumed from external marketing research and knowledge of the competitors' fiscal structure that the

Exhibit 9-1 Primary Targets/Job Counseling Agency Contract Plan

Target	Why Selected	Exchange
Local CETA program	Has funds to subcontract with our agency for summer job programming, skills testing, and work evaluation activities. This source of potential funds and contracts has not been used previously by our agency.	Agency offers professional training, established credentials, and a new source of assistance to CETA. CETA offers a respectable funding source, a ready group of clients, and a potential for added funding.
Public school systems	Has identified need for vocational counselors to back up school system counselors, acting in overflow capacity. School district can contract for per capita counseling arrangements.	Agency offers trained counselors who can work in schools as well as inner city locations near several large high schools; fee structure is compatible with school system's ability to pay. School system has a need and a problem that can be satisfied, offers new sources of clients, has adequate funding, and offers possible long-term relationship.
Local industry	Has occasional need for outside preretirement counseling; has occasional ability to place excess work assignments and contracts with handicapped persons represented by the agency; offers possibilities of work-at-home contracts.	Agency has clients who can assemble products in the agency workshop or at home; its staff can counsel industrial employees about retirement, other problems. Industry has funds to cover outside contracts or counseling; possibly can supply new board members or contribute to next agency fund drive.
Peer organizations	Are sources of new clients, but need to be reintroduced to our agency, rediscovering our services and staff potential.	Agency has certified, accredited counselors; maintains excellent feedback system; charges fees approved by the United Way. Peer organizations can supply clients, some funding, some promotion and publicity, as well as potential members of agency task forces or joint committees.
Foundations	Have funds to invest in experimental programs to help preretirees; need to be reeducated about benefits of job counseling services; interested in general field of the handicapped and their problems.	Agency has established reputation with experienced, active board of directors and staff; maintains good accountability for donated funds; can bring credit to foundations; can help promote their benevolences. Foundations need new outlets for grant awards; offer prestige; lend close identity to important community

Agency board of directors	Is relatively large and varied, with many community contracts; has not had thorough orientation to agency and thus is poorly informed about depth of services; needs stimulus from staff.	*Agency* offers prestige to board members, outlet for civic service and altruism, chance to expound ideas for community betterment. *Board* contributes time, influence, authority, skills, funds.
State legislature	Discusses and passes laws that directly affect operations and future of agency.	*Agency* provides data and information about its activities, problems and concerns; expert witnesses and testimony at hearings; support for bills; support for legislators. *Legislature* passes bills favorable to agency payment rates; supports sheltered workshops, licensing of facilities, and other issues; gets to know problems of agency.
United Way	Is both a major funding supplier and a source of ideas for growth, management, and development.	*Agency* collects funds for United Way campaign; performs services according to various UW guidelines; serves as adviser to UW board and volunteers on job counseling; works with UW information and referral division; acts as showplace to steer potential UW givers. *United Way* helps fund agency; advises it on management and other sources of contacts for community assistance; endorses agency planning and development efforts; finds board members and others to assist agency; brings community focus on agency.
Labor unions	Can influence members' attitudes toward agency and endorse its services to fellow unions.	*Agency* provides specific services to union members; can help unions build membership by offering more services; can enhance unions' reputation among their own members. *Unions* can join in cooperative programming with agency or experiment with new member services; can assist in broadening base of agency financial support or provide on-site locations for expanded agency services.

Exhibit 9-2 Secondary Targets

Target	Why Selected?
Professional associations	Can provide organized groups of caseworkers, counselors, and personnel directors who must be told about and shown agency facilities so they can inform clients about the agency; can set up speaking engagements before various organizations.
News media	Can assist in promoting and featurizing special programs; some media expertise probably needed on agency's board.
Church groups	Can help agency through pulpit messages, congregational announcement media and counseling activities, and church officials perhaps can participate in selected joint programming.
Agency employees	Must be kept informed about developments with outside contracts, new business opportunities, and activities within the professional community and community at large. This is a cooperative venture with the agency public relations division.

CETA organization and its well-endowed programming process might be the key to the new contract program. Hence, the agency chose CETA as its main target to inform and educate its managers as to the agency's programs and benefits and to learn as much about its policies and practices as possible.

In assigning a high priority to local industry, the agency gambled that its industrial contacts would be so well thought out and methodical, with careful consideration given to the separate exchanges with each of the 24 companies it wanted to contact, that for the first time in its long history it would make an impact in the local corporate world. Likewise, the agency, in designating its own rather influential board of directors as a major target, made the decision to explore the many exchange possibilities between it and its board, also for the first time. By choosing the school system, with its array of officials and bureaucrats, the agency was saying, in effect, that it planned to penetrate the local educational system, demonstrating how the agency could offer school children benefits heretofore unknown to the scholastic community. In designating peer organizations, the agency actually was commencing a plan to rebuild and add to its referral network that had retrogressed at about the same rate as the agency in general. As to the foundations, the agency previously had been of the opinion: "They never have any money for us." The marketing process at least will test the hypothesis and perhaps find it to be wrong. The agency board, the state legislature, the United Way, and the labor unions had not been analyzed previously as to their projected exchange potential; thus, for the first time the agency would be seeking to balance its offerings to these targets rather than expecting unilateral dealings with them, transactions in which the agency typically expected the balance to be tipped in its favor.

Secondary targets were ranked as follows:

Professional associations	10
Agency employees	8
News media	8
Church groups	4
Regulatory agencies	4

It is in the job counseling agency's best interests eventually to become known formally to several professional associations in its community. Strategies and promotional tools can be developed that will make such associations major sources of staff and board recruitment, information dissemination, and potential or indirect sources of referral. Agency employees are a key target because they can be inspired to act as casefinders, publicists, and supporters of agency actions and activities. News media outlets always are targetable. In this case they are not a primary target because the agency must address itself first to main sources of business and income. In turning to church groups, the agency seeks to penetrate up to a dozen local congregations that are known for their interest in social causes and that have large special interest groups among their parishioners. It will mark the first time the agency will have approached local churches in any organized manner.

After the preliminary sorting and breaking down, all targets, like the subobjectives, are sorted further to reach those that can best influence a marketing exchange. Under secondary targets, for example, a further breakdown of professional associations would be:

Tri-City Social Caseworkers Association	10
Job Development Society	10
Tri-City Chapter, Personnel Association of America	8
Areawide Manufacturers' Association	6

Using another subtarget (church groups), the breakdown would be:

Clergymen	10
Outreach workers	9
Homebound visitors	8
Church office managers, secretaries	6

A further refinement of targeting also must occur—the designating of contact persons associated with the target. Thus, under the secondary target news media we find:

Newspapers

1. The daily Planet	Clark Kent, reporter
	George Smith, medical reporter
	Sam Johnson, city editor
	Lynn Laue, director of public affairs
	John Allen, director of photography
2. The Weekly Comet	Carl Campbell, publisher
	Phil Walters, publisher
	Horace Pink, editor-in-chief
	Tina Haas, correspondent

Radio

1. WWOK	Richard Falk, program director
	Bill Nightingale, daily disc jockey
	Morton Hayes, station owner
2. WPLI	Arnie Watts, program director
	Matt Franklin, station owner

Television

1. KHHY	Frank Bailey, program director
	Barbara Swanson, assignment director
	Mary I. Campbell, reporter

Community, area magazines

1. The Islander	Jim Wanton, managing editor
	Martha Laue, news editor
	Sandy Miller, reporter
	Emilie Kohlstaedt, reporter

In designating media subtargets, the marketer placed primary importance on daily and weekly newspapers since they give more space to agency causes and concerns. The two radio stations carry the agency's first-run news, too, and play the agency's public service announcements. Neither the local television station nor the regional magazine pay much attention to the agency (or are expected to), so they are selected as the final subtargets.

SUMMARY

Target selection is crucial in marketing. Careful selection sets the stage for proper development of strategies, tactics, and the promotional tools with which to describe agency services to targets.

Marketers must remember that publics are groups with common, sometimes homogeneous, interests but if they are to be meaningful to the average organization, they must be divided or segmented. Within each segment or portion of the market are other groups that can be pinpointed further as specific targets.

As a rule, the total public first must be isolated, then segmented, then broken down into the final targets of opportunity. If this does not happen, the result often is wasted time and effort, distortion of the organizational objectives, and general agency confusion.

Marketers must make sure that their organization supports the marketing segmentation concept, generally known as market differentiation, and that each service the organization provides is linked with one or more targets. Marketers also must reexamine targets for information they may be able to pass along about the acceptance or rejection of agency services or programs. A reminder: targets change continually; as such, they must be under constant surveillance. In the process of targeting, target organizations, groups, or individuals are identified, ranked, and weighted, and key target personnel and potential exchanges are listed.

NOTES

1. Scott M. Cutlip and Allen H. Center, *Effective Public Relations* (Englewood Cliffs, N.J.: Prentice-Hall, Inc., 1958), p. 67.
2. William Lazer and Eugene J. Kelley, *Social Marketing: Perspectives and Viewpoints* (Homewood, Ill.: Richard D. Irwin, Inc., 1973), pp. 84-85.
3. Ibid., p. 85.
4. Ben F. Enis, *Marketing Principles: The Management Process* (Santa Monica, Calif.: Goodyear Publishing Co., 1977), p. 246.
5. David J. Schwartz, *Marketing Today* (New York: Harcourt Brace Jovanovich, Inc., 1977), p. 78.
6. Lazer and Kelley, *Social Marketing: Perspectives and Viewpoints*, p. 38.
7. Ibid., p. 39.

Chapter 10

Strategies and Their Use in Marketing

Strategies are the precursors to actions and run parallel to objectives; they are placed in a hierarchy just as are objectives and subobjectives. The difference is that strategies are related specifically to targets.

A strategy is "a method, plan or series of maneuvers used to accomplish a specific objective."[1] A tactic is "a plan, procedure or expedient for promoting a desired end or result."[2] The authors consider them to be synonymous.

Strategies are the creative part of marketing. The logical, deductive process used up to this point does not provide simple equations that tell the marketer what will or won't work to advantage. Imagination is a priceless asset; it is as important in marketing as anywhere else. Marketing has been depicted as a discipline forcing an ordered examination of facts and conditions about the marketplace, targets, and an agency's own internal operations. Encouraging creativity, marketing forces the organization to look at new ways to deal with target groups or organizations, stimulating selective exchanges with each target. While some agencies have many brilliant ideas, they operate in the realm of gimmickery, not marketing, unless they have designed strategies as carefully as their objectives.

STRATEGIES: SIMPLE AND COMPLEX

Strategies may be relatively simple or as complex as a jigsaw puzzle. To illustrate the former:

Case 1

A community recreation center serving families sought to use its health and gymnastic facilities throughout the day instead of mainly at noon, late afternoon, and evening hours when men and boys "took over the place." It encouraged women to use the 8 a.m.-to-noon opening, and at first there was some limited interest and activity. Within a year the agency decided that its strategy was only in its own interests rather than in those of its women members. With the use of an advisory group, it developed a new approach. A structured pre-school program was set up for the children of the mothers and, for the latter, a two-part plan of organized fitness and family life education classes was established. Thus, in half a day, mothers could enjoy both physical and mental activities and have their children cared for at no extra expense.

The strategy, of course, involved the participation of mothers in planning, the element of exchange and better service. The result: full utilization of the facilities, more income, and happier members.

An example of a more complicated project and multiple strategies:

Case 2

A health systems agency undertook a study to establish a new treatment program in drug abuse to replace an agency that had lost federal funding and had been dismantled. Normally, the agency might have conducted a special study, prepared a report and recommendations, transmitted it to the appropriate funding sources and authorities, and then awaited their response and implementation. The HSA's operational philosophy was that it would become involved in studies only if it also had responsibility for execution of recommendations.

The planning organization established these steps:

- *Involvement* of key funding and service agencies in the study operation

- *Precommitment* to some kind of action on the problem

- *Cultivation* of those likely to oppose or be lukewarm to creation of a new drug treatment program

- *Participation* of several key agencies in the study's staff work

- *Preparation* of a report that was nontechnical, graphic, and easily understood

- *Staging* of the study's recommendations so as to attract as much public support as possible

- *Pledging* of financial support from a few key resources as the recommendations and appropriate actions began to emerge

Obviously, the HSA used several strategies to ensure productive results. It acquired respect because its work was not conducted in a vacuum. It provided an exchange of benefits with several of the actors it had involved. Its chance of success was assured when it distributed responsibility and credit where it was needed and due.

A special relationship exists between the manager and the marketer in deciding what strategies to pursue in a marketing project. In a nutshell, the higher or more fundamental the objective, the greater the manager's responsibility to decide the main strategies. Conversely, lesser objectives have their accompanying strategies; others in the organization will be responsible for their execution, and the administrator may delegate strategy making down through the ranks. The executive is the dispatcher as well as the liaison between all levels of the organization and is the judge of a strategy's soundness and appropriateness.

"The best way to build a strategic framework is from the top down, not for any theoretical reason but simply because it works. 'Bottom-up' planning schemes provoke all the frustrations of pushing on a rope. They take a lot of time, often produce a lot of unhappy people, and seldom result in anything being done that would not have been done anyway."[3] Kastens thus points to the agency chief executive officer as the one responsible for basic strategy. The marketer (and the marketing team) should be a reliable source of objectivity in the marketing process, but in the long run the marketer is an adviser, not the policy setter. Of course, the more reliable the marketer's information and the more penetrating the studies, the more influence the individual will have on setting policies and strategies.

But it is the administrator who must decide the grand or basic strategy for marketing the organization or any major program or project within it. Peter F. Drucker writes that "strategic decisions—whatever their magnitude, complexity or importance—should never be taken through problem solving. Indeed, in these specifically managerial decisions, the important and difficult job is never to find the right answer, it is to find the right question."[4] The role of the CEO, therefore, becomes one of asking the right questions of the marketer and then helping to frame strategies in response.

MARKETING STRATEGIES AND CATEGORIES

Kotler states that three general marketing strategies can be identified and that one of them might be applied at any given time:

> *Undifferentiated marketing* occurs when an organization decides to treat the whole market as homogeneous, focusing on what is common

to all the members of the market rather than what is different; in this case the organization engages in no market segmentation. . . . *Concentrated marketing* occurs when an organization decides to divide the market into meaningful segments and devote its major marketing effort to one segment. . . . *Differentiated marketing* occurs when an organization decides to operate in two or more segments of the market and to design separate products and/or marketing programs for each.[5]

When addressing the identification of targets that have a bearing on the organization's efforts to implement the marketing objective, the authors have categorized the targets in various levels of relationships. Each category has a special influence on the ability of the agency or institution to operate in the most effective manner. Not all objectives are concerned directly with growth of service volume, of course. Nevertheless, having the confidence or trust of some target organizations is essential and may make the difference between growing and standing still. For example, an agency that depends on the United Way for only a small portion of its operating funds may find that the group's influence in the community may be of considerably more importance than the allocation itself because the organization has the impact of having a *Good Housekeeping* "Seal of Approval." A health systems agency that has helped obtain a certificate of need has the effect of franchising an existing or potential service area for a provider.

The authors believe that an agency has various market categories and must follow a strategy of differentiated marketing. But differentiated marketing applies in one or in many segments and in all projects, however narrow and limited in scope. More precisely, if targets are categorized in terms of relationships and objectives and then ranked by order of relative importance, they lead to a specially designed strategy to apply to each target. One or more objectives must be accomplished with each target. The strategy is our plan to accomplish the objective.

An enlightening exercise is to examine basic marketing strategies for an objective that seeks the growth of service volume for an organization. Using the commonly accepted business-industrial model, four strategies are considered: market penetration, market development, product development, and diversification.[6] Applications of these strategies follow:

Case 1. Market Penetration

A hospital-based glaucoma clinic that provides 40 percent of all such care to patients in the community might decide its main strategy should be to get physicians, senior citizen groups, and others to double or triple referrals. The effect would be to increase both the volume of referrals and the percentage of the service market.

The strategy is to get a bigger share of the business in its current sphere of operations.

Case 2. Market Development

A family counseling agency may open a new branch in an adjoining county, providing the same services as in its main location. A health maintenance organization serving employees of a large university might contract with city and county governments to make its services available to their employees, too.

The strategy is one of finding new targets to serve in the present service area or expanding that area to include new targets.

Case 3. Product Development

An information and referral service operated by a United Way may improve its operations by increasing its availability from normal daily office hours to 24 hours, seven days a week, by tying into the community's 911 emergency telephone network and by conducting training programs for personnel of service agencies to help them help others gain access to the human services delivery network.

This strategy calls for changing or improving an organization's services and effectiveness.

Case 4. Diversification

A Red Cross chapter might add the Heimlich maneuver (for freeing blocked tracheal passages) to its group of emergency training programs and then make it available to employees of restaurants and company cafeterias. A local bar association might prepare an adaptation of a Tel-Med service (a telephone program using tapes to respond briefly to a health question or problem) to present information on legal matters and to steer callers to its members.

The strategy is to find a completely new kind of service or program to offer to a target.

Although it is a matter of personal preference, the authors believe the average administrator will discover that these four strategies are listed in the proper order of priority. In other words, to penetrate the present market with present services should be more important than seeking new markets or diversifying the service program. One strategy should be a constant: improving and developing the organization's products and services.

GROWTH AND PROBLEM SOLVING

Seeking growth of an organization is a natural ambition. The human services agency manager is not different from counterparts in proprietary businesses. But growth is not necessarily the sole objective because the organization was not created for the single purpose of growth; it was created to solve human problems. In effect, the goal of an agency is to be so successful that there no longer is a need for it. As an example, tuberculosis was so prevalent at the turn of the century that, in some states, each county had its own sanitorium. Remedial public health measures and treatment were developed over a 40-year period so that the disease was nearly eliminated and, consequently, so was the need for special facilities. The National Tuberculosis Association (known for its sale of Christmas seals) changed its program emphasis and name. Now the American Lung Association, it deals with a variety of respiratory ailments but still sells seals annually.

Provider organizations often have an inherent objective that runs counter to pure growth: how to diminish the need for its services. In reality, there are few instances like polio and tuberculosis in which the need vanishes. The recent growth of drug abuse, teen-age alcoholism, and family violence has spawned a new generation of services and agencies. More often than not, the health or human services organization seeks to change the character of its objectives and services to meet evolving problems and needs rather than simply to grow in the same direction for which it was created.

There is an inextricable linkage in the marketing process among objectives, targets, and strategies. The marketer's real contribution is the ability to influence such linkage; the result is implementation of the entire marketing project. Thus, there is a similarity between objectives and strategies and a hierarchy for both.

EXAMPLE: SINGLE OBJECTIVE, SINGLE TARGET

As an example of a hierarchy of strategies, picture a hospital that derives 85 percent of its financial reimbursement from three sources: Medicare (39 percent), Medicaid (12 percent) and private pay insurance (34 percent). It has had a severe cash flow problem, not receiving full payment for its services soon enough to be able to make timely payment of its bills. From time to time the hospital has had to use its line of credit with banks in order to borrow money, at high interest, to meet its obligations. An auditor's analysis has indicated that part of the problem can be attributed to a high rate of retroactive denials of claims for reimbursement, meaning that the third party payer has refused to recognize the validity of certain charges, forcing the hospital to absorb the resulting deficits. The hospital's task of correcting the situation is simplified (or compounded) because the third party payer, for most of its private pay cases, also is the intermediary for the federal programs. It is the local organization for Blue Cross and Blue Shield.

The marketing project had, as a primary objective, the restoration of sound fiscal health to the institution. Subobjectives were identified. One of these and the strategies devised to implement it follows:

Subobjective

Within the next nine months, reduce the rate of retroactive denials for reimbursement claims by 50 percent.

Targets

1. The hospital's finance department
2. Blue Cross and Blue Shield
   a. Accounting division
   b. Policy committee

Strategies

In-House

1. Employ outside expert financial analyst to revamp policies and procedures.
2. Establish position of risk manager in hospital to seek reduction in operating costs.
3. Upgrade quality of finance department personnel and provide inservice training.

External

1. Seek appointment of Blue Cross representative to a joint committee to help develop new procedures to correct problems.
2. Prepare financial analysis presentation to be submitted to Blue Cross policy committee seeking changes in its procedures.
3. Seek support of local hospital association in addressing issues affecting mutual problems in reimbursement.
4. Identify issues and procedures that may be a source of relief by legal means (if all else fails).

The basic strategy approach is twofold: to address what are known to be obvious internal faults and to overcome an external situation that, in the eyes of the finance department, is really to blame for the difficulties. The strategy is to approach internal problems first, then tackle the intermediary who isn't being exactly fair in its dealings with the hospital.

Each strategy becomes progressively more specific and less grand in scope, less a policy than an action. The strategy is neither to conduct a public relations program nor to maintain the goodwill of the target. Each strategy, instead, is intended to take a step toward achieving the objective. The marketing strategist constantly asks the question: "What will it take or what must I do to get this or that kind of result?"

EXAMPLE: MULTIPLE OBJECTIVES, LARGE TARGET

The more complex the project objective and larger the target group, the more varied the tactics. The marketer can use the same basic strategy with the whole target group, but each member of the group will require some special approach. Following is an example.

The primary (and as yet unquantified) objective of one home health care agency that offers a combination of health and human services is to increase substantially the rate of referrals and volume of services in its eight-county operations area. Having categorized its targets, it has analyzed available information about the use of home care services by all target groups. It has ranked its targets by potential for increased business. Because of certain practicalities such as numbers of patients, availability of ready reimbursement, and the investment of staff and time required to produce new business, the agency picked hospitals as its primary target group. It has segmented 60 hospitals into priority groups for new business potential (Table 10-1).

This kind of segmentation may not be readily apparent to someone unfamiliar with home health services. Each category has a relationship to type of patient served, age group, and potential for payment or reimbursement for services the home care agency may provide.

Table 10-1 New Business Potentials

Priority	Number of Hospitals
A. Acute care hospitals with high Medicare occupancy	18
B. Rehabilitation hospitals	3
C. Short-term chronic care hospitals	3
D. Acute care hospitals with moderate Medicare occupancy	20
E. Mental hospitals	2
F. Acute care hospitals with high Medicaid occupancy	2
G. Veterans hospitals	2
H. Children's hospitals	2
I. Alcoholic rehabilitation hospitals	4
J. Long-term care hospitals	4

The following breakdown of subobjectives, targets, and strategies was devised for the marketing plan:

Subobjective

Within one year, to increase the number of referrals of discharged patients from hospitals by one-third and, subsequently, by one-fourth in each of the following three years.

Targets

All hospitals in categories A through D (in Table 10-1). (In effect, the agency chose to write off 16 of the 60 target hospitals as not being worth a marketing effort. At the same time, it was agreed to address the rest as one target group, but one at a time, taking them in order of the priority placed on them.)

Strategies

Basic: To concentrate on hospitals as a highly potential source for patient referrals

Secondary: To concentrate on segments of the target group where potential was judged to be highest

Tertiary:

A. Establish a pilot business-referral development project with the 18 hospitals in Category A.

B. Prepare a program of person-to-person contacts between the home health care agency executive and the CEOs of the hospitals in the pilot project.

C. Prepare a set of objectives for all hospitals but individualize them with emphasis on exchange of benefits to be sought.

D. Develop special tools and arrangements for use in carrying out the exchange between the hospital and the home health care agency.

At this point the pilot target aggregate was divided into 18 separate targets and a set of strategies was devised for each. Each target hospital was analyzed further, with the result that individuals in each institution became targets since it is individuals, not organizations, with whom the marketer must deal.

The marketer knows well the necessity of preparing for the initial contact as well as the continuing relationship with the targets. Rather than proceeding pell-mell in carrying out either the subobjectives or the strategies, the marketer is concerned with the following:

- assessing the possible interest and receptivity of the target to the marketer's proposals

- determining who is the right person to present the proposal (or who can help get a foot in the door)

- preparing a clear, attractive case that will stimulate a positive response

- providing a program with permanent benefits to both the target organization and the agency

The preparatory phase of the hospital program called for a marketing tool that would help facilitate the strategies to be used with the targets. A special profile was designed and completed for each target hospital with the help of knowledgeable staff persons from within the agency and from other community agencies. A sample profile for one hospital is shown in Exhibit 10-1. (All names and places listed in the profile are fictitious.) The profile is broken down as follows:

- *Identifying information (Numbers 1 through 7):* This includes the hospital address, name of administrator, type and number of beds, and names of chief professional officers.

- *Present referral information (Number 8):* An effort was made to determine the practical status of discharge planning in the institution, whether there was a plausible system of referral to home health care, and who was responsible for the referrals.

- *Statistics (Numbers 9 through 16):* Information about daily census, occupancy levels, and percentage of Medicare/Medicaid patients was available from one or more sources such as the local and state hospital associations, state health departments, or health systems agency. More difficult to obtain were data on referrals made to agencies other than the hospital with the marketing project.

- *Assessment of situation (Numbers 17 through 19):* More subjective judgment went into this section than any other. An effort was made to learn of attitudes, obstacles, and opportunities regarding the development of new business or greater numbers of referrals.

- *Suggestions (Number 20):* This is where the profile writer tries to provide clues for strategies that might be used with the target hospital.

The profile is designed to give the marketer a fair idea of the chances for success before planning strategies for the target. Through the profile, the marketer should have found several new leads instead of having to resort to a system of blind contact. For example:

- Analysis should identify the chief decision-maker in the hospital for home health care, perhaps the head nurse or lead social worker. There may be

Exhibit 10-1 Profile of a Sample Target Hospital

Hospital Profile—Home Health Care (HHC)
Referral Development

1) Hospital: St. John   Telephone: 842-3737

2) Administrator: George R. Cartwright   Title: President

3) Number of beds:

Med-Surg.	450	Obstetric	22		
Pediatric	30	Psychiatric	41		
Rehab	64	Other	0	Total:	607

4) Chief of Medical Staff: Amos R. Bridges, M.D.   Spec. Int.

5) Director of Nursing: Sr. Agnes C. Bennett, R.N.

6) Director of Social Services: Mary Nodean, M.S.W.

7) Director — Discharge Planning: Sr. Felicia Williams, R.N.

8) Present source/system for HHC referrals:
Discharge nurse confers daily with ward chiefs; meets twice weekly with selected staff and social service workers to review patient needs; candidates for home health care are referred to Social Service for handling.

9) Patient discharges (1979)   23,612

10) Average daily census (Nov. 1980)   566
11) Occupancy level (Nov. 1980)   93.3%

12) Percent Medicare patients (Nov. 1980)   39.4%

13) Patients residing in HHC service area   91.3%

14) Referrals to Home Health Care: Our agency Others Totals

	Our agency	Others	Totals
1977	257	131	388
1978	277	154	431
1979	304	175	479

15) Referrals as percent of discharges in service area (1979)
2.03 %

16) Formal agreement for home care benefits with Blue Cross:
x Yes   No

Exhibit 10–1 continued

17) Summary of our HHC coordinator's present operational activities (if any) with this hospital:
Coordinator (Jackie Nichols) calls on hospital weekly; discusses potential referrals with medical social worker; keeps hospital supplied with referral forms and brochures; does not know discharge planner.

18) Attitude of administration toward home care (if known):
Evident that administrator knows little about HHC, has not encouraged utilization. Discharge planner appears to serve perfunctory role — leaves judgment on referrals to social service staff; latter is more interested in making referrals to nursing homes.

19) Obstacles and opportunities:
Lack of promotion or advocacy for HHC and its benefits. Hospital could benefit from our wide range of services which would be applied to staff as well as patients.

20) Special notes/suggestions:
Chief of rehabilitation department is a member of our HHC board; rehab makes more direct referrals than any other unit. Our director of clinical affairs was long-time, highly regarded staff member of this hospital prior to joining us.

no real system of referral because of the agency's own, inadequate liaison arrangements.

- To a home care agency with more than 70 percent of its income derived from Medicare, a hospital in which such patients constitute less than 15 percent of the population would not be a prime target unless other forms of reimbursement were apparent.

- If the discharged patients referred for home health care are known to be 2 percent or less when the average for other such hospitals is 4 percent to 5 percent, then the target hospital might be an even better candidate for special efforts.

- A hospital with a low percentage of occupancy may be an unlikely prospect for new business because the administrator is concerned with keeping beds filled for as long as possible.

While the profile here applies to one particular project, the instrument may be developed for other fields and other agencies. Profiling has much precedent.

The top salesman in a business may maintain a detailed form describing a client's organization, key individual contacts, types of products needed, reorder dates, and competitors. The 5'' by 8'' file card in a political campaign headquarters contains enough information about voters to help plan innumerable strategies. The drug detail person who tells physicians about the company's products has a large amount of data about targets as well as a strategy to fit each doctor with whom the individual deals. A state health planning agency may keep a detailed file on each legislator as a tool for preparing a drive for passage of bills related to its special interests.

Once the information was gathered on its target hospitals, the home health care agency in this example decided to prepare special objectives for each hospital. Examples of the objectives for one hospital were to:

1. seek an increase in rate of referral for home care from last year's level of _percent to _percent of all discharged patients (a different percentage from each one).
2. identify status and responsibility for discharge planning in the hospital.
3. seek to improve staff attitudes and perceptions toward home health care as an appropriate mode of health care for its patients.
4. discuss with the administrator and top staff any potential working arrangements between the hospital and the marketing program.
5. determine the feasibility of increased (or new) utilization of home care coordinators, or other arrangements.
6. arrange meetings with other key personnel in the hospital to consider referral development possibilities.
7. provide inservice training presentations to key groups within the hospital: medical staff, UR (utilization review) committee, nursing staff, social service.
8. arrange a system to feed back service results to the referring staff member of the hospital.
9. offer potential services of the agency's coordinator as part of the hospital's discharge planning team.
10. develop formal contract or working arrangements between the hospital and the home care agency.
11. provide a kit of agency information for use by hospital staff including:

- list of types of services and hours available
- referral procedures
- patient pamphlets
- outline of inservice training programs

- memoranda to physicians for placement on patient charts
- after-hours or emergency telephone numbers

The objectives in this situation are to emphasize what the home care agency can do for the hospital and its patients, assuming that service benefits would be repaid with increased referrals.

Obviously, the successful marketer considers a number of strategic options as the occasion may suggest. Preparing a special tool such as the information kit, organizing teams to contact target individuals, and devising one or two special inducements all are in the interest of attaining the objective. Even if the marketer has assessed the targets correctly, there is no guarantee that a specific strategy will work because people do not respond in the same way to any given stimulus. The marketing strategy is, or should be, fluid and adaptable. It is the marketer who must respond to the target's wishes and needs, constantly seeking those things (values) that will lead to mutual exchange and benefit.

TYPES OF STRATEGIES

There are no restrictions on creative strategy making, a process that defies labeling and classification. What one person would call a grand strategy may not be all that grand to another. Books have been written only to discuss strategies: how to conceive them, apply them, evaluate them, make them work. This chapter seeks merely to stimulate the creative juices in the marketer's own organization.

In a monograph prepared to train personnel in health systems agencies, Leland Kaiser outlines a series of strategies to implement planning objectives.[7] While meant for health systems agencies, some of them are worth considering since they may be equally applicable to many human services agencies:

1. A *rational problem-solving strategy* assumes a smooth flow between fact gathering, developing plans or solutions to a problem, and implementation. This classic approach depends upon a reasoned response to reasoned plans. Its greatest drawback is a long history of ineffectiveness. It doesn't work by itself because it is too logical.
2. The *community development strategy* suggests that the organization mobilize efforts of many persons around a given problem or opportunity. They are helped to plan and implement their own objectives. This strategy is used by neighborhood associations that depend upon the concern of their members to get things done.
3. The *negotiation strategy* assumes that each organization has something of

value to exchange and that the home care agency is capable of bargaining without being put in the position of being a beggar.

4. The *joint investor strategy* involves bringing together a group of target organizations to pool their interests and resources to accomplish a particular objective. This also might be called the *coalition strategy*.

There are, of course, numerous strategies for particular projects or specific targets. They might include:

- offering inducements or rewards for the right response

- using leverage of relationships or of authority or, perhaps, obligations previously incurred

- assuming an advocacy role for the target organization

A secret to the use of strategies is in their blending. Since the same strategy may not work for all targets in the same group, they are mixed and applied according to the best judgment of the marketer. The marketer realizes that:

- Strategies are actions that are undertaken to produce a desired action from a target or target groups.

- There is a hierarchy of strategies related to the organization's policies; the more fixed the policies, the less easy it is to change strategies to accommodate targets.

- Strategies must be mixed and used differentially; the same substrategies are unlikely to get the same response no matter how homogeneous targets may appear to be.

- Strategies are flexible; they must be altered constantly to fit the situation.

Although strategizing is enhanced by an imaginative marketer, this is not to suggest that the individual must be a genius or a master innovator. Imagination is a fine attribute, but the main qualification is the simple ability to think through the process of exchange. What is it that the target group and target organization or individual want? What will make others react positively? What can be done to gain acceptance, credence? Such a process is more important than all of the flashes of brilliance that may strike the marketer. If nothing else, applied strategy is a direct response to a predetermined exchange.

SUMMARY

A hierarchy of strategies is employed by the marketer, who links and directs the shaping of strategies in accordance with the problems or opportunities presented by the target groups or individual targets. Success in an important project can't be achieved without a differentiated marketing strategy where specific strategies and tools are directed at each target. One vital tool is a profile of the target with which an exchange is sought. Strategies are the creative end of marketing, perhaps the most exciting part of the entire marketing process.

NOTES

1. *Random House Dictionary of the English Language* (unabridged ed.) (New York: Random House, Inc., 1973).

2. Ibid.

3. Meritt L. Kastens, *Long-Range Planning for Your Business*, (New York: AMACOM, 1976), p. 3.

4. Peter F. Drucker, *The Practice of Management (New York: Harper & Row, publishers, 1954), pp. 352-353.*

5. Philip Kotler, *Marketing for Nonprofit Organizations* (Englewood Cliffs, N.J.: Prentice-Hall, Inc., 1975) pp. 108-109.

6. Ibid., p. 166.

7. *Annual Implementation Plan,* Monograph prepared by Leland Kaiser, Ph.D., Professor at University of Colorado Medical Center, PACT Health Planning Center, (Denver: August 1978).

Chapter 11

Promotional Tools

Promotion is communication that tells potential users about an agency's services and attempts to persuade them as to the benefits they provide, benefits that should satisfy client wants and desires. Some services are tangible, others are intangible. Intangible services are "promoted on the basis of a very simple idea—an idea which receives universal approbation—consumer, user, client benefits. This is at the heart of promotion." Rathmell explains.[1]

In marketing, promotional tools carry direct messages to targets. Reflecting marketing objectives and strategies, tools are selected from an array of choices, then are funneled through any of four business communications or promotional channels: *publicity, advertising, personal selling,* and *sales promotion.* Tools can be as transient and fleeting as markets themselves.

Tools can be written (brochures, news publications and news releases, annual reports, business and personal letters, signs, posters, and such) or nonwritten (slides, films, videotapes, audiotapes, personal visits, staged events, media appearances). They have direct and indirect benefits for the health or human services organization. Tools can: (1) help acquire new business in accordance with the marketing plan; (2) serve as a surrogate agency spokesperson; (3) clarify agency positions, policies, procedures; (4) inform and educate targets; (5) help obtain funds; (6) address competition; (7) recruit staff and volunteers; (8) help form acceptable attitudes and opinions among targets; and (9) reflect the organization's managerial skills.

All tools should have some payoff or overriding organizational benefits. A tool is prepared for a specific purpose such as educating targets, clarifying a position, or raising funds. It should either serve its purpose or be scrapped. If the tool is well thought out, the benefits that will fall to the agency will be obvious.

CHARACTERISTICS OF PROMOTIONAL TOOLS

Most productive promotional tools:

- reflect marketing and organizational objectives and strategies
- are written or prepared for specific targets and communications channels
- carry at least one promotional message
- reflect or suggest service benefits
- reflect organizational purposes
- have a distribution plan
- have an acceptable tone, style, and character
- persuade or inform
- are concisely written, edited
- reflect both reader and management needs
- ask for some action or participation by targets

Tools must direct the targets from unawareness in order to convince a potential client to try the service, repeat its use, and recommend it to others. This flow is called the hierarchy of promotional effects. Specifically, the hierarchy consists of initial awareness, comprehension, a conviction to use the service, and actual service usage.

BASIC PROMOTIONAL TOOLS

Many administrators ponder questions such as: What promotional tools do we need? Is a brochure enough? Do we need a newsletter? Do we require a slide show or film? What about our bulletin boards? Must we prepare a traveling display?

Confronted by limited budgets, managers may ask further: If we have only so much money to spend on promotion, what should we do first? Such a question is answered more easily if the agency has marketing plans to promote and advance its most vital or most misunderstood services. If marketing techniques are used, a specific brochure or factsheet on the service almost always will be suggested. In fact, the contents of such a promotional tool will practically write themselves, the result of marketing research and the strategies developed to reach the targets. If there is no marketing plan, it is more difficult to decide on the appropriate promotional tools because the organization finds itself promoting a cause with no discernible communications direction or system.

Whatever its perceived promotional requirements, each organization should have a basic set of promotional tools that are directly inspired by marketing plans. Basic promotional tools, according to agency size or number of employees, are suggested by the matrix in Exhibit 11–1. The basic promotional

Exhibit 11-1 Basic Promotional Tools

Number of agency employees	Basic promotional tools to communicate with targets
1 to 10	All-purpose brochure
	News releases
10 to 25	Brochure
	News releases
	Internal newsletter
	External newsletter
	Public service announcements
25 to 50	Brochure
	News releases
	Internal newsletter
	External newsletter
	Public service announcements
	Factsheets for specific services
	Traveling displays
50 to 100	Brochure
	News releases
	Internal newsletter
	External newsletter
	Public service announcements
	Ethical advertising
	Factsheets for specific services
	Traveling displays
	Continuing sampling of user opinion
	Educational forums and events
100 employees and up	Brochure
	News releases
	Internal newsletter
	External newsletter
	Public service announcements
	Ethical advertising
	Factsheets for specific services
	Direct mail promotion
	Traveling displays
	Continuing sampling of user and employee attitudes and opinions
	Educational workshops, seminars, special classes, joint projects
	Annual social event to raise funds
	Videotape capabilities

tools of an organization usually consist of a brochure, news releases, and internal and external news publications. With notable exceptions, depending on agency size and its marketing situation, all other tools become secondary.

In its early stages, each tool should undergo a preliminary process resembling that of the marketing plan itself. The process includes steps to:

1. determine the perceived purpose of the tool
2. discuss marketing objectives to be reflected by the tool
3. determine the target(s) to be reached
4. devise applicable marketing strategy or strategies
5. agree on methods of distribution
6. designate the tool's writer
7. figure how production (layout, design, typesetting, art, printing, and mailing) will be handled
8. decide who will evaluate the tool as to its conformance to the marketing plan, and when.

The typical promotional tool also must reflect certain contents if it is to communicate its message to targets. The basic content of four major tools follows.

CONTENT OF MAJOR PROMOTIONAL TOOLS

All agencies require basic printed materials that state the purpose and nature of their services. Most people think of basic literature in terms of "the brochure," the consummate publication often called the ultimate extension of the administrator's ego. Some managers contend that a basic brochure is not necessary and that in its stead the agency can use a melange of items and concepts including matchbooks, pencils, balloons, ice cream socials, quality care, or word-of-mouth advertising. Despite all of these options or distractions, the authors believe that the basic brochure is a necessity for a good organization, that it is a simple confirmation of the agency's existence, that it is indicative of an interest to become a part of the greater community, and that it is responsive to community and client wants and needs.

The Basic Agency Brochure

The basic brochure should contain much of the following material to transmit a comprehensive message to existing or potential targets:

1. What are the purposes of the organization? These purposes should be explained as they are reflected in articles of incorporation or agreement, bylaws, or mission statement.

2. What services are offered? Services should be described according to categories, such as treatment, counseling, outreach, education, or research.

3. What benefits do services provide to targets? This should cite especially benefits suggested by clients and potential clients during the marketing research phase of the market plan, not benefits perceived by agency managers without consulting potential or existing targets.

4. What is the agency's referral network? Can a client self-refer? Is referral restricted to counselors, caseworkers, or professional organizations? How easy is it to refer a new client? Is any extraordinary paperwork involved?

5. How do potential clients make initial contact with the agency?

6. Who do prospective clients first talk with on their initial visit or contact with the agency? What happens after the initial contact?

7. Who uses the agency's services?

8. What is the typical treatment routine for the average user of agency services? How many appointments may be necessary? How long is a typical period of treatment or service? Are services performed in one or more locations? Will there be unusually long waiting periods for services? Which staff members are likely to see clients?

9. How do patients pay for the agency's services? Sliding fee scale, cash only, credit cards, third party payers, charity policy?

10. When are agency services available? What are the hours of business, including after-hours on weekdays, as well as schedules during weekends, holiday? What provisions are made for emergency treatment, counseling, crisis intervention?

11. What happens after the agency's services no longer are appropriate or come to an end? What routine follow-up is practiced by agency staff? Where does the agency normally refer clients who are finished with its services but who require help elsewhere?

12. What constitutes the agency professional staff?

13. How is the agency managed and governed? What is the background of agency managers? Does the board represent a cross section of community interests? Is there a strong voluntary service program?

14. Where is the agency located? Where are branch offices? Is there an advantage in agency location(s) in terms of client traveling time? Do all sites offer full services?

15. What outside organizations are affiliated with the agency? How do such affiliations bring benefits to clients?

16. How does the agency relate to, or share facilities with, other agencies in the community or region?

17. Which organizations certify or accredit the agency?

18. What key memberships does the agency hold? What are organizations with which the targets would be familiar, such as the United Way?

If artwork—photographs or illustrations—is to be used in the brochure, it should depict typical clients (targets) in the process of using agency services (typical service scenes). A cross section of agency staff disciplines should be represented in the art.

"The effectiveness of a brochure has nothing to do with how much money is spent," Weld Coxe comments. "The very best brochure can be a handmade affair composed of original photographs and typewritten. Such a presentation is perfectly capable of holding its own against the most expensive product of the printing industry—if the message is there. . . . "[2]

The News Release

A news release is mailed or distributed on the agency's letterhead or on a special news release letterhead, which also should list the principal services if it has a hard-to-define name such as The Family Guidance Association, The Human Service Group, or The County Social Services Department.

Any message or announcement in the release should be of interest to targets identified in the marketing plan. The release, always factual and impersonal, also should modify or reflect a given market strategy as well as the stated marketing objectives. Benefits that will accrue to the target should be stated in some way. If targets, objectives, and strategies can't be identified, the reason for issuing a release, other than for agency ego, should be challenged.

The release can contain information about a current condition of the agency (finances, employee force, staff, board, or volunteers) or its future (a new service, a party or celebration, a long-range plan or policy). Whatever the subject, the copy must relate to a key target of the agency: clients, contributors, legislative supporters, professional staff, employees, volunteers. For the most part, releases should not be prepared on past events, with the exception of fund campaign results, hearings, and some other officially sanctioned occurrences.

Releases, the shorter the better, can be written by a PR staff member, a marketer, the administrator, a secretary, a staff assistant. In some small towns, the release can be dictated by phone to the news media, provided a rapport exists between the agency and the news people.

The gist of the message is summarized in the first paragraph, with some releases brief enough (such as an announcement of a new administrative staff or board member) to be self-contained in that one paragraph. Editors usually appreciate such terseness.

The writer must be identified in the release, along with the date it was written. Special instructions for publication should be indicated in the top right corner.

Artwork such as illustrations, photos or other graphics can accompany a release but must be thought out in terms of the targets who will see the story. Artwork must be identified separately, with the source and release date on each piece.

The Internal Newsletter

Internal newsletters can be many things: informative, impersonal, personal, instructional, authoritarian, propagandistic, manipulative, inexpensive, direct, informal, formal, intimate, casual. No matter how it is viewed, an effective internal newsletter can be a strong promotional tool, one that should tell much about the organization's integrity.

Employees usually are the primary marketing target for the internal newsletter. Articles should be planned to relate to strategies that can maintain morale, sharpen attitudes, inform, or clarify a situation. Targeted articles in a hypothetical internal newsletter might be:

1. A discussion of agency-related issues and concerns that may appear in local media in the near future.
2. Announcements of new policies, procedures, and why they were adopted. How will the average employee benefit from such policies or procedures? Were employee opinions and feelings considered when changes were made?
3. A discussion about employee perquisites.
4. Educational opportunities within and outside the agency
5. Departmental profiles, such as noteworthy things various departments are doing. How do departments respond to agency client needs, expectations?
6. Successful community outreach projects and the clients who have benefited from them.
7. Stories about the agency's growth. Monthly or quarterly statistics and for interpretations, usage trends, commentary on new program implementation, interviews with the administrator and chairman of the board.
8. Stories that suggest the employee's role as an agency referral agent or client finder. How can employees provide their friends, relatives, neighbors, and others with news and information about agency programs, services, job opportunities, and events? Are there incentives for finding new clients?
9. Stories about how employees can work with the agency's key referral organizations.

10. Articles that explain agency marketing strategies or objectives. Indeed, internal newsletters can be written around strong marketing themes: What do our social caseworkers do? What is the future of our battered adult program? How do we work in partnership with City Hall? How can we achieve more branch operations? How can we learn from the people who use our services? What doesn't the community know about us?

11. New or renewed agency certifications, accreditations or affiliations and what they mean to employees and clients.

12. Grants, donations or extraordinary efforts on the part of volunteers. How do employees benefit from each?

Written by one person (PR person, marketer, office secretary, administrator, or a volunteer), a typical newsletter contains two to four pages. Typed on the office typewriter, it can be reproduced on the office photocopy machine, then mailed to employee homes. Of course, the newsletter can be more elaborate, depending on agency size and budget. A newsletter can reproduce instant photographs, snapshots, pen-and-ink sketches, crude graphs, or anything that will help the agency achieve its marketing objectives with the employee target and that matches the aesthetic tastes and traditions of the organization.

The External Newsletter or Newspaper

An external newsletter is appropriate if the organization has a referral network that embraces several substantial referral sources, a caseload of 200 or more clients, and a multidisciplined staff with counterparts in related or competing agencies. These are not ironclad guidelines, of course, since there are circumstances that would impel a smaller agency to want an outside publication—a special fund-raising drive, a special cause to lobby, a controversy to air. External publications must mirror marketing objectives and be directed to specific targets; the only alternative to such a structure is labor and communications wasted on unknown readers. Stories should reflect or contain information obtained through the organization's marketing research efforts. They should possess a future cast, where possible, forgoing mention of past events, historical analogies, and large doses of agency philosophy.

Hypothetical external publication topics might be:

1. A focus on specific agency services. How do services benefit community targets? How do service components reflect needs or expectations of targets?

2. How referral agencies can increase professional relations with the agency.

3. How the agency trains its staff to meet needs, wants, expectations of clients. How is training updated periodically? How do referral agencies, clients, or community groups participate in agency educational activities?
4. How outside groups can join with agency leaders or volunteers to help solve the agency or community problems.
5. How the agency maintains quality control. What does quality control mean to referral organizations, clients? What are the standards for quality control that the agency must meet?
6. How agency conserves costs and energy to benefit clients and the community in general.
7. How the agency reacts to a new idea from an employee, volunteer, or referral source.
8. What new services, departments, or branches are planned; how they reflect either agency or areawide planning.
9. What myths surround the agency, and how they are deflated.
10. What the functions and current projects of the agency board of directors or lay advisory board are.
11. How the agency compares with similar agencies in other areas of the country. Where is the agency ahead of the times? Where does it show leadership? Which of its ideas have been replicated elsewhere?
12. How outsiders can contribute to the agency. Cash, long-term pledges, voluntary efforts, equipment donations, referrals?

SECONDARY PROMOTIONAL TOOLS

When working from a marketing plan, the marketer first ponders the use of the four basic promotional tools and the appropriate promotional channels. If the marketed program or service does not mesh realistically with targets and strategies that have been ordained for the agency, auxiliary tools must be considered. For practical purposes, some auxiliary tools are listed, not alphabetically but according to what the authors consider to be their communications usefulness. By usefulness is meant their ability to transmit a message to a target as rapidly and directly as possible. This list is based on our experiences with health and human services agencies. Other marketers will have their own lists of auxiliary tools. Here is the authors':

- factsheets
- special business letters
- direct mail
- meetings, symposia, seminars, workshops, forums
- handbooks and manuals

- public service announcements
- comment forms from clients
- questionnaires and surveys
- displays, fairs, and exhibits
- information racks
- bulletin boards
- films and audiovisual items
- speakers' bureaus
- feature stories
- inserts and enclosures in mailings
- hotlines (telephone)

- open houses and tours
- videotape programs
- news conferences
- regional and local magazines
- posters
- public address systems
- annual reports
- billboards
- contests
- signs and allied graphics

CHANNELS OF COMMUNICATIONS

Marketers generally agree that the four main promotional channels in human services organizations are advertising, publicity, personal selling, and sales promotion.

Advertising

Advertising does not play as strong a role in promoting human services as it does in hospitals and other health services. But some human services groups have used paid advertising in newspapers and regional publications to promote youth and counseling services, fund-raising events, and day-care centers; to assist the sale of hearing tests and aids; to obtain applicants for testing and screening operations. Direct mail advertising has been more helpful to human services organizations because targets can be pinpointed more easily within a selective direct mail project. A counseling group or a "Y" may send mail advertising its programming to neighbors, members, and small businesses that lie within certain census tracts, or a day-care center may send a mailer to parents who reside in a 20-block area or to politicians who represent the city in the state legislature.

Another offshoot, the public service announcement (PSA), is a popular advertising mechanism. Typically, the public service announcement is transmitted over radio or television at almost any time during a 24-hour period. The PSA (1) usually relates one main benefit of the organization, (2) amplifies that benefit in the copy, and (3) requests some action by the listener: a phone call, a letter, a visit, participation in an event. In some areas, there is so much competition for air time that radio and television program directors tend to broadcast only PSAs that are produced professionally, that entertain well, or that communicate the clearest messages. Stations are likely to compare PSAs offered by the health or human services agency with spot announcements from commercial advertisers. So organizations should take heed: PSA production can be expensive and, once produced, the spot may not reach the designated marketing target because of the station's prerogative of inserting it anywhere it chooses in the program schedule.

Publicity

Publicity is the most enduring promotional channel, the least expensive and easiest to use. Publicity embraces news releases and features, speakers' messages, and press conferences. Agencies find countless outlets for news releases in daily and weekly newspapers, in regional tabloids and magazines, in an ever-growing number of radio stations, and in some television stations (more likely in smaller communities). Administrators find that in many areas broadcasters compete actively with print media for local news, frequently requesting organizations not to overlook them in news distribution. Agency people also are discovering that scores of local and area organizations want speakers both to educate and to entertain their audiences. It is evident that consistent use of the publicity route is more prevalent among smaller organizations.

For larger agencies, a more strategic balance among all four promotional channels should be sought because in some locations print space or air time for human services news has been squeezed to the vanishing point in large newspapers and radio stations and has nearly disappeared on television because of the expansive coverage of crime news, sports, the weather, politics, and the economy. Thus, the larger agency must seriously explore other channels such as advertising, personal selling, and sales promotion.

Personal Selling

Personal selling channels are as popular among human services organizations as they are among hospitals and other health providers. Personal selling deals primarily with the influence on existing or potential targets of one or several individuals who represent the organization. This channel's scope is wide: it includes personal salesmanship; word-of-mouth messages, pleas, or endorsements; referral relationships; and consultant activities on the agency's behalf. In personal selling, these scenes might occur:

1. A family planning center administrator visits with key persons in the center's referral network to discuss ease of referral, obstacles to referral, or new programming.
2. Families of potential home health care clients are visited by an ageny supervisor and encouraged to refer relatives to the agency.
3. A social caseworker from a rehabilitation service performs extra duty by helping to establish a telephone hotline for blind persons.
4. Members of a Planned Parenthood program describe their agency's services in an organized way to potential members who are either friends or neighbors.
5. A staff marketing director from a psychological clinic visits the homes of clientele to assess their needs and to find other potential clients.

Personal selling often is the most pleasurable and self-rewarding channel of promotional communication because it permits key individuals to experience personally the impact that the agency is making in its target areas. Active, positive feedback is a primary attribute of this channel. Rogers and Rogers point out:

> One of the most important differences between mass media and interpersonal communication is that feedback is facilitated by the latter . . . communications is not a one-way flow of a message from a source to a receiver. The receiver also generates information and messages for the source and, in fact, such interaction is necessary for communication to thrive.[3]

Sales Promotion

The fourth channel, sales promotion, includes a variety of printed items and programming designed to promote and persuade potential and existing clients rather than merely to educate them. Most sales promotion pieces ask for decisive action by the reader. Sales promotion may include brochures and persuasive special mailings that also are part of the organization's direct mail advertising program; attractive application or survey forms that may be left in counseling offices, schools, churches, public transportation, or shopping malls; special invitational programs on how to take advantage of the organization's services; agency open houses; note pads, matchbooks, pencils, pens, and other novelties that nudge target recall of the organization's name; posters; special films or slide programs; displays; and well-situated information racks.

CONTROLLED MESSAGES

Managers should know which promotional tools they can reasonably expect to control and which tools may slip from their grasp. An organization that controls its outside messages usually can expect its targets to receive the information intact. Messages beyond the organization's control are likely to be rewritten, rearranged, and possibly misinterpreted somewhere along the promotional channel before reaching the designated targets.

Among controlled tools are print advertising, public service announcements, newsletters, brochures, slides and films, letters, billboards, information racks, public address systems, displays and exhibits, and staged events. All of these can be produced intact by the organization without media or middlemen making any changes in the final product that reaches intended targets.

News release preparation should be approached with caution since the organization cannot expect that its original message will look the same in a newspaper or come across the same on the air as it does in a secretary's typewriter. It is the professional journalist's privilege to rewrite news releases or canned feature articles in order to conform to the newspaper's policy on contributed non-staff material. (Many newspapers have a policy that all such submissions must be rewritten by staff members even though the organization's efforts in describing its news may have been flawless.) Agencies whose releases are intended for radio or television cannot be assured that their thrust will be broadcast in a way that management's primary message will be heard in its entirety. It is not unusual in these cases that the messages will be cut, edited, and altered by 25 percent or more. And although speakers' remarks for broadcast interviews or panel appearances may be rehearsed meticulously, there is no assurance at all that the interviewer will follow the interviewee's line of thought.

In personal or face-to-face communication, such as in some forms of personal selling, there often is a 50 percent chance that the organization's message will not be received as intended because of the receiver's biases, feelings and emotions, distractions, third party influence, differing viewpoints, and other factors. Examples are numerous: public hearings and forums where emotions can influence the direction of events; personal surveys that are conducted by representatives of the organization or outreach persons; certain speeches or panel appearances where the audience or other participants are apt to interrupt, divert, or confuse the speaker.

With so many tools, four channels, and so many approaches to choose from, the average agency often asks for guidance, particularly if costs and budgets are influencing factors. And, they usually are. This chapter has dealt with basic tools most agencies use rather than the more elaborate and expensive tools. Regardless of the size of the organization or the extent of its promotional resources, marketing calls for a deliberate, focused application of tools, even penny pinching if the same results can be achieved.

The marketer, perhaps better than the manager or public relations director, knows that tools are applied to their targets sparingly. The marketer does not bombard targets with dozens of approaches when one or more well-created tools will suffice.

Here are some of the guidelines the authors use with clients who are investing in promotional tools as part of their marketing operation:

1. *Design the promotional tool solely for the target or target group you want to reach.* Avoid trying to cover the universe with your message when you are interested mainly in the immediate neighborhood.

2. *Keep tools time-limited.* Don't print 10,000 brochures when your initial main distribution is 2,000. (How many times have stacks of unused printed pieces been removed from agency cupboards?) Times change; so do telephone numbers, addresses, programs, personnel. Think of the short-term and long-term future when budgeting for tools.

3. *Make sure that each tool reflects the aesthetic tastes and cultural background of the target.* A slick, thick, four-color brochure is apt to startle potential contributors who may wonder if their help really is needed. On the other hand, a sloppy, poorly mimeographed report presented to the same people may appear to have been done by a poorly run, unbusinesslike organization.

4. *Establish an order of priority for all tools.* If the budget is important, decide on the one, two, or three tools you cannot do without. Make judgments: will the stickers to be attached to doctor's office telephones be more productive to the agency than renting a booth at the youth job fair? Will 50 personally written letters be more effective than 250 fliers?

5. *Seek quality in the production and use of your tools.* Quality is not synonymous with expense. It means the way in which the tool is written, designed, and distributed. If need be, look outside for volunteer or paid assistance. Quality of tools is one way to distinguish the organization from competitors.

6. *Don't forget marketing's main premise: exchange.* Most tools should convince the target that they can or will receive something from the organization. Exchange should be evident from the benefits listed in the tool.

7. *The tools should provide a return on investment.* Many tools are aimed at bringing in new clients or patients; many others, such as questionnaires to former clients, are intended to yield clues for improvement of services. A tool should not be used as a throwaway item.

8. *Give as much consideration to the deployment of the tool as you did to its production.* Should the beautifully written annual report be mailed to the business offices or to the homes of civic leaders? Should the new ten-minute agency film simply be made available to everyone, or should someone personally get it into every service and civic club in town?

A marketer cannot make a firm contribution to the organization without becoming serious about the use of tools. It is the marketer who determines the critical tools and not the tools that determine what the marketer can do.

SUMMARY

Promotional tools are part of every organization. They can direct messages to marketing targets based on the organization's objectives and strategies. Tools have many purposes and identifying characteristics. They help to effect the exchange process that is so vital to marketing.

The brochure most often is the agency's primary promotional tool, followed by news releases, internal and external news publications, and a variety of auxiliary tools. Ideally, tool preparation is preceded by a preliminary planning process similar to that used in developing the basic marketing plan. All promotional tools have definable contents that will assist the target in making an exchange with the organization.   Tools are assigned to any of four promotional channels: advertising, publicity, personal selling, and sales promotion, with publicity the one used most consistently among human services groups. Tools are subject to changes by outsiders if they are not prepared by the organization with an eye toward complete control of the message. Guidelines on the agency's investment in tools are helpful to any marketer who wants to maximize their contribution to the total marketing picture.

NOTES

1. John M. Rathmell, *Marketing in the Service Sector* (Cambridge, Mass.: Winthrop Publications, Inc., 1974), p. 96.
2. Weld Coxe, *Marketing Architectural and Engineering Services* (New York: Van Nostrand Reinhold Company, 1971), p. 142.
3. Everett M. Rogers and Rekha A. Rogers, *Communication in Organization* (New York: The Free Press, a division of Macmillan Publishing Co., 1976), p. 2.

Chapter 12

Making Internal Adjustments for Marketing

In the wake of a successful marketing project, a careful examination of the agency should suggest the need for internal adjustments—a fine-tuning of services, administration, communications, and performace—even if the organization appears to be managed skillfully.

There is nothing new or magical about internal adjustments; they occur with or without marketing. Neither is there any special sequence that occurs or a place to say, "Now is the time to rearrange everything." Marketing helps furnish reasons for adjustments; the benefits are seen more readily than if the agency were conducting business as usual. The larger the organization, the more complex its service pattern; hence, the more frequent the changes.

Some internal adjustments are simple but necessary housekeeping chores. Some adjustments may merely eliminate organizational weaknesses that slow the agency's effectiveness in functioning in the marketplace. Some examples:

- Bylaws of a speech and hearing center are rewritten because market research suggests expansion of the service area to four additional counties and representation from those counties on the agency board of directors.

- A family counseling agency, encumbered by 20 standing committees on its board, revamps its bylaws and halves the number of committees. Thus, it frees staff and volunteer time, allowing the board to focus on more important issues.

- A nursing home chain installs a computer software package in its finance office, enabling it to produce daily information on patient costs and charges, personnel utilization, and other subjects.

There are other adjustments that the marketing process might press on the organization in the interest of strengthening the agency's ability to operate, serve, and compete more effectively. Some changes are more innovative and productive. For example:

- A large health systems agency establishes an incentive program for professional staff members who must carry out specific objectives listed in its annual implementation plan. Quarterly progress reviews result in a rating of staff performances, and three awards are made: first prize is attendance at a conference of the winning staff member's choice; second prize is a dinner for two at a local restaurant; and consolation prize is a letter of commendation for the individual's personnel file.

- A Goodwill Industries organization, faced with changing driving habits of customers for its resale goods because of a shortage of such items and the high cost of auto fuel, concentrates its discarded goods collection points and resale shops in major shopping centers. It had found through a survey that people were more likely to utilize those locations than ones in poorer neighborhoods.

- A home health agency decides that its principal target for educating people about its services should be physicians who are likely to refer patients. It hires a retired drug company detail person who previously had contacted physicians on a daily basis to promote and explain the firm's products.

THE IMPORTANCE OF SEQUENCE

At first glance it appears that these actions, or adjustments, are simply good responses to ideas generated within a progressive management. "These kinds of changes happen all the time," it might be said. "What makes them different?" In relation to the marketing process, the answer is that the sequence of market research, setting objectives, picking targets, and setting strategies has a specific consequence. The adjustments are calculated, not whimsical. The results may be measured within a reasonable time. The idea may be tradition-breaking in the usual way of doing business, but it is worth trying. To illustrate, this example dissects one organization that, with a new approach and some internal adjustments, reached a better level of effectiveness:

The Agency

An area agency on aging serving eight counties; this was a nonprofit organization responsible for planning, developing, and funding (in part) services to elderly citizens through the Older Americans Act. It was located in a metropolitan area, with a substantial portion of its service domain being rural in character.

The Problem

For more than five years, the agency had been unsuccessful in its seven out-lying counties in finding existing service organizations, civic groups, or churches to sponsor hot meals, homemaker programs, transportation, and other needed services. The reasons were: (1) few potential sponsors and (2) reluctant acceptance of direction, even a skepticism, on the part of rural people when the agency's staff members came out from "the big city" to organize services.

The Solution

The agency concluded that using staff who did not live in the concerned counties was ineffective, and that acceptance of new services, although highly needed and desired, never would be achieved without deep involvement of the affected population. It proposed establishing separate, incorporated service organizations in the outlying counties, each responsible for promulgating interest in the problems of the aged and working with the regional council in program development. None of the counties had any central organization that might have addressed the specific problems or objectives.

The Internal Adjustments

The regional council replaced existing staff and hired new members who actually resided in the rural counties, assigning them to work at each of the newly established service organizations. Guidelines and objectives were set forth by the regional council, but each county's operation took on a character and productiveness of its own.

The Results

Greater organization and involvement of the elderly in the rural counties ensued. Human services, civic, and religious groups in each county participated, accepting the goals of the regional council. There was encouragement for, and new funding of, services by the United Way and Title XX organizations as well as discovery of local resources for serving the aged. Finally, the frustration of trying to develop services known to be needed but without community backing was ended.

In this example, the internal adjustments were comparatively few, but are worth citing. They involved:

- a change in the method of winning the interest of people in difficult-to-reach areas

- the creation of subsidiary or branch operations
- geographical redeployment of staff assigned to service development
- revised staff requirements that related solely to principal place of residence
- administrative redistribution of staff costs

Some policy matters were changed, of course. The creation of an independent service corporation was a decision that only the board of directors could make.

MARKETING AND EVOLUTIONARY CHANGES

Some adjustments take years to make. This evolutionary process is described next.

A local human services organization, supported by an ample endowment fund, operated as an educational resource to deal with alcoholism. Its early efforts were evangelical—to promote understanding of alcoholism and to seek moderation in its use. Educational efforts were beamed primarily to young people. The agency's program included distribution of materials, school lectures and educational film production.

After ten years of repeated programming, the endowment fund trustees (separate from the board of directors) hired an outside consultant to evaluate the program. Two findings emerged: the agency's educational thrust was being duplicated by other organizations in its service area, and the impact of the program was unmeasurable since there were no baselines on teen-age drinking available from any source. There was, further, a belief among school officials that the abuse of alcohol had grown substantially over those ten years, though little evidence could support such a contention.

To the credit of the trustees and the flexibility of the endowment fund, the agency was allowed to venture from its unproductive path. Its first adjustment was to move from a solely educational function to the provision of direct services. A department was created to provide counseling to alcoholics and their families. Over five years this department accounted for two-thirds of the total volume of agency services. The agency acquired considerable respect for its work and growing expertise among its staff.

The trustees again asked consultants to assess progress and to identify future service directions. Imbued with an orientation to marketing, the consultants helped the organization explore a marketplace that the original trustees and board would not have imagined. Among the discoveries were new target markets in and near the service area:

- employers concerned with employee alcohol problems
- growing use of alcohol and drugs among high school youth (the original target group)
- emergence of alcohol and drug abuse problems among youngsters in middle schools
- greater prevalence of alcoholism among women

The written policy objectives of the organization required only slight adjustments to enable the trustees to broaden their concern to cover drugs other than alcohol. Nor was it difficult to address new target populations. The program was aided further by the discovery of the availability of funding from sources outside its own coffers, which were being depleted slowly.

Another adjustment was that the agency moved from a position of dispensing only its own funds to using them as seed money or to match grants from other major financial resources. It retained much of its own money for experimentation rather than simply using it for direct services; such a stance would have been unthinkable when the agency was young.

As target groups were delineated more clearly, the agency gradually adjusted its operations. It enlarged its client counseling capacity by:

- widening the age range of its clients
- increasing the number of women clients
- serving hard drug users

The agency installed a methadone clinic in a branch location and created a residential alcoholic treatment program. It contracted with several companies to provide counseling to their employees who were troubled by alcoholism. A change that was suggested (and rejected) was a proposal that the agency serve as the hub of a designated mental health catchment area. The trustees were not prepared to meet such a challenge, perhaps because of biases and misconceptions about mental illness as well as a desire to stay within the original goals of the organization.

Adjustments made in the marketing approach produced an agency quite unlike the one that had opened nearly 20 years earlier. In retrospect, only ordinary changes were made after the initial engagement of outside consultants. Changes effected by the subsequent marketing approach were far different, bringing more benefits to both the agency and the community.

THE BENEFITS OF HAVING BENEFITS

The organization that responds to marketing has to make internal changes in view of its potential with target groups. It is much easier to do this when readily apparent benefits are at hand. Two brief examples of perceptive and successful service operations illustrate the situation.

- A large nursing home develops an outreach program in its main service area. It uses its counseling staff for periodic calls on senior citizens living nearby who are affiliated with the churches from which the nursing home derives much of its support. Regular contact helps to discover problem situations that then are referred by the nursing home to various community resources. The institution also provides limited in-home health care services for which it is reimbursed. Organizational objectives, to help the elderly remain as self-sufficient as possible, are met by having people stay in their own homes. At the same time, the nursing home's credibility is well established for those who, at some future time, will be forced to seek care there.

- A small rural nursing home improves the quality of its patient care remarkably by the simple installation of an incentive program for employees. The plan helps reduce turnover and improves patient-employee relations. Once a month, a committee of both groups meets to discuss mutual interests and ways to improve the patient care program, food, and housekeeping. An employee of the month is named and rewarded with a day off with pay. A year-end drawing among past winners results in one employee and spouse receiving a one-week, all-expenses-paid trip to Florida. The sage administrator buys a number of benefits for the nursing home with a rather low-cost investment. These benefits include patient participation in the home's operations, employee stability, better service to patients, less apathy on the part of both groups, better morale, and good community relations.

SUMMARY

Marketing, by its very nature, requires internal adjustments; it forces change. Change should be welcomed and encouraged, but it must harmonize with the application of marketing principles. Some adjustments are mundane and easily identifiable, others are evolutionary. The marketing process continually identifies them.

The key to making adjustments is staff involvement at different levels within the agency and staff motivation by management. Marketing objectives determine all internal adjustments. They must be clear and understood by all concerned.

Chapter 13

The Marketing Plan

Formalization of the marketing plan results in a written document or documents. No two plans are alike. Some are short, some long; some are windy, some paper thin. Each plan reflects the marketing objectives of the organization.

Some organizations that recognize marketing do not prepare formal plans; they simply deal with marketing elements on a fragmentary, often illogical, basis, getting results that often are sketchy or suspect. Formal plans are avoided at times by some organizations because a plan to them is tantamount to a promise to perform on the marketer's part, with subsequent judgment as to the success of the program.

For nonprofit organizations, the authors suggest initial plans that lay out one year's marketing activity rather than longer programs that might prolong results of the agency's initial marketing efforts. A formal plan, it is said, "puts an end to the intuitive approach to decision-making and to informal planning to meet day-to-day challenges."[1] Plans usually are prepared by the marketing, public relations, planning, or development director; administrator; a board committee; or others. Frequently, they are assembled by consultants or advertising or public relations agencies. Generally, a separate marketing plan is prepared for each service or bundle of services.

As we have cautioned, the organization does not construct an all-encompassing marketing plan for its aggregate of programs and services. Such an undertaking might be calamitous. Consider a typical hospital in such a situation. From what is known about the construction blocks of marketing, how could a hospital logically prepare a plan to market to the entire community? How could the hospital successfully and economically promote all of its services with the same focus to all targets and publics? How could it develop strategies that would be uniformly effective with all targets? How could the hospital's promotional tools be applicable to all targets? A master marketing plan for the total institution simply won't work.

There is nothing to preclude the energetic health or human services organization from compiling its separate marketing plans into one umbrella document. If the organization has one marketer or one public relations person interested in marketing or a planner with a marketing inclination, it is unlikely that it can implement more than two or three detailed marketing plans a year. This chapter later presents an example of how implementation of one marketing plan for a hospital emergency department can consume the time of one marketer as well as others in the hospital management structure.

Anyone with an interest in marketing may experience the joy, and the tribulations, of building a marketing plan. Many nonprofit organizations ask for contributions and ideas from department heads, first-line supervisors, and line employees as marketing research and planning is carried out. "Where there is broad and continuous participation in the development of plans, communications is made much easier. Those who contribute input to planning will be more receptive to its outputs."[2]

In many organizations, plans are approved by the administrator and shown, at that executive's discretion, to the board. Since a marketing plan is a management tool, it does not always require board approval. On the other hand, the board communications, marketing, or planning committees may participate in plan development and thereafter be vitally interested in the entire board's reaction to its content.

Marketing plans are being altered constantly. Most plans are written for one year, with their target designations always under scrutiny and their strategies continually shifting. Timetables within the plan suggest that the manager establish listening and observation posts during the implementation period.

MARKETING PLAN ELEMENTS

1. Though optional, a summary of the marketing plan that provides the administrator and/or the governing board information for quickly grasping the key ingredients quickly is useful. These key ingredients would be: (a) main suggestions and strategic recommendations, (b) the marketplace and how the marketing plan might change it, (c) what the marketing plan will cost, (d) the principal marketers, and (e) how the plan will be measured.

2. The current business situation or a statement of fact about the health or human services organization is essential. This section should include something about internal and external factors, competition, patient attitudes toward services, how services are distributed, how they are promoted or advertised, patient needs or wants that they are designed to meet, and attributes of the services that help satisfy those wants. Share of market, if known, and pricing policies must be stated. It also is well, in

summarizing the situation, to be sure that the project to be marketed is in harmony with the primary mission or charter of the organization or lies within its bylaws and objectives.

3. A statement of the marketing objectives is a key factor. A marketing plan can have one objective or many. No matter how many objectives, they usually are considered as the core of the plan, the ultimate criteria for judgment.

4. Problems and opportunities involved in carrying out the marketing project should be listed.

5. Targets should be defined. From the objectives, says Eldridge, should come "pinpointed targets to shoot at so that the success of the program can be measured factually through the closeness with which performance approached the targets."[3]

6. Strategies to implement the objectives and reach the targets should be presented.

7. Promotional tools and devices to carry out the strategies should be recommended.

8. Monitoring and measuring the effectiveness of the marketing plan should be provided.

Despite what may seem to be adequate preparation, a marketing plan is not immune to failure. Some plans fall short for reasons such as: "lack of a real plan; lack of adequate situation analysis; prepared without adequate participation of supporting functions; unrealistic goals; plan not adequately sold during and after preparation; unanticipated competitive moves; unanticipated product or service deficiencies; or acts of God."[4]

Two marketing plan extracts are presented in the following sections so that readers may get to know differing approaches to building a plan. A hospital emergency room is used as one example because it easily highlights the inherent challenges of social marketing. The second involves an employee assistance program developed by a family help center. All names have been changed.

A MARKETING PLAN FOR THE APEX
HOSPITAL EMERGENCY DEPARTMENT

After a review of last year's patient statistics at Apex Hospital, it was agreed that the marketing manager undertake a program to increase patient usage of the emergency department by giving that unit some of the qualities of St. Henry's Hospital, which is universally admired by all the other hospitals in the city. Appropriate elements of the marketing plan follow. (The initial summary of the marketing plan, which often is used as a quick recapitulation for the reviewing officer, is omitted here.)

Situation Analysis

The Apex Hospital emergency department is one of eight such units in the city. Last year, 8,040 patient treatments were recorded in the emergency department, with 32 percent of those patients admitted to the hospital as inpatients. The emergency department is staffed around the clock by contracted physicians.

Three other hospitals in the northern part of the city—and tangential to our service boundaries—have emergency departments. Last year, Memorial Hospital recorded 12,982 treatments, North General 6,754, and St. Henry's 14,420. A closer look at each of the three competing hospitals follows:

1. *Memorial Hospital:* This hospital has 415 beds, eight emergency department carts, and ten emergency room physicians under contract. The emergency room is located within four blocks of Interstate 60 and is convenient for ambulance deliveries. Since it is the oldest hospital in the city, many persons go to Memorial by force of habit. Most of its physicians prefer to send their patients to Memorial or St. Henry's, although many doctors share staff membership among all of the hospitals. Memorial does not promote its emergency department actively; that is, it has no printed emergency room brochure, no advertising, no public service announcements, no wall rack information in the visitor's waiting room. A patient survey two years ago indicated that users of the Memorial emergency room substantially approved of the way patients are moved from waiting to treatment areas. Patients did not object to the billing methods. Emergency room visits to Memorial have been increasing at the rate of 3 percent annually.

2. *North General:* The hospital had 160 beds, a four-cart emergency department, and continuous physician staffing. Though this hospital has not experienced an increase in emergency room patients for about two years, it has not promoted the use of the emergency department, preferring instead to call attention to other services such as nuclear medicine and same-day surgery. There seems to be little administrative concern about the plateauing of emergency department visits. The hospital does not have a triage nurse near the emergency room, so department personnel must accommodate all new patients by giving them some priority. This system often breaks down under pressure, so patients complain. Several of the emergency department doctors speak such poor English that an orderly or a nurse must, in effect, translate the doctor's instructions to patients. No written information is distributed to patients about emergency room practices and protocol, payment or follow-up instructions and care. The wait-

ing area is small, with no television set, telephone, or coffee machine. So far as is known, the hospital has not surveyed its patients as to their attitudes and opinions about the emergency room.

3. *St. Henry's Hospital:* With 520 beds, St. Henry's is the largest hospital in the city. It receives many trauma patients in its emergency room because of its affiliation with St. Henry's Medical School, the comprehensive training of its emergency room physicians, and its designation as official state trauma center in its region. There are 12 carts in the emergency room, as well as three general examination rooms, a room for ob/gyn, and a cast room. Staff physicians, interns, and residents supply the facility around the clock. Despite its success, the hospital promoted the use of its emergency facility aggressively with brochures, speakers, news articles, tours, and special mailings to doctors. Its treatment total rose by 22 percent last year. A wall rack in the waiting area contains four attractive fliers on emergency room practices and procedures, what to do when leaving the emergency room, preventive health tips, and "St. Henry's Hospital in Review." A coffeepot is kept hot at all times; two pay telephones, a soda machine, a newspaper machine, and up-to-date news magazines are available in the waiting area. The hospital computer system permits the emergency room to track each patient treatment, including waiting time in labs and x-ray. Printouts are distributed at weekly staff meetings so that employees can review the progress of patient treatment. As they leave the emergency department, all St. Henry's patients receive dismissal instruction sheets, which they must sign as having read, as well as an attitude survey form to take home and complete.

In terms of estimated share of the market (according to year-end and month-to-date statistics furnished by the Metropolitan Hospital League), Apex Hospital emergency department visits constituted 14 percent of the total number of persons who visited emergency rooms in the city last year. Other share-of-market statistics are: Memorial Hospital 19 percent, North General 12 percent, St. Henry's 22 percent, Loadstone 9 percent, VE Arms 16 percent, Certs Central 10 percent, and Shoreless Seas General 8 percent.

For the most part, the Apex emergency facility has grown naturally since it opened 28 years ago and its complete remodeling two years ago. No true effort to sell the facilities has been made, however. The department rarely is mentioned in the Apex external publication and news releases about the facility are nonexistent. Until our market research, it had not been documented precisely that the emergency department accounts for 32 percent of all admissions to Apex Hospital, a statistic that has been maintained for at least five years. Our research indicates that the average user is 38 years old, male, white, employed in a trade, lives in the neighborhood, and comes to the emergency room with a nonemergency condition such as a contusion, flu symptoms, or abdominal pains. However, research also indicates an extraordinary number of infants and children are being brought to the Apex emergency area despite the absence of a pediatric unit in the hospital. The charge for each patient's emergency room visit to Apex ($62) is near the $64 average for all hospitals in the area.

Last year, Apex did not allocate any funds to promote its emergency department. On the other hand, it is estimated that St. Henry's spent about $3,500 for a brochure and a 30-second radio public service announcement that describes the hours and location of its facility. Memorial Hospital, which did not have any written promotional material last year, spent approximately $550 on a dinner party for five executives of local ambulance services as well as $700 for a mail survey of its medical staff members regarding emergency department referral preferences and practices.

Apex hitherto had not identified any target markets for its emergency room, preferring instead to cater to the general public. For the first time in 28 years, our market research provides profiles of average users and where they reside. None of the competing emergency department managers was able to show us a user profile, although St. Henry's said a study planned for later this year would provide such information.

So far as is known, users of Apex's emergency facilities want to be able to use the hospital as a free clinic. Most users are nonemergency patients; 35 percent do not have physicians of their own. Most know about the hospital because it is close to home or in the neighborhood. On occasion, a friend, relative, or business associate either had used Apex or had heard favorable comments about it and recommended it to the patient. Only 34 percent of Apex's emergency patients last year were judged by staff physicians and R.N.s to be true emergency cases. Consumer wants that the Apex emergency room apparently satisfies are closeness to patient homes, availability as a surrogate family physician, 24-hour availability, and a policy that accepts all patients regardless of their financial ability to pay for treatment.

Problems and Opportunities of the Apex Emergency Department

Based on interviews with all emergency department personnel, randomly selected physicians who refer to the emergency department, ambulance drivers and owners, competing emergency facility supervisors, and patients, our research indicates that the Apex emergency facility is confronted with the following problems:

1. Physicians' language problems make it difficult to converse with patients.
2. Its services are not promoted to any of the hospital publics.

3. Hospital employees do not understand emergency room policies and have misimpressions of the services.
4. The emergency room offers no specialty services or equipment.
5. There is no explicit system for moving patients from the waiting area to the treatment area to ancillary services and back again to the outpatient area for billing and checkout.
6. The waiting area is not sufficiently supplied with convenience items.
7. Emergency room physicians seem to lack leadership as well as allegiance to the hospital.
8. Waiting time for tests from the laboratories seems to be about twice as long as national norms tell us they should be.
9. Ambulance drivers and paramedics know little about the emergency department.
10. Emergency room statistics are not retained for more than two years and do not provide an adequate profile of users.

Identification of these problems suggests opportunities that may present themselves to the emergency department. Among them are opportunities to:

1. pinpoint the users of the facility in order to determine likely prospects for emergency room services
2. mail written information to designated targets, encouraging them to use the facility
3. lay the groundwork for further study of the patient movement system, with a view toward reducing patient waiting time
4. educate Apex employees so that their misimpressions will be cleared and they will tell others—relatives and friends, especially—about the Apex emergency room
5. reexamine the status of the emergency room physicians and provide them with more communications with the clinical and nursing directors, chief of staff and others
6. view the emergency department as a competitive division of the hospital
7. obtain new equipment and provide new services and specialities
8. upgrade the quality of emergency room physicians as well as work on improving their ability to communicate with patients
9. increase substantially the hospital's share of the emergency patient market in the community
10. improve the morale of the facility's staff
11. reorganize or refurbish the patient waiting area so that it offers more services and items to soften the waiting period

Marketing Objectives for the Emergency Department

The overall marketing objective is: "To increase the market share among emergency room users from 14 to at least 18 percent within the next 12 months and to carry out information and promotional programs to support efforts to raise the patient volume."

Three primary objectives have been established by the emergency room staff, working closely with the marketing team. These are to develop:

1. a specific promotional program to explain to users and potential patients (persons outside the hospital family) the emergency facilities and services available
2. a communications program within Apex Hospital to inform physicians, employees, auxiliary members, and visitors about the department
3. new arrangements for contracts and agreements with outside groups that may wish to use the emergency facilities

Subobjectives of the three primary marketing objectives, with suggested deadlines, are:

Objective 1:   *Develop promotional programs (responsibility of the marketing director).*

    1-A Survey emergency room information/promotion programs at 10 other hospitals. (Deadline: Feb. 15)

    1-B Identify features, benefits of Apex emergency department. (Deadline Feb. 20)

    1-C Develop promotional tools and programs to reach targets of opportunity. (Deadline: April 1)

    1-D Distribute promotional tools and informational programs to reach appropriate targets of opportunity. (Deadline: May 15)

    1-E Monitor acceptance among targets of emergency department information and promotion programs. (Deadline: Nov. 15)

    1-F Determine changes to be made in program to reach targets. (Deadline: Dec. 10)

Objective 2:   *Develop an in-hospital communications program to explain the emergency department.*

    2-A Determine staff members, physicians, auxiliary members who must be reached. (Deadline: Jan. 15)

    2-B Determine schedule of programs or devices to reach in-hospital targets. (Deadline: Feb. 1)

2-C Implement first program for physicians. (Deadline: March 1)

2-D Implement first program for employees. (Deadline: March 15)

2-E Implement first program for auxiliary members, volunteers. (Deadline: May 15)

2-F Monitor acceptance by in-house targets. (Deadline: Nov. 15)

2-G Determine changes to be made in programs to reach targets. (Deadline: Dec. 10)

Objective 3: *Develop at least 10 new agreements or contracts with local companies that might use the emergency department facilities.*

3-A Determine from hospital records the companies and/or organizations whose employees now use the emergency facilities. (Deadline: March 10)

3-B Research potential companies, firms, and organizations that might send their employees to Apex for emergency treatment. (Deadline: May 25)

3-C Design a program to inform doctors, nurses, and appropriate executives of potential client companies or organizations about the Apex emergency department. (Deadline: June 15)

3-D Implement a program of visitations and promotions with local companies that are targets of opportunity for the emergency department. (Deadline: July 15)

3-E Monitor progress of company visitation program. (Deadline: Oct. 15)

3-F Determine future of promotional plans with local companies. (Deadline: Nov. 15)

Marketing Targets of the Emergency Department

Primary targets: (Note—The marketer also must determine the exchanges that are to be transacted between the hospital and the target. If no exchange can be determined, no marketing opportunity exists, and the target should be deleted or rethought.)

1. *Patients and/or potential patients*
2. *Apex Hospital physicians* (all staff physicians, including emeritus rank and medical consultants)

3. *Employees and volunteers* (all full time and part time employees as well as those who have retired within the last five years)
4. *Neighborhood and church groups* (all churches, service clubs, educational groups, school offices, and senior citizen groups)
5. *Ambulance services* (owners, managers, key drivers, dispatchers, and paramedics of all private and public ambulance services)
6. *Large and medium-sized companies and organizations*
7. *Other health and human services organizations such as nursing homes, home health agencies, HMOs, and counseling services.*

Since the initial marketing plan for the Apex emergency department is to be for one year only, the marketers feel that it is not practicable to list secondary targets now. In the second year of the plan, secondary targets such as news media, government leaders, and fire and police organizations will be designated for promotional and educational efforts. Parallel with the development of the initial marketing plan, the public relations department at Apex Hospital will keep local media informed about activities and programs related to the emergency room.

Marketing Strategies for the Emergency Department

Three basic marketing strategies will be used in the marketing plan:

1. *Market penetration:* Through various programs designed to reach physicians, hospital employees, neighborhood groups, ambulance services, local companies, and other health groups, the hospital wishes to expand the volume of its business annually and to increase its share of the patient market by a minimum of 4 percent.
2. *Market development:* Since Apex has completed enough preliminary research to determine that there are many potential patients who are unaware of the hospital's emergency services, the marketing plan will help find new pools of patients, perhaps expanding simultaneously the present service boundaries.
3 *Product or service development:* New or improved services will be provided in present emergency room markets.

Strategy development by targets: (key to overall marketing strategies: * market penetration; ** market development; *** product or service development).

1. *Patients and/or potential patients*
   * A. Mail questionnaire to every tenth emergency department patient (responsibility of the marketing director).

** B. Mail emergency room brochures to residents of three nearby census tracts (marketing and PR directors).

* C. Interview patients at random in emergency room on continuing basis (marketing director).

*** D. Reexamine emergency room triage nurse function and assess observation values and techniques required for the position (ER supervisor; director of nursing).

*** E. Employ a pediatrician for at least part time duty in the emergency room in response to volume of children seen in the facility (chief of staff).

*** F. Revise waiting room architecture by installing rest rooms, coffee counter, built-in wall racks, and seating in order to make the area more attractive and comfortable for patients, visitors (administrator; others).

*** G. Prepare master dismissal instruction sheet to hand to all patients when they leave the emergency room (ER supervisor; chief of staff).

2. *Hospital physicians*

* A. Hold informational meetings for various sections of the medical staff, including medicine, surgery, orthopedics, ENT, urology, and psychiatry (chief of staff; administrator; marketing director).

* B. Schedule physicians' open house in the emergency department (marketing director; ER supervisor).

*** C. Realign emergency room committee of the medical staff (chief of staff; administrator; appropriate ER committee members).

*** D. Reexamine basic clinical policies and procedures of the emergency department and rewrite where required (chief of staff; director of nursing).

*** E. Begin program to obtain board certification for majority of emergency room physicians (chief of staff; administrator).

*** F. Appoint physician-in-chief in the emergency department (chief of staff; administrator).

* G. Hand deliver or mail new emergency room brochure and factsheet to all physicians (marketing director).

* H. Put emergency room policies and procedures in all physicians' hospital mailboxes (marketing director).

* I. Begin program of mailing acknowledgement letters to physicians who refer more than ten patients to the emergency room each year (marketing director).

** J. Orient new staff physicians regarding the features, benefits, policies, procedures of the emergency department (chief of staff; ER supervisor).

* K. Attend general staff meeting to review emergency room patient usage and efforts to obtain ER patient referrals from physicians (administrator; chief of staff; ER supervisor).

*** L. Purchase new equipment for the emergency room, especially in pediatrics (chief of staff; administrator; ER supervisor).

3. *Employees and volunteers*

  * A. Hold series of open houses (coffee, cookies) to introduce employees to emergency room personnel, facilities (ER supervisor; director of nurses; marketing and PR directors).

  * B. Distribute emergency room factsheet to employees as part of the payroll envelope (PR director).

  ** C. Publish emergency room issue of the hospital's employee publication (PR director).

  * D. Visit employee department meetings to describe emergency room and how employees, friends, relatives can use it or recommend its use (director of nursing; marketing and PR directors).

  ** E. Distribute emergency room brochure and factsheet at auxiliary annual meeting (marketing director; director of volunteers).

  ** F. Send brochure to former employees (administrator; marketing director).

*** G. Begin program of sending ER staff members to special outside continuing education courses (ER supervisor; personnel director).

*** H. Hold all-staff meetings to exchange information and data about the ER and to trade ideas, opinions (ER supervisor).

4. *Neighborhood and church groups*

  ** A. Visit key clergy at all churches in area to determine how churches can assist in promoting the use of Apex emergency department (marketing director).

  ** B. Visit all senior citizen and retirement clubs; determine how clubs can help promote the use of the emergency department (marketing director).

  ** C. Visit presidents of all key service clubs and business organizations (marketing directors).

*** D. In the Apex emergency room, hold a session for senior citizen club officers and shut-in visitors from local churches on how to use the emergency facilities (ER supervisor; administrator; marketing and PR directors).

  ** E. Hand carry brochures to all key churches and senior citizen clubs for distribution by their officers (marketing director).

  ** F. Mail emergency room brochures to all members of key service clubs, with cover letter from hospital administrator (marketing director).

  ** G. Visit public school district office as well as individual public and parochial school principals to determine policy for sending students to the Apex emergency room (marketing director).

***H. Form senior citizens advisory committee on the use of the Apex emergency room and how such services can be understood better by the elderly (administrator; marketing and PR directors).

5. *Ambulance services*
   * A. Visit owners, directors, key employees of all services, leaving copies of policies, procedures, and ER factsheet (marketing director).
   * B. Hold cocktail party/dinner for ambulance owners, executives, and key personnel (administrator; ER supervisor; chief of staff; marketing and PR directors).
   ***C. Invite ambulance services to participate in the senior citizen session on use of the emergency room (marketing director).
   ***D. Hold training session for paramedics (ER supervisor; director of nursing).
   * E. Revisit all appropriate ambulance executives in their offices (marketing director).
   * F. Send year-end letter of gratitude to ambulance executives (administrator; marketing director).

6. *Large and medium-sized companies and organizations*
   ** A. Visit physicians, nurses, and appropriate executives of such organizations (marketing director).
   ** B. Phone nurses or doctors of all companies not visited personally (marketing director).
   ** C. Mail emergency room factsheets, brochures, and policies and procedures to companies, along with cover letter from Apex administrator (marketing director).
   ***D. Hold employee health and safety forum for employees of selected companies at their offices (ER supervisor; ER physicians; marketing director).
   ** E. Phone key referral companies to determine their reactions, opinions as to emergency room services (marketing director).
   ***F. Appoint a specialist in industrial medicine to emergency room committee (chief of staff; administrator).

7. *Other health and human services organizations*
   * A. Mail policies and procedures as well as emergency room factsheets to all appropriate organizations, with cover letter from marketing director (marketing director).
   ** B. Visit all organizations that are potential referrers to the emergency department in order to provide up-to-date information on the facility and to ask for referrals (marketing director).

*** C. Cooperate with a convention center by offering emergency services at large local conventions or meetings (marketing director).

* D. Phone all organizations to thank them for referrals and encourage them to continue referral patterns (marketing director).

* E. Update local information and referral organizations about Apex emergency room; visit such organizations in person (marketing director).

Promotional Tools

The following promotional tools are required to help promote the Apex Hospital emergency room to various targets in the next 12 months:

1. emergency room brochure
2. emergency room factsheet
3. basic advertisement
4. questionnaire for patients
5. clinical policies, procedures
6. cover letters for accompanying tools, mailings

Monitoring Emergency Room Marketing Plan

The subobjectives of our three primary objectives require monitoring so that any necessary corrective action can be taken in the second year of the plan. By October 15 of the first year, we are to chart the progress of our efforts to acquire new contracts or relationships with companies regarding the use of the Apex emergency department by their employees and constituents. By November 15, we are to monitor target acceptance of our promotional strategies as well as acceptance by Apex employees and volunteers of in-house promotional efforts on behalf of the emergency department.

Here is how we propose to measure the effectiveness of the initial marketing plan for the emergency department:

1. *Develop and evaluate promotional programs.*

   - *Seek continuous feedback* from Apex administrators, key supervisors, emergency department personnel, physicians, volunteers, patients, and others as to the effectiveness of messages and communications about the department.

   - *Check monthly hospital statistics* as to emergency room patient visits; compare with last year's figures; check with similar sets of figures from other hospitals.

   - *Study questionnaires* completed and returned by emergency room patients.

- *Check for increase/decrease in patients who originate from the three census tracts immediately adjacent to the hospital.*

- *Evaluate results and recommendations of informal interviews with emergency room patients and their relatives or friends.*

- *Review questions asked by Apex physicians about the emergency department* in sectional meetings of the medical staff and at the physician open house in the emergency room; determine which ideas or suggestions have been converted into action programs and which should be converted.

- *Determine if there has been an increase in staff physician referrals of patients to the emergency room in the last year.*

- *Review emergency department usage and statistics* with norms established by the local and state hospital associations or the American Hospital Association.

- *Break down usage of the emergency department by senior citizens, service clubs, membership, church members, and other categories,* using information taken either from the questionnaire or from the random patient interviews.

- *Determine increase/decrease in ambulance deliveries to the emergency room in last year.*

- *Compare benefits and features of the Apex emergency department as envisioned by the marketing department with actual benefits/features mentioned by patients in the questionnaires or interviews.*

2. *Develop in-hospital communications programs to explain the emergency department.*

- Determine percentage/number of full time and part time hospital employees who were treated in the emergency room this year as compared to last year.

- Assess briefly the attitude and morale of the emergency department staff to determine what effect the marketing campaign has had on job performance and job outlook.

- Review questions and comments obtained through programs for employees, volunteers, and auxiliary members to determine which points were implemented or resolved.

- Determine, if possible, how many referrals of patients were attributable to employees or volunteers.

- Determine usage of emergency department this year by former employees and their families.

3. *Develop ten new agreements or contracts with local companies.*

- *Determine number of companies with contracts or agreements one year ago.*

- *Determine number of new agreements/contracts this year.*

- *Determine probable contracts or agreements that can be expected by the end of the year.*

- *Review examples of resistance to the use of Apex or reasons for decisions not to use the facilities.*

On the basis of attitude tracking, analysis of patient traffic in the emergency department, market share analysis, a possible repeat of some parts of the market audit operation, budget reviews, and continuous feedback, the marketing department of Apex Hospital will take corrective action either to adjust the marketing plan during the year or to recommend new actions for the second year of the plan.

An example of another marketing plan is ASSIST, a (fictitious) new program established by a nonprofit human services agency operating outside the walls of an institution but also serving the special needs of a major metropolitan community.

FIRST-YEAR MARKETING PLAN FOR ASSIST, THE EMPLOYEE ASSISTANCE PROGRAM

ASSIST is the name assigned to the new employee assistance program (EAP) developed by the Family Help Center. EAPs have their roots in major corporations that have established in-house programs to help employees afflicted with alcoholism. Later, these programs were expanded to deal with other personal problems. Many companies, however, find that costs and staffing can be minimized when remedial services are contracted for outside. Because of this belief and a growing corporate interest in helping employees and thus protecting the company personnel investment, many EAP service corporations have been started, most of them proprietary. In recent years, however, nonprofit health and human services groups have started their own EAPs as an alternative to usually more expensive corporate programs.

The Family Help Center's EAP resulted from a marketing feasibility study. An initial analysis identified business firms and governmental and labor groups with in-house programs as well as profit and nonprofit organizations that provided contractual services to company employees. The Center concluded that a promising market would exist if it could develop an approach and service package that differed from potentially competing groups. With appropriate review by its directors, ASSIST was given three years to prove its promise.

The following is from ASSIST's first-year marketing plan.

Description

Preventive in nature, ASSIST is designed to quickly identify troubled employees whose job performances are impaired and to motivate them to seek an effective remedy for their problems with the least disruption in personal living and work routines. Typical problems brought to the attention of the EAP relate to marital discord, single parenthood, divorce adjustment, alcohol or drug abuse, child care, teen-age stress, legal issues, and personal finance management.

Program Objectives

1. To offer preventive services through early problem detection and intervention
2. To offer a competent, full range of services to employee organizations as a natural extension of the Center's community service role, without duplication or diminishing current service delivery
3. To offer client organizations a nonprofit alternative to purchase of services from proprietary groups

Program Design

From the outset, the Center did not consider replicating another EAP. Most so-called EAP competitors provided only information and referral services: that is, for a fee, they would interview employees, assess their needs, and refer them to a community agency for service. The Center's goal was a comprehensive program beginning by helping management spot the troubled employee and ending with resolution of the employee's problem.

ASSIST components are:

1. *Management consultation*

   - Assessment of need and job performance

   - Review of personnel policies and procedures

   - Analysis of special service requirements, employee demographics, special working conditions

- Designation of a company EAP coordinator

2. *Program development*
   - Consultation with key company personnel

   - Preparation of EAP program policy

   - Preparation of referral system

   - Development of guidelines for confidentiality

   - Establishment of joint management-union committee, if applicable

   - Preparation of publicity programs

3. *Management-supervisory training*
   - Explanation of EAP goals, objectives

   - Distribution of manuals and employee aids

   - Discussion of program benefits

   - Demonstration of constructive confrontation

   - Instruction on referral techniques

4. *Employee orientation*
   - Explanation of EAP goals, benefits

   - Trust building between ASSIST and employees

   - Provision of details on how to obtain service

5. *Employee services*
   - Problem assessment interviews

   - Continuing counseling

   - Special service arrangements (e.g., day care, temporary homemakers, financial or legal counseling)

6. *Ongoing training and communications*
   - Provision of brochures and other educational materials to employees and supervisors

   - New employee orientation

   - Additional training for supervisors

7. *Program monitoring*
   - Quarterly service statistics reports

- Client satisfaction measurement via outcome interviews
- Periodic informal reviews with management
- Formal semiannual program review

Service Costs

ASSIST was offered to employers on the basis of four pricing options:
1. An annual per-employee charge for a full-service program
2. A lower annual per-employee charge for one or two assessment interviews with each referred employee, with provision for an hourly fee for those requiring more than two sessions. The employer would be charged for continued service with such employees.
3. Same arrangement as above except that some cases would be paid through the company's medical insurance plan
4. Special fees for supplemental programs such as extra supervisory training, education for living classes or day care

Targets

A total of 180 firms was categorized as follows:

- Companies currently using other services of the Center
- Companies with insurance provisions for payment of outpatient treatment for mental health problems
- Companies with in-house EAPs
- Companies known to have an interest in creating EAPs

The first-year targets consisted of 25 organizations with 1,000 or more employees, 25 with 500 to 1,000, and 25 with 100 to 500. These groups were refined further as to their union and nonunion status and put in an order of priority, based on management-labor relationships and attitudes toward improving employee working conditions.

ASSIST Staff

The Center assigned specific staff persons to implement ASSIST. Some, including the administrator, began on a part time basis. The latter was sent to an extensive training program on effective selling sponsored by the local sales and marketing executive group. Other staff members participated in training in treatment of alcoholism and drug abuse, personnel administration, and supervision. With cooperation of the local central labor body, a training program was planned for union stewards in companies where the EAP potential showed promise.

An advisory committee was created to work with the ASSIST staff. It consisted of representatives from the Center's board of directors who were familiar with management and administrative practices as well as others in the community who held positions in business, labor, sales, marketing, and personnel administration. The advisory committee was charged with: (a) assisting the development and realization of ASSIST; (b) providing a broad base of community opinion for program and policy formulation; (c) interpreting the program to appropriate organizations, business, and industry; and (d) guiding ASSIST staff in understanding employer administrative procedures and problems.

The Center joined ALMACA, the Association of Labor Management Administrators and Consultants on Alcoholism. Staff also was assigned to work with other nonprofit EAP providers in order to acquire mutual working arrangements.

Tools

ASSIST's initial marketing tools were:
1. A *general brochure* for distribution to prospective employers
2. Inclusion of ASSIST in *community service directories*
3. *Print advertisements* on ASSIST for use in selected local publications as well as in company employee publications
4. A *recommended interview format* for use with local communications media
5. A *personal introductory letter* to initial target groups from the president of the Center
6. A *prospectus* about ASSIST, tailored to each prospective employer client
7. *Business cards and stationery*

Besides these traditional tools, other methods were used to introduce ASSIST:

1. A *chamber of commerce EAP forum* was held, at which the Center described ASSIST.
2. Twenty-five initial target firms were invited to a *cocktail party* that heralded the program's kickoff; slides, charts, and printed materials were introduced during the party.
3. ASSIST staff and advisory committee members participated in two local *television panel shows*.

4. A team approach—advisory committee and staff—was used in making *personal visits* to CEOs in the initial target group.

Other program tools developed by ASSIST for distribution within client companies included posters, employee brochures, referral forms, training manuals.

Monitoring

Twelve objectives were established for ASSIST's first six months, 11 for the next six months. Progress reports were reviewed quarterly by the advisory committee and the Center's executive director. The ASSIST administrator reported on progress at weekly meetings of the Center's management group.

SUMMARY

No two market plans are alike. Some may be simplified, such as the authors'. Others may be much more detailed. The authors believe in formalizing the plan instead of having no written document at all.

A marketing plan in detail points up an undeniable fact about the marketing procedure: It takes time to do it right. If one person in marketing were to have primary responsibility for the marketing of the Apex Hospital emergency room, for instance, it is conceivable that 10 to 12 hours per week over one year of that person's professional time could be spent carrying out all steps of the plan. Such detail indicates to any reasonable person that most health or human services organizations must choose very carefully the projects to be applied to marketing and to be reasonably assured that those projects will contribute to the institution's general revenue and objectives.

Marketing plans, at least at the outset, should be prepared for one year and should relate to specific projects, not to the total programming of the organization. There can be institutional commitment to total marketing but the agency cannot be marketed in toto—all of its dozens of potentially qualifying projects and programs notwithstanding—in one unifying, inclusive marketing plan. Such a task would be the undoing of the marketer or anyone else in the organization who sought to undertake such an adventure.

Marketing plans are coordinated by specific persons but most managers and key supervisors can contribute ideas. Most plans include a situation analysis, statement of marketing objectives and overall strategies, recommendations for promotional tools, list of problems and opportunities, definition of targets, and monitoring steps.

It often has been said that nonprofit organizations are casual about gathering information on how certain projects or programs are doing or how their institution is faring in the marketplace. Public relations programs with their emphasis on news and events, community relations programs with their stress on projects that are thrust unilaterally on community groups, development programs with their intent on gathering pledges and gifts for the institution—all of these disciplines usually do not provide a barometer reading on how the institution's programs actually are functioning, succeeding, or failing. Marketing has identified this requirement to find out how the institution is faring and, as a discipline in itself, is able to perform a function that has not existed before in a systematic way.

NOTES

1. David F. Hopkins, *The Short-Term Market Plan* (New York: The Conference Board, Inc., 1972), p. 3.
2. Edward S. McKay, *The Marketing Mystique* (New York: American Management Associations, 1979), p. 150.
3. Clarence E. Eldridge, *Marketing for Profit* (New York: The Macmillan Co., 1970), p. 215.
4. Hopkins, *The Short-Term Market Plan*, p. 19.

Chapter 14

Appraising and Recycling the Marketing Plan

How many times has this or a similar tag line been seen at the end of a study or a long-range plan: "This document represents a new beginning, one that will assure a strong and effective organization for years to come." When so much work has gone into development of a major plan, it is difficult for its authors to avoid the temptation to predict its outcome and to pat themselves on the back.

A marketing plan, in contrast, is deliberately fluid, flexible, nonbinding. Rather than say, "We *recommend* that such-and-such be done," the marketing plan says "We will do this particular thing, but if it doesn't work, we will do something else that may help to achieve the result we want." A market plan is a proximate road map that the marketer follows but adds to when an occasional landmark, a short cut, or a better way to arrive at the objective are spotted.

RESILIENCY A KEY FACTOR

Marketing plans, unlike study reports or long-range plans, are revised as implementation occurs. They are designed with the knowledge that they may be effective for a few months or a year or two at most. But as client and patient preferences change, as uncontrollable events occur, the marketer must be resilient enough to change strategies, tools, and, quite possibly, targets.

Monitoring of the implementation of the marketing plan should be built into the agency's management information system. The marketer, the department manager, or the project head should make regular progress reports to management. Such reports should indicate the effects of the implementation steps and how the marketer has sought counsel on particular problems.

Evaluation of each strategy used, of the special tools employed, and of any internal adjustments are critical to the marketing plan. What works and what doesn't? What did the marketer forget? What should be added to the plan?

Recycling the marketing plan is, of course, updating the implementation, comparing results with standards, and inserting all the necessary changes and control to keep the plan on course.

An example of evaluation and recycling is found in one of the marketing plans discussed in Chapter 13. ASSIST was the employee assistance program operated by the Family Help Center. Here are excerpts from a report to administration on ASSIST's first six months:

General Progress

ASSIST is working well as related to the agency mission and the stated goals for the program. Ten of the 11 objectives set for the first six months have been accomplished. The center is clearly established as an EAP provider in the field. . . . The center is becoming known in business, industry, and among labor unions.

We clearly have a salable product. None of the 48 previously targeted organizations for EAP services have closed the door on negotiations. At least 12 companies have shown an interest in further discussions. Four companies definitely want to deal with a nonprofit agency. Most of the 48 company representatives stated that they were impressed with the cohesiveness of our program, the diversity and the quality of services available, the plan for continuity of care, and the geographic accessibility to the counseling units. Six contracts are in operation; a seventh is in process. Two in-house corporate EAP programs are contracting with us to provide supplemental services.

Specific Problems

Unforeseen when we were designing our EAP and the marketing plan was the current state of the economy. Most economic advisers forecast a steep and long recession through this year and well into next year. The economy already has impacted on the promotion of AS-SIST; for example, Convoy, Inc., a fictitious heavy machinery manufacturer with 2,400 employees, is holding up further negotiations pending some recovery in its sales and production.

The next six to 12 months will, no doubt, be a slow growth period for ASSIST. We have examined this matter with some care; some members of the marketing team have questioned the wisdom of trying to proceed under present economic circumstances.

Marketing Plan Revisions

Our studies indicate that unemployment and threat of unemployment, health and family problems, and alcohol and drug abuse increase during inflation and economic stress. In other words, both employers and employees need ASSIST more than ever before.

We propose the following revisions in the marketing plan, effective immediately:

1. Sales and marketing efforts for ASSIST should be increased by 100 percent (contact 100 companies instead of 50).
2. A new priority on target firms and organizations should be established. Do not concentrate on automotive or automotive-related industries; seek out medical, chemical, and service organizations; also seek out midsized firms where the developmental process for ASSIST takes less time.
3. Our basic promotional brochures and tools should be revised to reflect the importance of helping employees in this national period of high stress.
4. Our experience of taking six to eight months to develop and finalize new contracts should be reduced by one-third; this can be accomplished by assigning a team from our finance, personnel, and legal divisions to prepare a formal procedure to expedite contract approval within the Center.
5. The ASSIST manager should be provided an additional staff member to increase sales efforts with targeted groups.
6. The Center, under the name of ASSIST, should sponsor a series of free workshops for laid-off employees, personnel managers, union stewards, and others to address the various needs of families and individuals; such a program will have business promotion benefits for ASSIST as well as provide a community service.

The marketer for ASSIST demonstrated ably the essence of the marketing approach:

1. capitalizing on a change in business environment that might discourage the fainthearted
2. showing resiliency and an ability to change upon discovery that a large, early targeted market group (the automotive industry) seemed to be in collapse
3. recognizing that some promotional tools weren't conveying the correct message

4. retargeting markets by classifying firms according to (a) the impact of the economy on their business, (b) the time required to put a program into operation, and (c) other intelligent factors
5. using imagination in seeking new ways and means to reach prospective clients (e.g., the stress workshop)
6. displaying courage in asking for more investment in the marketing program rather than waiting until the times were ripe and facing the probability of more competition.

Some smaller marketing plans require only some fine-tuning here and there. For example:

- A United Way organization reduced the size of special teams making campaign cultivation calls on corporate executives from four to two when it found that some CEOs reacted adversely to the formidable appearance of large teams.

- A community planning council held up the distribution of service directories to labor unions when it realized that the printing union emblem inadvertently was missing and would cause an adverse reaction. (It reprinted the directory covers with the emblem at extra expense, of course.)

- A multiservice center established in a public housing project was little used, subjected to vandalism, and resented by tenants until the sponsor provided jobs for some of the tenants. Its program became effective because of a new sense of ownership on the part of the residents.

A marketing objective may remain the same but the plan and its component targets, strategies, and tools may be altered radically, depending on the size and depth of the operation. The marketing plan is good so long as it works; when it doesn't, it is recycled with all of the changes that appear to be obvious.

EVALUATION BY SELF-APPRAISAL

Marketers have not discovered the perfect method of measuring, assessing or appraising a plan's impact on the agency, its clients or patients, or on society at large. Business and industry use computerized and other technical systems to assess, control, and implement marketing changes; these seldom are available to the average health and human services organization.

The authors are confident that the self-appraisal approach to evaluating and controlling the marketing plan's effectiveness can be helpful to most nonprofit organizations. A self-appraisal seems to be more suited to nonprofit agencies than do industrial techniques such as top management observation, reliance on continuing reports from accounting, periodic business reviews, or complicated performance reports.

To assist readers in developing their own self-appraisal forms, some of the key checkpoints that must not be overlooked are indicated next. Readers will find others.

Marketing and Its Effect on Our Agency

1. Are our efforts in marketing developed to help the agency or to satisfy the needs of clients?
2. Is our marketing staff suitable to the tasks we seek to implement?
3. Do our marketing people work well with others in areas such as planning, public relations, or fund-raising?
4. How has the concept of marketing taken hold within the ranks of management?
5. Is there professional respect for marketing within the agency?
6. Do we really know our marketplace?
7. What opportunities are we missing?
8. What are we doing in marketing that is special?
9. Is the agency making a profit in areas where marketing is used?

The Marketing Planning System

1. Are our marketing plans reaching their stated objectives?
2. Are the original market targets as critical now as when the plans were developed?
3. Which strategies need overhauling or scrapping? Which new strategies do we need?
4. Are we maintaining a running log or checklist for the correction of our marketing plans as they are being implemented?
5. Do our marketing plans complement the organization's short-range and long-range plans? Do they honestly reflect the annual work program?

The Promotion and Support Systems

1. Do our promotional tools help the marketing effort?
2. Does promotion concentrate strongly on benefits for clients or patients?
3. Do promotional staff members accept the often minute promotional details that relate to the implementation of strategies?
4. Are the proper people representing the agency in contacts with various targets?

5. Do agency personnel understand why we have a marketing program?
6. Is there a balanced mixture among available promotional channels—personal representation, publicity, advertising, and sales promotion?
7. How are agency feedback and client or patient suggestions integrated with marketing plan changes?

Once the self-appraisal (actually a system of interviews, checks, and group discussions) is completed, the marketer must make immediate changes or prepare an implementation schedule for the changes. A remaining question is: How often is the marketing operation inspected? There is no indelible rule. Some appraisals occur continually, some weekly, others on a monthly, semiannual, or annual basis. Once an organization finds a credible self-evaluation format, it should continue with it, reaping the dividends that it surely will bring.

SUMMARY

Marketing plans are fluid and nonbinding and are changed according to new intelligence received in the marketing department. This requires that the marketer be resilient, gritty, and willing to shift to new strategies and tools midway through a marketing plan's implementation.

No hard-and-fast rule applies to the measurement of marketing plan effectiveness, although the self-appraisal approach may be very suitable to health and human services organizations. Using this approach, the agency, in a series of group discussions and staff interviews, examines the effectiveness of marketing within and outside of the organization, especially as to its ability to convey the benefits of services to clients or patients.

Chapter 15

The Marketer and Marketing Team

Most of this book is a chapter-by-chapter description of how the marketer approaches the tasks. The marketer is described as objective, possessing some research skills (or at least being capable of asking the right questions), able to write somewhat clearly, politically astute, capable of coordinating multiple activities within a single project, and maintaining the skills and cool manner of a first-class manager. Little wonder that readers may ask how such persons are found and employed. Are there such people? Do they come trained and equipped to do the job? Can the agency afford them? How does it use them in the organization?

Chapter 16 discusses the conversion of the public relations specialist into a marketing specialist. In some organizations, notably hospitals and health education agencies, the public relations role has been long established and is closer to marketing than perhaps any other specialty except planning. The marketer obviously must have an understanding of both arts but, more importantly, know how to use both. In organizations without funds to employ either professional public relations or planning specialists, some other way must be found to use marketing.

Installing marketing in a health or human services institution should be approached with some thoughtfulness by the chief executive officer. Not only is the responsibility one that must fit well in the table of organization, but its complete acceptance within the organization—by staff, board, and other volunteers—must be programmed to help the marketer start off on the right foot. To use and deploy marketing without confusing, threatening, or drawing ridicule from the existing constituency, the CEO should examine the following:

- placing the marketing responsibility within the staff

- orienting the organization to marketing concepts

- designating the marketer and determining the individual's qualifications

- using the outside marketing consultant

- using the in-house marketing team
- building and maintaining marketing momentum

PLACING THE MARKETING RESPONSIBILITY

Few organizations in health or human services are prepared to accommodate marketing as a staff function. Much of what the marketer should address is handled by public relations or planning people. Some hospitals have created the position of director or vice president for marketing; so have a number of health systems agencies, but the latter tend to label the function as "director of plan implementation" to signify the intent to execute the proposals and objectives specified in their annual implementation plans. A social service agency employs a program director who may supervise agency activities but who also may be the principal source for service development. An associate director may carry administrative functions, some of which are closely aligned to marketing. If marketing is to become a continuing system, just where should it fit in the staff structure?

To begin, the CEO will want a close and direct relationship with the marketing program. The executive needs to control it. The marketer, in turn, needs leverage and access to management's resources. Since implementation is a focus of effort, the position should carry more responsibility than that of a planning director. It uses the tools of public relations but doesn't command all of its activities, particularly those of a purely traditional mode. Marketing is not a fund-raising position as might be applied by the title of "development director."

Marketing has a very definite connection to all of these programs, yet transcends all of them. The authors do not suggest that the marketer should assume the responsibility for all three positions but believe the individual should be able to call upon each for expertise and, perhaps, even have first call on their services. We would suggest further that a well-qualified, clearly defined and clearly understood marketing program probably would hold a position rating higher than planning, public relations, and fund-raising or else that all three functions would answer to the director of marketing.

Correct placement of staff personnel has been the subject of debate in hospital administration since the first vice president for marketing was named by a Chicago area hospital in 1975. Some public relations persons have felt threatened by the idea of reporting to a marketer who might embody all of the undesirable traits of the huckster. They have been fearful that their communications and counseling role will be usurped by someone pledged to "sell" or "hype" the organization's wares regardless of the effect on image or reputation. Some professionals lacking an exposure to marketing have been skeptical about the professional propriety of establishing such a position in a service institution.

But as more administrators acquire training or exposure to marketing, these fears and the fallacies begin to evaporate. The important thing is the understanding and acceptance of the marketing function, not its particular title in the executive ranks nor its place in the staff pecking order.

Often, the PR director will be the director of fund-raising as well. An associate director will be designated as the principal long-range planner and the executive will do a little of everything. It is better that the institution appreciates and knows how to use marketing than to be stalemated over the relative position of marketing in the staff organization. However, we believe that the more deeply the agency becomes involved in marketing, the more desirable it is to have one place where coordination of various projects and assignments is maintained and followed continuously. When two or more marketing projects are under way, such coordination becomes imperative.

ORIENTING THE ORGANIZATION TO MARKETING

Consultants working with health and human services managers often receive curious responses when they suggest that marketing be applied first to a specific project and be experimented with before it is made an operational fixture. Enlightened and enthusiastic as an agency manager may be, the consultants should expect to meet some resistance, skepticism, and more than a few misconceptions. Therefore, it is important to give some attention to its proper introduction among agency personnel and, of course, among volunteers who set organizational policies. From our experience with clients we have found that the first reactions to the idea of marketing generate these types of questions:

- What has marketing to do with delivering services to people who are ill or in need of other kinds of help?

- Isn't this just another difficult, time-consuming, work control system similar to management by objectives?

- Doesn't this require expertise we don't have or cannot afford?

- What will marketing do for us that we haven't tried already?

Occasionally, we find an institution whose basic operations are in such poor straits or whose image is so blurred that it is grasping at anything new to provide an escape from its woes, or worse, simply trying to find a way to convince the public that the institution is worthwhile and needed.

The authors have attempted to get people to understand marketing before they plunge into it by using a three-step orientation process:

1. Orientation of Top Management

A two-hour or three-hour outline and discussion is held on marketing principles and techniques and their application to health and human services organizations. This gives managers an opportunity to explore possibilities in their own departments or in special project objectives. They can question or express reservations. They also learn that marketing embodies a system of implementation that they generally have not followed in normal operations. A goal of this session is to seek a collective commitment to marketing as well as to identify a few program objectives that will be worth experimenting with as starters.

2. Orientation for Selected Committees

A similar orientation is held for a group representative of the board of directors and the agency's planning or program committee (if one exists), and including members of a departmental or special project committee to which marketing is to be applied. Again, the purpose is to achieve some understanding and acceptance. It is not at all unusual to find an appreciation of marketing among these persons because many business executives have grown up with marketing. Such an orientation also protects management from appearing to move precipitously into uncharted waters.

3. Orientation of Staff

Much depends on the size and nature of the organization. A very large institution's staff has no need to be brought into the marketing orientation. A medium-sized (25 to 75 employees) agency is intimate enough so that everyone may have some part to play in the implementation of most major projects. The "grapevine" in any organization is bound to carry information (correct or otherwise) from one end to the other. It is important that marketing be introduced properly with the declaration that everyone has some role in the process. Special training conferences or retreats are an ideal method of introducing a marketing program.

In addition to this device, which many organizations might find difficult to use, other orientation methods include:

- several half-day sessions for key persons in selected departments or units
- continuing inservice training courses for all personnel spread out over a period of months

- use of a brochure about marketing that explains its principles, how it is to be used in the organization, what projects are involved, and who carries marketing responsibility

Staff orientation can occur in several ways. One of the most successful, in our experience, was done by a large multiservice organization in Ohio. Once management had announced its intention to use marketing, an orientation program was planned. The administrator had been in that position for a little more than one year and had decided to use the occasion as an opportunity to bring together a cross section of personnel for the first time. A meeting place was selected away from the main office.

Approximately 10 percent of the entire staff (45 persons) spent two days in a retreat atmosphere. The group consisted of all first- and second-echelon managers, department heads, selected professionals, paraprofessionals, and clerical staff members. The purpose of such diversity was to convey the concept that marketing was not an elitist function or confined to any one department. Further, the ideas forthcoming from all participants proved to be stimulating to the entire group and contributed a healthy balance to discussion.

Generally, this kind of approach has been awarded by professionals quickly grasping the fundamentals of marketing and adapting rather rapidly to its techniques. This should not be too surprising since it is the nature of human services that professionals must deal constantly with human behavior, seeking to change it in order to help people help themselves. Marketing is no less concerned with influencing behavior.

THE MARKETER AND NEEDED QUALIFICATIONS

A critical decision for the chief executive officer is the assignment of the marketing function in the management structure. There is no ideal to be put forth. A person whose training has been in business or industrial marketing theoretically should be able to adapt to any professional field, but this is not always so. On the other hand, a person trained in social administration, health planning, community organization, community development, or other derivations of these disciplines may have been exposed already to marketing courses. Several schools of hospital or health care administration have long mandated marketing courses for students; other professional schools provide electives on the subject.

Failing the in-house availability of the ideal person, an agency or institution would do well to select an individual with a sound base in a major profession and then provide the person with experience or education in marketing. Some of the ways that this can be done include:

- taking business courses or marketing training in local or nearby universities

- attending seminars and courses in social marketing

- providing part time consultation to the marketer from universities or firms experienced in social marketing

- acquiring a library of books and articles on marketing

- participating in activities of the local professional marketing association

The organization that employs a person with marketing skill, but who is without experience in health or human services, can use the same tools in reverse; that is, expose the person most thoroughly to the workings of the agency and its dominant professions. This would include:

- orientation to daily operations of each department of the agency or institution

- participation in management meetings at all levels of the organization

- participation in appropriate inservice or staff development programs

In the authors' opinion, the qualifications of the marketer, apart from academic training and field experience, are a separate consideration for the CEO. Here are a few suggested assets that the individual should possess:

- an ability to organize work well

- an ability to command respect from all levels in the organization

- an ability to write well

- a sense of creativity

- a better than an ordinary degree of political sensitivity

- an ability to convene and run meetings expeditiously

- an ability to maintain little professional bias toward any segment of the organization

- an ability to mediate differences between groups having a variety of interests and loyalties

The title of the position should reflect the appropriateness of the responsibility as well as help gain recognition within the organization. Be realistic. A "director of marketing'' might be less appreciated than a ''director of planning and development,'' although one title would be no more descriptive of the person's duties than the other.

The marketing function is sufficiently important that the person holding the position not be insulated from top administration. If not immediately below the CEO in the staff organization chart, then the marketer should report to an associate director or vice president. The important point is the availability of and access to the CEO at all times, reflecting both the desirability for close communication and the relative importance that the CEO attaches to the function. Communication within top management is absolutely essential to the marketer. It should not be hindered by artificial or rigid lines of authority. The marketer should be part of the top management team. Still, the individual must be far enough removed from line or direct service responsibility to devote as much time as possible to the job.

USING THE OUTSIDE MARKETING CONSULTANT

A consultant should possess all of the qualifications listed for the marketer. In addition, other skills are needed, including an ability to conduct research, competence in public speaking, and management skills. Ideally, the consultant should have had exposure to the professional field of the organizational client, but this is not as important as having a knowledge of marketing and its techniques. Many consultants are skilled in business/industrial marketing but far fewer are experienced in social marketing.

Hiring marketing consultants is as much a matter of selectivity as if the organization were to need financial, architectural, or legal assistance. It depends on what is to be done, how important the particular project is, and how the consultant can be used most effectively.

Once the organization acknowledges that marketing is sound and that its key personnel should be exposed and oriented to its use, there are a few appropriate uses of the marketing consultant. The authors take the position that the organization can and should be helped to help itself, that agency personnel must make key decisions and perform the work, and that outside assistance is valuable only up to a point.

There are several ways to use a marketing consultant:

- Ask the consultant to provide marketing training for staff and volunteers.

- Request intermittent or regular consultation with the in-house staff person responsible for marketing.

- Contract with the consultant for a specific project that requires special knowledge of the subject rather than solely of marketing.

- Ask the expert to develop marketing plans for separate projects for execution by different units or departments of the agency.

The selection of a consultant is a matter of individual preference as well as exposure or experience in social marketing. With the exception of larger firms that dominate the management and financial side of health and human services consulting, most consultants are known because of their work within a region or because they have a particular service specialty. Since much of their success in acquiring work stems from satisfaction by former clients, they become known primarily by word of mouth. There is no formal system of acquiring consultants in social marketing. Trade and professional associations generally maintain lists of approved or recommended consultant firms in other fields. These lists are based upon information passed on by previous clients. Today, any national listing of marketing consultants would be a short one indeed.

Consultant fees in marketing vary with firms, of course. They are not different from practices in other consulting fields; that is, they vary according to the demand for service, the caliber of the specialists involved, and the work expected. Most consultants charge a per diem fee plus expenses for short-term activity. For a given project, an agency can negotiate a block fee that also covers expenses. A retainer for regular consultation is not unusual. In any event, the consultant can be expected to specify in writing the services, materials, and assistance the expert will provide and to detail expected costs and fees. Reports and written documents depend on the desire of the contracting organization. In other words, the organization engages a marketing consultant under the same business terms as it would any other supplier of goods or services.

USING THE IN-HOUSE MARKETING TEAM

Because the authors believe that successful social marketing depends on the commitment and enthusiasm of the staff, we advocate the creation of an in-house marketing team for major, single projects. A team approach is standard in most agencies; it is especially helpful in marketing since, we stress, no individual has sufficient information on targets or target groups, relationships, and strategies that is complete enough to implement a marketing plan, let alone prepare it. Further, marketing project components may well require interdepartmental participation. Knowledgeable paraprofessionals and support staff can bring a leveling effect as well as a realistic view of clients/patients, the manner in which services are being provided, the operations of the agency itself, and views of other matters that may be different from those of professionals who dominate the organization.

Criteria for the selection of individuals to serve on the marketing team include:

- knowledge or background of the specific marketing project or subject
- existing or past relationships to potential target groups in the project
- special interest in the project in addition to having knowledge that is useful to the project
- leadership qualities
- management indication of their strong potential for job advancement
- enthusiasm for working with peers and others
- innovative thinking, flexibility in approaching work

Representation from a cross section of staff will produce strong participation and prevent overprotection of special interests or fiefdoms.

A description of duties and procedures can be developed to guide the marketing team(s). There can be and often are several marketing teams working concurrently in the agency. The size of the teams will vary but should remain sufficiently small to expedite activity. Depending on the scope of the project, the principal membership should run from four to about 15 persons.

Exhibit 15-1 presents a general instruction form that can be used in marketing team operations.

Exhibit 15-1 Instruction Form for Marketing Teams

Tasks and Responsibilities—Marketing Teams

General Charge:

Each marketing team will be responsible for addressing a specific project designated by management. The project will be concerned with a problem or opportunity confronting the agency and/or will impact on accomplishment of our broad goals and objectives. The team will apply a social marketing systems approach to the project or program with the intent of producing a plan (written to the extent practicable) that will implement the objectives that will be determined for it. The marketing plan will include specifications on costs, personnel requirements, and implementation strategies and will fix various responsibilities for the project.

Specific Charge:

Each marketing project will be preceded by a specific charge to the

Exhibit 15–1 continued

marketing team; an initial analysis may be undertaken prior to beginning the project and the team's efforts.

Leadership:

The team leader is the person selected by management to assume overall direction of the marketing effort. Reason for selection: special interest or qualifications in the subject matter; direct supervisory responsibility for the program within the agency; potential for staff promotion or managerial opportunities.

Team Member Qualifications

Members will be knowledgeable of the agency and its operations and will have demonstrated ability to work with others on a program. They must have the ability to analyze a situation and to set forth clear, measurable, and reasonable objectives. They must have the willingness to follow a disciplined approach toward implementation of project objectives and know where and whom to approach for help. A team member need not have been exposed to indepth marketing training or experience.

Authority:

The team leader is vested with full authority to develop and coordinate marketing activities for the project.

Reports will be made to the executive director or to a manager who may be assigned the responsibility for directing the agency's marketing efforts at a later date.

Any matter related to conformance with present agency policy, development of a new policy or program, or investment of new financial or staff resources must be submitted to management and, subsequently, to the board of directors for approval. The marketing plan and its details must be approved by management.

Team Assignment:

The team leader will convene members on a "working basis;" that is, the group is not to be just a "think group" but one in which individual assignments are made and executed. The size of the group is flexible and will consist of those who may bring substantial assistance to the project. It could include any employee, volunteer

Exhibit 15–1 continued

leaders, advisory committee members, or even professionals from outside the agency who have special expertise.

Consultation and Support Services:

The director of the research department, the director of planning and development, and the director of public information will participate on call. Other staff members, such as the director of finance, may be brought in occasionally for special purposes and advice. Outside consultants will be available to advise on development of the marketing plan in accordance with arrangements made by management. However, such consultants are to provide counsel rather than to take over responsibility for production of the marketing plan.

Financing:

Any special financing required for implementation of the marketing plan must be detailed in advance and submitted to management for approval. Expenses for research, special promotional tools, etc., if not extraordinary, will be absorbed within regular departmental budgets.

Timetable:

Deadlines are dependent on the urgency of implementation desired by management. There should be broad objectives that have dates attached; they will be subject to review monthly. As marketing procedures are defined, "production" dates should be placed on each item. A sense of timing is an important essential to marketing efforts.

Suggested Steps in the Marketing Process:

1. Convene marketing team; discuss charge, project situation, rationale for a social marketing approach; set up ground rules and procedures, dates for regular meetings; develop checklists.
2. Review, revise, and agree on approaches recommended in initial analysis of project.
3. Define primary objective of project (which may differ from #2); detail secondary objectives; review against agency's stated objectives and current policies.

Exhibit 15–1 continued

 4. Identify key target dates for project.
 5. Identify all possible problems and opportunities related to project. (Detail barriers and how to overcome them.)
 6. Review research activities according to outline (as modified).
 7. Initiate and conduct special research projects as required.
 8. Concentrate on identification of targets, proper analysis of their importance, ranking and sequence to implementation of project.
 9. Identify exchange and sources of influence, advocacy, leverage that are related to target organizations.
10. Review targets; place in their proper sequence for implementation of strategies.
11. Identify internal adjustments needed with agency operations: policies, staff deployment, service fees, and so forth.
12. Hold progress report meetings with management to discuss findings, key decisions to be made, and preliminary recommendations.
13. Decide on tools that must be developed and used in implementation; arrange for their production.
14. Produce written marketing plan with provision for periodic adjustments.
15. Evaluate effect of strategies at key dates; be prepared to determine measurable results.

BUILDING AND MAINTAINING MOMENTUM

Management should find it propitious to give special attention to an assembled marketing team or group. The CEO should meet with the members at the outset and at several key points to ascertain the degree of progress and to provide encouragement. At the same time, the resources of the organization should be made available and some leeway given with respect to normal agency demands for meetings, written information, and other procedures. If extra funding is required, it should be made available readily. If staff time and schedules would be enhanced by rearrangement to allow full team participation, it should be done quickly.

Recognition of special efforts on the part of persons who are working on the projects besides performing their normal activities is important, is in good practice, and should be expected. Management's job is to promote enthusiasm, reduce red tape, show interest, open doors, and aid in getting results. It would be well worth the effort to provide marketing teams with as much incentive as possible, particularly when the system is new to the organization.

In our experience, we have found that when only one or two projects are undertaken, the marketing teams tend to get all of the management support needed, enjoy the challenge of tackling a direct goal with a new system of implementation, and achieve a sense of pride and accomplishment over and above that from the day-to-day work in which they also are involved.

SUMMARY

Marketing is not undertaken simply by naming someone to the job or announcing to the organization that it now has a new system or method of implementing its objectives. The nondescriptiveness of the term "marketing," the misconceptions of the system, and even the fears on the part of some staff specialists dictate that the organization take some care in orienting staff, board, and committee members in just what marketing is, how it works, and what it can do for the agency or institution.

Placement of the marketing specialist in the management structure and where that expert must be situated to be effective have been discussed. Certain attributes are highly desirable besides having someone with training and experience in marketing concepts and techniques. The organization also should consider the use of marketing consultation from the outside but not expect that this alone will suffice. The work still needs to be done within the organization.

A marketing team approach is a highly effective way of bringing staff talent and resources together on a project. Selection of the team members also is important, and their criteria have been analyzed. Also suggested is a sort of track to guide the marketing team as it sets forth on its task. Finally, the contributions of the marketing team should be recognized and rewarded according to performance. Management has to show its interest and concern and then provide the muscle that will help the team do its job.

Chapter 16

Introducing Marketing into the Agency Public Relations Operation

Not long ago a popular figure in social marketing addressed a meeting of hospital public relations directors. The seminar sought to explain how social marketing applied to a hospital. Several of the public relations persons faulted the speaker. "How dare you suggest that a hospital needs a full time or even a part time marketing person?" one asked. "That action would rob public relations directors of their rightful positions. This profession has finally established itself as critical to hospitals, and now you want to change it all. You should be ashamed. You don't know hospitals."

Although we sympathized with the hospital people, we wondered why an astute public relations person would not want to assimilate enough marketing knowledge to become marketing oriented. One problem is that public relations itself has become rooted in the nonprofit sector, developing its own problems, issues, and concerns, forming its own associations, issuing its own newsletters. In some hospitals and in human services organizations, public relations still is feeling its oats. In many organizations, the concept of a staff public relations director, let alone a marketing person, has yet to be sold to management or to the board of directors.

Customarily, the public relations staff in a health or human services setting performs such functions as:

- planning for, gathering raw material for, writing, editing, and proofing news releases and publications, promotional and informational publications, reports, and other aids

- contacting communications media regularly with story ideas, tips, background items, explanations, rebuttals

- issuing instructional publications for employees and prospective employees, clients, potential donors, government and regulatory agencies, community groups

- developing audiovisual, film, and videotape projects
- conceiving, arranging for, writing, and placing institutional advertisements and public service announcements,
- collecting and sampling comments and complaints
- working with graphic designers, typesetters, photographers, and printers
- helping plan and conduct special events
- "caring for and feeding" the board public relations or communications committee
- spreading goodwill in all quarters
- maintaining the archives and clipping file

In recent years, many agency public relations practitioners are finding that much of what they have been doing is marketing directed, especially in strategy development, preparation of promotional tools, and some targeting. In the average health and human services agency, public relations usually forgoes the critical preliminary marketing process, the marketing research, the internal adjustments, and the objective-setting stages that are part of marketing.

DIFFERENCES BETWEEN PR AND MARKETING

A baker's dozen of comparative points (Exhibit 16-1) distinguish marketing from public relations, at least in health and human services.

CASE HISTORY: PUBLIC RELATIONS

A large family guidance and social service agency located in an older, blue-collar neighborhood in a medium-sized city had a constituency that was primarily young and middle-aged adults with problems with marriage, finances, interpersonal relations, and vocations. Elderly clientele constituted only about 10 percent of the agency's caseload. At an administrative staff meeting, the administrator said to the public relations director, "Can we put on more programs for the elderly around the neighborhood?"

This request inspired the public relations director, whose previous link to the elderly had been through news releases and the agency annual report. He went about his initial program plan as follows: He phoned the local Red Cross chapter "to see if they had any programs for old people." He phoned the Cancer Society "to see if they could send someone out to talk to old people." He

Exhibit 16-1 Sizing Up Marketing vs. Public Relations

Marketing	Public Relations
A planned system of achieving objectives	A tool, vehicle, channel to communicate messages favoring the sender
Very directive in method	Most often generalized in method
Internal management of time, effort, and investment	Often reactive to public statements, events, occurrences; sometimes dictated by whim instead of by management planning
Target oriented	Public oriented
Strategy oriented	Dependent on will, as well as mood, of media persons
Selective in use and investment in tools	Reliance upon traditional promotional publications and publicity; not too selective in tool preparation
Focused on knowing client or patient desires	Focused on knowledge of management predilections, directives, likes, and dislikes
Focused on exchanges of values	Focused on hopes, threats, incomplete actions, and decisions
Accent on controlled promotional channels	Accent on partially controlled promotional channels
Based on a marketing plan or system	Based on a possible publicity plan, budget, or orders from management
Heavy stress on projects, programs	Heavy stress on publications, publicity
Judged by project completion, thoroughness, interrelationships with internal and outside groups	Judged on ability to produce publications, change agency image, amass newspaper clippings, and draw grateful thanks from patients/clients
Often reports directly to highest administrative officer	Often reports directly to an associate executive director

phoned a Meals on Wheels outlet "in order to see what they had to offer in the way of programs." He phoned the local branch of the Heart Association "to see if they could send someone out to talk about hearts." He checked to see if localites from the Diabetes Society "could furnish a speaker and some brochures." He asked if the local American Association of Retired Persons (AARP) "could furnish us with someone to talk to our group." To his relief, he learned that all of the groups he phoned would be happy to supply speakers and collateral literature.

He arranged a six-month speakers program, then determined how to attract audiences. He discovered that his best promotional thrust was through news releases to city and weekly newspapers. Logistically, he arranged for chairs and a head table, ordered coffee and rolls, and waited for the first guests to arrive. Twelve came. A similar attendance pattern repeated itself at all subsequent programs in the series. After the last program, the public relations director wrote off the series as one in which "there is just not much interest locally."

In supervising the series, the public relations officer operated on the supposition that all resources "are out there in the community and that they will respond automatically to any request of ours" All the speakers, he figured, would arrive at the agency fully prepared with plenty of information, enthusiasm, and handouts. They did, of course. It was the agency, though, that was a victim of the speaker program gone sour. In effect, the agency had acted merely as a broker for the services of the groups whose representatives had appeared. The public relations director would take the platform, deliver a welcome ("I congratulate you on your attendance"), introduce the speaker, and thank the audience for coming. In none of his introductory or presiding remarks did the director mention how his agency meshed with the speaker's organization, how the agency planned to follow through on points or recommendations made by the speaker, how the agency could reinforce the speaker's remarks, or how some of the agency's services can supplement the guest's services.

During the series, agency management thought it was performing a good deed for its neighbors. But was it really a good deed, a tangible service, or was it just a series of happenings soon to fade into memory? Was the time and expense in planning, coordinating, organizing, and implementing worth it for an average of 12 persons per event? What did the agency receive in exchange for the programs? Not very much.

CASE HISTORY: MARKETING

Let's take a situation in an almost identical family guidance and social service agency. The agency marketing director concluded that a partially untapped market in the community consisted of persons 65 years of age and older who were relatively healthy and ambulatory. She discussed her conclusions at an administrative staff meeting. "Show us a plan," said the administrator. The marketer developed a simple marketing plan. Reviewing the agency philosophy, bylaws, and stated objectives for clues to an official posture toward the aged, she was able to provide raw data for staff discussion. She also reviewed client origin data, client profiles, and census figures; she checked with neighboring clergymen to determine the extent of their parishes's needy elderly. Through internal and external research, she reasoned that a market existed for agency-sponsored speeches, delivered either by outside groups such as the Cancer Society or Heart Association or by an agency representative speaking on behalf of the agency or of the agency and outside groups combined.

Next, she wrote four or five marketing objectives for the speakers program, gaining their approval from the administrator. She differentiated from among 14 separate targets. Included as targets were (all names are fictitious) the Fifth Street Baptist Church Retired Men's and Women's Clubs, the Golden Geezers Social Club from the same church, retirement clubs from five local companies, four dining centers sponsored by the Area Agency on Aging, and several senior citizen organizations near the agency. For each target, she noted the exchanges that would exist between the target and the agency. She eliminated a few prospective targets after deciding that in some of the potential relationships the agency would gain and the target would not.

In talks with managers from at least 20 local human services organizations, she sensed that a straight speaker approach would not assure a repeat audience, that audience participation was important, and that routine talks should be broken up tastefully. Instead of offering a lecture type speech at each program, she opted for screening exercises, panel discussions, role playing, quizzes, closed circuit television, slides, educational field trips, and workshops. Later, she developed outlines for marketing tools to be involved. Included were news releases, invitations, public service announcements, posters, small ads in weekly papers or church newspapers, and printed program schedules.

After management approval, she began to implement the plan and drew 45 persons to her first public meeting. She was happy with the turnout; so was her administrator, who began to attend the sessions. At each of the five subsequent meetings, the crowds became larger. In most instances, the agency developed enduring ties with the organizations that supplied speakers and materials; several cooperative, permanent programs for agency clients were developed.

These case histories show how public relations persons planned some events with fingers crossed, expecting more or less an automatic, reassuring response from target audiences. When such responses weren't forthcoming, the public relations director discovered that he had no written plan to review or strategies to revise. He paid the piper later because he approached the speaker assignment too casually, eliminating steps that were pivotal to establishing a memorable program.

There was no interest on the public relations director's part in examining the agency's attitude regarding the aged, no interest in conducting research, no interest in determining from senior citizens themselves their enthusiasm for the nature and possible content of the proposed programs, and no fascination at all for experimenting with unusual approaches to new markets and their differentiated targets. Further, the public relations director had no written guidelines. Each element of his program was improvised, with most parts unconnected to others.

The overall project was implemented simply because it was assigned from above. When asked at the end of the sessions what had been accomplished by the presentations to the elderly, the public relations director said, "We achieved six distinct programs, lots of goodwill, and some new friends for our agency. Maybe some of them will use our agency if they ever have a need."

Conversely, the series planned by the marketing director drew about 300 people for the six sessions. "We have created what amounts to a new constituency among the older people who have come here." said the pleased marketing director, who reports:

> We have all of their names, addresses, and phone numbers. When they were here in our agency, we got them to list their interests and what additional programs they'd like to have. They told us of others in the community who would like to be invited, and they gave us names of clubs and organizations that should be contacted. What did we get as a result of our efforts?
>
> 1. When we distributed information on our main facility and branch office (at each meeting), we got 67 new persons as clients during a six-month period.
> 2. We obtained the services of 14 male and female volunteers who are spending one to two days each week at the agency.
> 3. We were able to draw from our group to form an older adults advisory committee to our agency board of directors. They already have met three times and suggested that we contract with the local Council on Aging for a funded education program here and set up an elderly dining center in one of our branch sites.
> 4. We have ideas for 28 additional senior citizen programs that we will present or cosponsor in the next two or three years.
> 5. We have developed tangible relationships for the first time with 12 other health and human services agencies with which we either were not acquainted or knew very little about. Many of them have programs or services for the aging.

6. We attracted the attention of a local sick room supply firm, which sent observers to two of our meetings and now wants to help finance half of next year's sessions.
7. We expanded our mailing list from 590 to 2,800 names, thanks to names submitted by those who came to our sessions.
8. Our overall agency visits by clients have increased by 11 percent in the first four months of this year. The majority of the increases represent senior citizens whose addresses lie within the postal zones from which we draw the most clients and which we call "our neighborhood."

A review of the results of the well-planned programs suggests that when a marketing person carefully plots an exchange, that exchange usually occurs. The public relations director, on the other hand, did not forecast exchanges; he merely wanted to conclude the series and call it a day.

In the next decade or two, it is inevitable that there will be more marketing than public relations in health and human services agencies. Public relations will not necessarily be diminished in importance, but it will take on a marketing flavor and a marketing posture. Marketing will add a strong dimension to the public relations person's already demanding job. It will seek to differentiate its publics, focus more closely on projects, set priorities, and jettison the thought that it must have simultaneous and grandiose programming to suit all constituents at the same time, an impossible situation to bring about. Existing agency public relations directors first must isolate their marketing from their public relations tasks, then gradually fuse their activities in a marketing direction.

APPROACHING THE TRANSITION TO MARKETING

How can the public relations director in a health or human services agency begin the transition to marketing director? Since one prescription for change would not fit everyone, the authors offer some general steps that could be useful:

1. Read the literature on social marketing in books and in journals, especially in hospital journals. For the most part, hospital-related marketing closely resembles human services marketing.
2. Review agency public relations projects for the past two years. Which projects were completed, how much planning time vs. writing time, how much time reacting to problems, how many projects were more closely associated with the needs of the administration or the board than the needs, wants, or desires of clients or potential clients? How many pro-

jects were canceled or dropped before completion; with how many out-side agencies did PR cooperate on PR projects; how accessible was the administration to the public relations director; what PR projects drew the most praise, the most flack?

3. Estimate how much solicited and unsolicited advice public relations has offered management in the last two years. How often was such advice followed? Who are the persons who sought such advice? To whom are unsolicited suggestions offered?

4. Name the departments or sections of the agency with which public relations is most closely associated; the least associated.

5. Complete a written profile of the public relations department as a basis for transition into marketing. (Exhibit 16-2 presents an outline for such a profile.)

Exhibit 16-2 Public Relations Project Assessment Profile

1. Number of separate public relations projects started and completed in last two calendar years:_____

2. List all public relations projects started and completed in the last two years:
   _____
   _____
   _____
   _____

3. Estimate how your time is divided in one calendar year (by percentages):
Thinking and deliberating	___%
Fact and data gathering	___%
Writing	___%
Conferences with staff	___%
Conferences with management	___%
Meetings in community	___%
Traveling	___%
Total marketing activities	___%
Total public relations activities	___%
Wasted activities	___%

4. List the public relations projects in the last two years that you personally initiated:
   _____
   _____
   _____
   _____

5. How many public relations projects were assigned to you by the agency administration? ____ How many did you finish? ____

6. What were the main reasons for not finishing a public relations project in the last two years?
   _____
   _____

7. List agency departments or sections with which you have close ties:
   _____
   _____

Exhibit 16–2 continued

8. List departments or sections with which you have infrequent ties:

_____

_____

_____

_____

9. How often do you personally confer with the administrator?

_____

10. How often would you *like* to confer with the administrator?

_____

11. List three projects in the last two years that drew the most compliments: _____

_____

_____

12. Which projects drew the most criticism?

_____

_____

_____

13. Were any communications-oriented projects assigned to departments other than yours in the last two years?

___ Yes ___ No

If Yes, explain: _____

_____

_____

14. What opportunities exist for increasing the respect for your department in the eyes of administration? the board of directors?

_____

_____

_____

15. What obstacles exist?_____

_____

_____

_____

When this profile has been completed and summarized, use a separate sheet to consider how marketing elements could be involved in current projects. Our *program marketing potential index* (Exhibit 16-3) has been prepared for such a purpose.

Exhibit 16-3 Program Marketing Potential Index

1. Name of public relations project:_____

2. Expected project completion date: _____

3. Purpose of project:_____

4. Description of project:_____

5. Could marketing research enhance this project? __Yes __ No

   Comments:_____

6. Could the setting of marketing objectives help the project
   __ Yes __ No

   Comments:_____

7. Which publics are employed in this project?

8. Could the publics be broken down further into marketing
   targets?   __ Yes __ No

   Comments:_____

9. Who will benefit more from the public relations project, agency
   or clients? _____

   Comments:_____

Exhibit 16–3 continued

10. If a marketing exchange had been considered, would the public relations project have begun?   ___ Yes ___ No

    Comments:_____

    _____

    _____

11. List the strategies devised to carry out the public relations project:_____

    _____

    _____

12. Would the strategies have been the same if a marketing plan had been prepared for the project?   ___ Yes ___ No

    Comments:_____

    _____

    _____

13. Which promotional tools are used or are anticipated in the public relations project? _____

    _____

    _____

14. Would different or modified promotional tools be employed if a marketing plan were applied to the projects?   ___ Yes ___ No

    Comments:_____

15. List the anticipated benefits of the completed public relations project and state who would benefit:

    _____

    _____

    _____

16. Indicate if the benefit list would expand or shrink if a marketing plan were applied to the project.

    _____

Exhibit 16–3 continued

17. Estimate how much of the basic raw material or information for the public relations project was based on opinion, feelings, problems, or concerns of agency clients: ___%

18. How did the public relations project originate? Was it suggested by:

___ administration?   ___ someone in the community?
___ board of trustees?   ___ staff members?
___ clients?   ___ others?
___ public relations dept.?

19. How much access to administration have you had or do you expect to have on the public relations project?

20. If a marketing plan were used, would you have any more access to the administrator or members of administration?

                                                                    ___ Yes ___ No

Comments:_____

21. In general, would a marketing approach make the public relations project:

More beneficial to targets or publics?   ___ Yes ___ No
More challenging for yourself as
        public relations person?   ___ Yes ___ No
More challenging for your public
        relations staff?   ___ Yes ___ No

MAKING THE MARKETING DECISION

After the profiles and forms have been completed, a decision about the transition to marketing can be made more easily. The next step involves the public relations person who must make the decisions: Do I believe in marketing? Will its benefits mean more to the organization than those brought by public relations alone? Can public relations and marketing work together? Will the marketing recommendations interest or stimulate administration? If the public relations person answers these questions affirmatively, a memo should be written to the administrator with the following elements to:

- define marketing for health and human services agencies

- contrast between public relations and marketing in general

- contrast between public relations and marketing as it is applied to the agency

- summarize the last two year's public relations programming at the agency (attach profiles, if necessary)

- discuss how some of the public relations results could have been augmented or enhanced by a marketing approach (attach index forms, if suitable)

- recommend two initial marketing projects for the agency

- provide hypothetical marketing plan outlines for the two recommended projects, including preliminary marketing process, brief initial analysis, research required, several possible objectives, possible targets and strategies, promotional tools, and timetable

- indicate how public relations will continue to play a role even with marketing in place

- recommend any possible staff changes under marketing

- recommend a budget for the initial marketing operations

If the memorandum and recommendations are received favorably the public relations office will be free to take on marketing programs and begin a business adventure that is surrounded by professional challenges and rewards. If the recommendations are rejected, the proposal should be analyzed carefully and resubmitted later. Because of marketing's affinity toward the views and feelings of agency clients, it will be unusual for recommendations for an initial marketing thrust to be turned down by contemporary managers.

SUMMARY

Social marketing differs from institutional public relations in its planned system to achieve objectives, direct methods, targets and strategies, selective use of promotional tools, accent on client needs, exchanges, controlled promotional channels, and simplistic project measurement.

Marketing could very well supplement or replace the public relations role in health and human services, with most public relations persons and administrators gradually accepting marketing. In the transition from public relations to marketing, the public relations staffer must look at the PR operation and determine how it would fare under marketing. The authors recommend several forms for these exercises.

By adding marketing responsibilities, the public relations director provides a new dimension for that role. (The existing public relations functions of the agency are not swept aside by marketing, but they are evaluated and used more selectively than in the past.) Simultaneously, marketing should bring new benefits to the agency as well as to its employees and clientele.

Index

About the Authors

ROBERT RUBRIGHT is president of Rubright, MacDonald & Co., a health and human services marketing, development, and planning firm, and The Home Health Consultancy, a company that starts, evaluates, and markets home care programs. Both firms are located in St. Louis. In addition to consulting activities, Rubright is an active marketing and communications workshop presenter and an after-dinner and convention speaker. An authority on American humor, he frequently presents programs at colleges and universities, as well as company and institutional banquets and meetings. He has served as president of boards of directors for several hospitals and human services groups. He holds degrees in English and journalism (Westminster College, Fulton, Missouri, and University of Wisconsin-Madison).

DAN MACDONALD is executive vice president of the United Way of Greater Indianapolis. Prior to that, he was the executive of the Community Service Council of Metropolitan Indianapolis for two years. He served for ten years as head of the Health and Welfare Council of Metropolitan St. Louis, was director of the area's Hospital Planning Commission, and founding director of the comprehensive health planning agency, the Alliance for Regional Community Health. As co-founder and partner of the Home Health Consultancy and Rubright, MacDonald & Co., he was active in consulting on a full time basis until 1978. His fund-raising and health and human services planning background includes ten years as executive of Omaha's United Community Services and four years in Champaign-Urbana, Illinois, with Community Chest, United Health Fund, and Council of Social Agencies. He holds degrees in journalism and social administration (Marquette University and Ohio State University). He is the author of *A Guidebook for Establishment of a New Agency in Home Health Care.*